The Politics of Wage-Price Decisions: A Four-Country Analysis

The Politics of Wage-Price Decisions

A Four-Country Analysis

**Murray Edelman
and R. W. Fleming**

University of Illinois Press

Urbana, 1965

Acknowledgments

This manuscript could not have been prepared without the aid and assistance of Ellen Bussey and Leonora Stettner. In gathering data and conducting interviews they showed greater resourcefulness than we had a right to expect, and in addition gave us the benefit of their very considerable background knowledge of the countries which were under study.

Gloria Pirzio Ammassari was an invaluable research assistant on the Italian part of the study.

Among the people who were helpful in making contacts for us or in commenting on parts of the manuscript we would like especially to thank Philip Arnow, Thomas Bowie, Kurt Braun, Professor E. H. Phelps Brown, John Correll, Robert Frenkel, Luigi Giugni, Desmond Hirshfield, Len Murray, Jacqueline Rutgers, Hans Schrinner, Edward Scicluna, Adolf Sturmthal, Douglas Taylor, and Vidkunn Ulriksson.

A very large number of people in management, labor, government, and academic circles in all four countries patiently answered our questions. We appreciate their cooperation even though we cannot name them here.

For funds and time to do this research we are greatly indebted to the American Foundation on Automation and Employment, Inc., which made it possible for us to employ assistants and to undertake much of the necessary travel, the Center for Advanced Study of the University of Illinois, which gave us reduced teaching loads, and the Guggenheim Foundation, which supported Mr. Edelman's work in Italy for several months.

None of these people or organizations bear any responsibility for inadequacies or errors in our findings and conclusions; they did what they could to steer us toward the truth.

Contents

1   Introduction

For the first time since the Middle Ages it is widely taken for granted that national governments have a serious responsibility to maintain some minimum of stability and purchasing power in the incomes of the people, including a responsibility to deal with the extreme case of income failure: unemployment. Wherever a substantial group lags seriously behind others because of imbalances in wage, price, and employment trends, governmental officials can expect political attacks and sanctions. A closer tie between private economic decisions and public economic policies has brought with it a tight interplay between income trends and politics. As measures to create full employment usually threaten wage-price stability, these two economic problems are often transformed into a political dilemma. Large-scale injections of public funds into the economy or stimulation of private investment through easy credit policies will usually stimulate production and increase jobs, and there is accordingly strong pressure to resort to these devices when unemployment is high. Strong political pressures oppose these policies too, however, for they are likely to bring rising wages and prices and fears of a runaway inflation.

Because governments have this new responsibility, serious and sometimes heated discussion has been common in the industrially advanced countries in recent years regarding an equitable formula for deciding how the national income is to be shared. Everywhere there is talk of productivity as a guide line for wage increases, of

fair shares or codetermination, of automatic wage increases to keep
abreast of rises in the cost of living, of economic planning or "programming," or of an "incomes policy."

One reason governments have been placed in this modern dilemma is a growing recognition that individuals and private organizations often cannot protect themselves against dangers to their
incomes flowing from international trade, acts of foreign governments, wars, crop failures or fluctuations, market speculations, labor
surpluses, labor shortages, or monopolies. What could once reasonably be thought an economic issue, to be worked out among managements, unions, and individual workers, has become a pawn
of political interactions, diplomatic developments, and interlocking
organizational interests. A second reason governments are expected
to do something is the simple fact that they *can* do more than they
once could. Men know more about the impact of various kinds of
economic intervention, and private groups are quick to demand what
will serve their interests.

Most wage and price decisions are still made basically by management and labor organizations, but there is constant two-way influence
between what the private organizations do and what government
does. The influence is sometimes overt and obvious. More often it is
subtle, based upon a sharing of values among men in private and
public life or upon fears or hopes regarding future governmental
interventions or private decisions. Public officials often forestall
private claims by anticipating them, just as management and labor
organizations may modify their wage-price claims and tactics to
forestall overt governmental intervention.

In this study we have tried to learn what has made workers, union
officials, managements, and governmental agencies in four Western
European countries act and react as they did regarding wage decisions and price decisions related to wage decisions. It is a study of
organizations and of politics: of the gamut of interests, organizational
pressures, and political pressures that explain decision-making in this
field. What happened depended on the actions and reactions of many
groups and power centers, all intertwined with each other. Their
various daily activities determined demand, wage push, wage pull,
administered prices, and competition. These were people acting, not
"forces," though it is often tempting and sometimes useful to think
in metaphors and to reduce men's acts to economic indexes. Fortunately, the technical economic data have been rather thoroughly

explored by others, notably the OECD, and we could fit their work
into the broader picture of policy-making processes.

We have examined the private institutions involved, the circumstances under which they have displayed common or opposing interests, and their tactics and strategies. This has involved an examination
of the bearing of their structures, constituencies, and leadership patterns upon both their market tactics and their political objectives.
The present inquiry was partly stimulated, in fact, by our suspicion
that developments in the world that came into being after World
War II are changing the character of management and labor organizations and the very meaning of collective bargaining. Preliminary
research suggested that many managements have found it expedient
to increase wages independently of union bargaining power, even
though the rhetoric of union-management conflict has changed very
little. We suspected that the willingness of managements to make
wage concessions has often not been so much a function of union
power as of foreign and domestic product markets, political objectives,
and tight or loose labor markets. We wonder whether bargaining itself
is not often (certainly not always) becoming a ritual that perpetu-
ates rank-and-file loyalties on both sides, while the outcomes of negotiations flow from organizational imperatives that sometimes push
management and union officials in the same direction. In the following pages there is considerable evidence for these hypotheses, and
some exceptions to them. Problems of political feasibility appear to
place roughly identifiable limits upon the powers of labor, management, and public organizations to influence and enforce announced
policies respecting wage and price levels.

We have examined the governmental institutions involved and
the patterns of governmental intervention, in an attempt to identify
the circumstances in which labor and management interests have
been supported or opposed and, so far as possible, the political and
economic impact of different forms of intervention. Always we have
been interested in the interplay between private and public action
and in the functions served in this process by ideologies, political
parties, public administrative agencies, strikes, and personalities.

One is quickly impressed with the extent to which all the interest
groups involved in wage-price decisions rely, consciously or uncon-
sciously, upon gestures and talk that serve to reassure or neutralize
adversaries, their own membership, and the general public. A very
high proportion of the legislation, speeches, bargaining, and even

legal contracts revolving around these policies turn out to be significant for the symbolic reassurance they convey, for they frequently
have little or no concrete impact upon wage or price levels. This
phenomenon is all the more remarkable in an area which seems at
first encounter to be reducible to objective exploration and statistical
comparisons. We have tried to understand these symbolic implications and to analyze their bearing upon political and economic
developments.

The countries whose postwar wage-price politics we consider are
Italy, West Germany, Great Britain, and the Netherlands. In respect
to the degree of governmental influence upon incomes policy they
form a spectrum, ranging from minimal, indirect, and occasional
controls in Italy to something close to displacement of collective
bargaining by the decisions of public and semipublic agencies in
the Netherlands. Two of the countries have a recent history of
dictatorship, while the other two have long been among the most
democratic countries in the world. In respect to postwar political
institutions they vary widely and again form a kind of spectrum.
Italy has a multiparty system and displays a strong clash of political
ideologies. In the Netherlands religious differences and significant
contrasts in program among four political parties have been com-
promised through give and take and widespread self-restraint. England has a two-party system and enjoys a basic political consensus
which has been compatible with energetic pluralism on economic
issues. Germany has been steadily moving toward a two-party system
and greater political conformity and homogeneity. The labor movements of the four countries correspond to these political patterns
rather closely, ranging from politically divided movements in Italy
and the Netherlands through a unified movement tied to the Labor
Party in England to a unified German labor movement hesitant to
become involved in politics at all. This institutional diversity, together with some pertinent cultural differences among these countries, furnishes a basis for comparison and contrast that we hope
is revealing.

The study concentrates upon the postwar years and especially
upon the period from 1948 to 1963. Our purpose is only incidentally
to chronicle the pertinent wage-price developments of these critical
years; we are more concerned with drawing lessons and formulating
hypotheses of general applicability about the impact of economic
and political changes upon wage-price decision-making. In the four

countries we studied, these years saw marked changes in inflationary pressures, in unemployment levels, and in political alignments and alliances. It is therefore an appropriate era for this kind of analysis.

One purpose of this inquiry is to contribute to political theory. All public policy is the result of the interplay of people's values and interests, usually brought into some kind of focus by private organizations.[1] In this field we have analyzed in some detail the manner in which people's interests are reflected in the decisions of both private and public agencies, the influence of the agencies upon each other, and the impact upon both private and public decisions of specific economic developments.

The study should also make some contribution to an understanding of the potential for wage-price stability. In their invaluable study for the OEEC of the problem of rising prices Fellner and his associates said, "We are convinced that the most difficult problems involved in securing greater stability of prices are fundamentally political — in the broad meaning of that word."[2] If we have learned anything about the political possibilities and limits of formal and informal controls, with and without participation of the bargaining parties, we will at least have attacked the right problems. We hope that this inquiry throws some light as well upon the current American problem of wage-price restraint, and we direct some attention to the contrast between the United States and the European countries in our concluding chapter.

Clearly, some pertinent events are left untouched or are only lightly touched. This is inevitable with a research design which expressly recognizes the relevance of a wide sweep of human activity for wage-price developments and which tries to specify and explore the total transaction. We thought it better to run this risk, however, than the risks inherent in a design which would have permitted full and rigorous probing of a segment of human activity too narrow to explain the events with which we are concerned.

In view of the focus of this study, it should be clear that it was not intended to contribute, except perhaps incidentally, to the important debates on the determinants of economic growth and the economic determinants of inflation.

---

[1] Cf. Arthur F. Bentley, *The Process of Government* (Bloomington: University of Indiana Press, reprint, 1949); David B. Truman, *The Governmental Process* (New York: Knopf, 1951).

[2] William Fellner, *et al.*, *The Problem of Rising Prices* (OEEC, 1961), p. 12.

Our field work in the four countries we have studied was conducted between October, 1962, and July, 1963. The procedure in each country was to interview knowledgeable persons in the labor movement, the business world, the government, and the universities. We conscientiously tried to check data and allegations about the positions of various groups by continuing the interviewing until we were satisfied that the inquiry was exhaustive. We have also consulted documents, opinion polls, and other published and unpublished data whenever they were relevant and available.

This area of public affairs is certain to remain vital and controversial in view of institutional and economic trends already well advanced. We trust this inquiry will have value as a history of the years in which new decision-making institutions began to make the old private-public and political-economic dichotomies obsolete, and that it will also help to broaden discussion of the wage-price issue so that there is more realistic assessment of the possibilities and consequences of political and organizational acts.

2   Italy

If any single theme has characterized Italy's postwar wage and price developments, it has been the fading of old ideologies and decision-making structures and their replacement with ferment and the beginnings of new structures. By the early 1960's the political polarization into left and center that had become Italy's international hallmark was dissolving. The united front of industrialists that Fascist corporatism had spawned had been seriously breached. The political in-fighting among ideologically hostile union federations was being dampened by technical and economic cooperation among them. The legendary paternalism of Italian management was still in evidence but was painfully being forced out of its old shapes and perhaps out of existence in the more advanced firms. The Italian unemployed were finding work. The peasants and the underemployed and underpaid workers of the South were moving North, with their old cynicism intact but with new opportunities waiting to change their lives, their incomes, and perhaps their politics.

This chapter describes and analyzes the values, pressures, and tactics underlying wage-price decisions in postwar Italy and must do so in the context of the structural and ideological changes just listed. Its plan is to begin with the more stable social structures as they existed at the start of the period and then to consider how changes occurred; how these in turn generated private and public wage-price policies; and how the latter in their turn fitted into and promoted new structures.

I

Rural life had long set the tone: static social classes, little mobility, industry run on lines that were closer to the feudal than to the paternal. This structure had been the most stable of all; but the breakup of the old power centers, in government and in industry, slowly in the South and rapidly in the North, was a phenomenon of the years with which this study deals. A recent symposium on "Values and Myths in Italian Society in the Last Twenty Years"[1] listed as the prime social change of the period the movement from a predominantly agricultural society to an industrial one. In the decade of the fifties alone the proportion of the labor force in agriculture dropped from 39 to 32 per cent. In the process there was a massive shift of people from the underdeveloped South to jobs in the industrial North or in other European countries. Between 1951 and 1961 there was a net increment of 1,029,000 people in northwestern Italy and a net loss of 1,866,000 from southern Italy.[2]

Even as the power structure was changing, however, old assumptions and attitudes toward government, industrial management, and the elite generally remained very much what they had long been. A recent survey of popular attitudes and activities respecting government found widespread doubt among Italians that there is any possibility of effective participation in political activities. Government, both at the local and the national levels, is chiefly seen as a hostile force against which the common man must try to protect himself as best he can. There is little interest in political programs and problems; the fact that a very high proportion of the Italian electorate actually votes is due chiefly to the law which makes voting compulsory and imposes mild penalties for failure to vote.[3]

This view of government is part of a generally skeptical and hostile view toward those who run things: employers and landlords, bureaucrats and politicians, and often the Church. In the face of the attempts of these people to exploit you, you have to be shrewd and

---

[1] "Valori e Miti nella Società Italiana dell'Ultimo Ventennio (1940–1960); Conclusioni," *Tempi Moderni*, 4 (October–December 1960), 19–26.

[2] Cf. Stefano Somogyi, "Variations in the Italian Population in the Decade 1951–1961," *Review of the Economic Conditions in Italy*, XVI (July, 1962), 291–300; *Problemi e Prospettive dello Sviluppo Economico Italiano* (Rome, 1962); Note to Parliament by Minister of the Budget, Ugo La Malfa, May 22, 1962, p. 28.

[3] Joseph La Palombara, "Le Partecipazione Politica e i Partiti in Italia," *Tempi Moderni*, 5 (January–March, 1962), 62–65.

resourceful or you cannot live. The "Protestant ethic," the view that work is in itself wholesome and a moral duty, is not a common ideology here, for work has too often and too visibly benefited the elite and not the worker. Law is regarded with anxiety and often with contempt. Organizations should be viewed with suspicion, even when they ostensibly help the common man. Unions, for example, are a place a man might go when he is in trouble, but it is pointless to be seriously involved with them at other times.[4]

These attitudes were unquestionably a realistic response to the conditions under which most Italian peasants and industrial workers lived for generations; they became especially realistic during the twenty years of Fascism, and they doubtless remain realistic for many today. That the industrial upsurge and economic growth of the last ten years has not changed them is shown not only by the questionnaire mentioned earlier, but by an actual decline in membership in political parties and unions.

Such attitudes are especially strong and most often reinforced today in the economically and socially underdeveloped South. The North-South imbalance is itself a major structural aspect of all economic decision-making in contemporary Italy, and has remained so throughout the years with which this study deals. Vera Lutz estimates that in the 1950's per capita income in the South was about 45 per cent of what it was in the North. Industry there is very largely small scale, with almost 60 per cent of the industrial workers exclusive of construction employed in plants of ten or fewer persons, while in the North this is true of less than 25 per cent of the industrial workers.[5] Other measures of industrial development and efficiency, living standards, and culture show the same backwardness.[6] Differences in the earnings of workers are especially marked. Labor costs, including social security charges added to contract wages, are about 25 per cent lower in the South than in northern plants, and the difference in actual earnings is substantially greater than that because earnings in the South remain closer to the minimum contract

---

[4] Joseph Raffaele, *Labor Leadership in Italy and Denmark* (Madison: University of Wisconsin Press, 1962), p. 81.

[5] Vera Lutz, *Italy: A Study in Economic Development* (London, New York, and Toronto: Oxford University Press, 1962), pp. 91, 93.

[6] Cf. Shepard B. Clough and Carlo Levi, "Economic Growth in Italy: An Analysis of the Uneven Development of North and South," *The Journal of Economic History*, XVI (September, 1956), 334–349.

rates than is true in the North and are sometimes below them.[7] Using the Ministry of Labor's figures for de facto hourly earnings during the first three months of 1958, Lutz calculated that in the chemical industry the spread between earnings in Liguria, where wages were highest, and Sardinia, where they were lowest, was 32.1 per cent. In the shoe industry, where the size of units is smaller and where the southern economy is therefore better represented, the spread between the top region, Lombardy, and the lowest, Sicily, was 54.4 per cent.[8] These heritages from an unfortunate past remain an important fact of life for all who must try to win a following for political proposals, industrial programs, and union claims in Italy today. Their influence will be apparent in much of the account that follows.

The collective bargaining structure of the first postwar years reflected an old Italian tradition of national bargaining to set minimum rates. National bargaining stems partly from the Socialist origin of Italian unionism, with its emphasis upon the interests of the masses rather than the labor aristocracy, and it was reinforced by the Fascist corporative system, under which national "syndicates" comprising both employer and labor organizations fixed wage levels and working conditions. Its prevalence is also due in part to the fact that Italian industry includes a far higher proportion of small- and medium-size firms than is true of the United States or the more mature Western European economies.[9]

On the employer side the bargaining has been conducted by a small number of peak organizations: Confindustria[10] for industry, Confagricoltura[11] for agriculture, and the General Trade Confederation[12] for commercial enterprises. Confindustria has a membership of some 107 regional associations and some 103 national "trade" associations. Collective bargaining agreements are usually for "categories" of workers: multi-industry or cross-industry groupings, such as metal mechanics and chemical workers. The appropriate trade

---

[7] Cesare Vannutelli, "Topical Aspects and Problems of Italy's Wage Policy," *Review of the Economic Conditions in Italy*, XIII (March, 1959), 23–24.

[8] Lutz, *op. cit.*, pp. 230–231.

[9] In 1951, 56 per cent of the persons employed in industry were in units consisting of ten or fewer employed persons or of the self-employed plus family helpers. See III Censimento Generale dell'Industria e del Commercio, November 5, 1951.

[10] Confederazione dell'Industria.

[11] Confederazione Generale dell'Agricoltura.

[12] Confederazione Generale del Commercio.

associations of Confindustria do the actual bargaining, subject in theory to the policies prescribed by the confederation's executive organs. As dues paid to Confindustria by individual firms are roughly proportional to the number of their employees and to the total payroll of the firm, the confederation is not likely in practice to exert sanctions against the giant firms even when they fail to toe the Confindustria line on wage or other issues. Only on labor matters, including wages, is Confindustria policy binding upon its members, even in theory. The confederation has no authority to intervene in pricing policy and claims that it does not try to do so.

On the union side there was a single union confederation, CGIL,[13] from 1945 to 1948. Tensions that were primarily political rather than economic in character thereafter split it into three major confederations with differing political orientations. CGIL, with roughly 2,800,000 members, is allied with the Communist and Socialist parties. CISL,[14] with approximately 2,300,000 members, has ties to the Christian Democratic Party. UIL,[15] with roughly 700,000 members, is tied to the Social Democratic and Republican parties.

The structure of the Italian union movement has mirrored both its economic frustrations and its political and organizational orientations and commitments. In all of the national confederations, CGIL, CISL, and UIL, centralization has been the keynote of both economic bargaining and political negotiation, and weakness in bargaining power, in turn, has been at the root of the centralization. As will appear in some detail below, bargaining in the fifties served chiefly to set minimum rates the marginal firms could pay. Both for this purpose and for ideological and political appeals, bureaucratic control at the top of the union confederations was called for and was maintained.

On paper each of the Italian union confederations have, it is true, had many local and provincial level units: provincial and communal chambers of labor corresponding roughly to American state central and city central bodies, and communal and zonal category unions corresponding roughly to American local unions. Except in the large cities, these organizational units have typically been staffed with a single parttime employee or not staffed at all, and they have had little or no money with which to operate. Even the national "cate-

---

[13] Confederazione Generale Italiana del Lavoro.
[14] Confederazione Italiana dei Sindacati Lavoratori.
[15] Unione Italiana del Lavoro.

gory" unions, corresponding to American national and international unions, have typically been highly dependent for money and staff services upon their parent confederations. This has not been true, however, of the CGIL metalmechanical, textile, chemical, agricultural, and sharecroppers unions, of the CISL unions in the metalmechanical, textile, and chemical industries, or of the UIL chemical workers union.

In the forties and fifties interconfederal agreements, applying to all workers in the industrial sector of the economy, were frequently concluded through negotiations between Confindustria and the union confederations. They dealt with such sweeping matters as the sliding wage scale for cost of living adjustments, skill differentials, and family allowances. Wage bargaining by industry was carried on by the category unions, with varying amounts of staff help and advice from the parent confederations.[16]

This highly centralized pattern has begun to be modified significantly for reasons that are considered below.

Immediately after the war, workers flocked into the unions in relatively large numbers. Among the reasons were a hope that union membership would make it easier to find a job; enthusiasm for the heroic role of the Communists and Socialists in the partisan movement during the war; and the high-keyed political infighting within the united union confederation before 1948, which gave the various political parties a strong incentive to increase their respective followings within it. Since 1948 there has been a sharp decline in union membership, and only about 40 per cent of the Italian workers are now organized. The political splits in the labor movement and the increasingly economic and technical orientation of the unions have made it easier for Italian workers to revert to their historic distrust of organizations and bureaucracies. A marked shift in the demand for labor from manufacturing to service industries has further contributed to the unions' problems. In 1953 white-collar workers comprised 15.02 per cent of the employed labor force; in 1962 they comprised 20.58 per cent.

A related factor that has limited the maneuverability of the union organizations is their financial weakness. A recent writer referred to the payment of union dues in Italy as "a process complex, occult,

---

[16] For a thorough account of the structure of the Italian union movement, see Maurice F. Neufeld, *Italy: School for Awakening Countries* (Ithaca, N.Y.: Cornell University Press, 1961), pp. 502–515.

and infrequent."[17] It is rumored that CGIL is better nourished by its affiliated political parties than CISL or UIL, but all the confederations get outside help. For many years the American unions have contributed money to UIL and CISL, especially the former. Fiat and Montecatini, the two largest Italian companies, allegedly long helped support these same confederations as part of their fight against CGIL, and it is likely that UIL still receives subsidies from this source. The Ministry of Labor makes some funds available to the unions for vocational training.

In the early 1960's the checkoff of union dues began to spread in Italy. This development is strengthening the treasuries of the national unions substantially and must now be counted as a major new factor in Italian industrial relations, even though a high percentage of workers have found ways to evade this system, too.

Although particular wages and prices are set by managements, unions, or both, the positions of these groups are inevitably influenced in all countries by actual or possible governmental interventions, direct and indirect. Any account of the basic structure for price-wage decisions must therefore consider the structure of influence in political parties and public administrative agencies.

Ever since the end of the war and the fall of the Fascist regime, Italy has had a multiparty system which makes the range of political opinion look rather more scattered than it actually is. The parties which bid for votes form a wide gamut. On the extreme right there are a Monarchist Party and a Fascist Party called the Italian Social Movement. The Liberal Party represents the views of an important segment of big business and uses the rhetoric of nineteenth-century laissez-faire ideology. The Christian Democratic Party, in the center, includes within its capacious ranks its own spectrum from far right to moderate left: groupings united chiefly in their political flexibility and in their confessional tie to the Catholic Church.

Just left of center are the Republican Party and the Social Democratic Party, both supported chiefly by middle-class professionals and intellectuals interested in political or economic reform; and in the case of the Social Democrats, at least, by Tammany Hall-like party professionals interested in spoils. To their left is the Socialist Party, leftist in orientation among European Socialist parties and until recent years tied to the Communists in a "unity of action" pact.

---

[17] Raffaele, *op. cit.*, p. 81.

Finally, there is the Italian Communist Party, the largest and probably the most moderate Communist party west of the iron curtain. Other parties have run slates in particular postwar elections and then faded from view, temporarily or permanently.

This scattering of parties permits the expression of a wide range of enthusiasms, but gives an unduly pessimistic impression of the possibility of mobilizing sufficient political support to permit a government to operate. The fact is that political opinion has been polarized into two major political groupings through most of the postwar years, and not into seven or eight. The Christian Democratic Party served as the base for one of the nodal groups and the Socialist and Communist parties as the base for the other. These three have also been the only parties to receive a substantial proportion of the vote in the postwar elections, as Table 1 shows.

From 1947 to 1962, the Christian Democrats remained in control of a succession of governments by forming coalitions with one or more of the small parties closest to it: the Liberals, Republicans, and Social Democrats. In the hectic first two postwar years even the Communists were represented in the Cabinet, but the fundamental polarization of opinion into center and left and the intensification of the cold war made the continuation of this sort of coalition impossible. The fascist and Monarchist parties have occasionally kept a conservative Christian Democrat in office as Premier for short periods by supporting him in Parliament, but that kind of alliance has also proved consistently unstable, and these rightist parties have in the main played the role of ineffective gadflies.

In the early sixties a new flexibility on the part of the Socialist Party created an important break in the polarization. For the first time there was a possibility of forthright state intervention in the economy supported by a new kind of political majority on the peninsula. This development therefore had key importance for current and future wage-price policy. It stemmed from the decision of Pietro Nenni and his supporters in the Socialist Party to break their long-standing unity-of-action pact with the Communists and support a center-left government of liberal Christian Democrats, Social Democrats, and Republicans. This new alliance of the non-Communist left represented the votes of a larger proportion of the population than any previous postwar government, except the one that included the Communists before 1947. It suffered from some inner tensions, however; these are considered later.

Table 2-1.[a] Percentage of Popular Vote Captured by Principal Italian Parties

	Constituent Assembly 1946	Chamber of Deputies 1948	Provincial Elections 1951–52	Chamber of Deputies 1953	Provincial Elections 1956	Chamber of Deputies 1958	Provincial Elections 1960	Chamber of Deputies 1963
Christian Democrats	35.2	48.5	35.9	40.0	38.9	42.3	40.3	38.3
Social Democrats	–	7.1	7.6	4.5	7.4	4.6	5.8	6.1
Liberals	6.8	3.8	3.5	3.0	4.2	3.5	4.0	–
Republicans	4.4	2.5	2.4	1.0	1.1	1.4	–	1.4
Communists	19.0	} 31.0	18.3	22.6	} 35.2	22.7	23.3	25.3
Socialists	20.7		11.8	12.7		14.2	14.4	13.8
Monarchists	2.8	2.8	4.0	6.8	} 8.5	4.8	–	1.7
Italian Social Movement (Fascist)	–	2.0	6.9	5.9		4.8	5.9	5.1

[a] Tables in *Italian Affairs*, III (1954), 194, and VI (1957), 23; *Compendio Statistico Italiano*, 1962; *Il Messaggero*, May 1, 1963.

For the analyst of the politics of wage-price policy, it is important to notice that the complex, fragmented party system of Italy can be a rather sensitive instrument for registering changes in the enthusiasms or fears of even a relatively small segment of the voting public. The American cliché that a vote for a minor party is a vote thrown away becomes obviously hollow here. In the 1963 Parlimentary election campaign, for example, the small Liberal Party right of center was correctly pointing out that a vote for it would strengthen the hand of the Christian Democratic Party in its bargaining with the Socialists about center-left policy. This sensitivity is heightened, moreover, in the measure that the party structure ceases to be polarized into two clearly defined camps that can stalemate each other but cannot compromise with each other.

Still another facet of the basic structure for making wage-price decisions lies in the organization of the executive branch of the government. Italy has a parliamentary system of government, and the tenure of postwar premiers and cabinets has depended, as just noted, upon their ability to hold together a coalition of political factions commanding a majority of the votes in the Chamber of Deputies.

Fiscal policy, an instrument for direct influence upon prices, is therefore a resultant of bargaining among party factions, for the annual budget, more clearly than any other single governmental action, synthesizes and symbolizes the policy directions of the state and is jealously watched by all the party leaders. The Budget, Treasury, and Finance Ministries are especially important in preparing and defending fiscal policy proposals. Their heads are appointed by the Prime Minister and approved by Parliament as a part of the overall bargain involved in forming a government.

Monetary policy is formally laid down in its broad lines by an Interministerial Committee on Credit and Savings[18] and by the Treasury Ministry. In practice the Bank of Italy, through its formal authority to recommend measures to these agencies and to carry out their directives, has very wide powers, and the Governor of the Bank of Italy has been the key figure in the postwar formulation of such policies. An administrative council (Consiglio Superiore) consists of the Governor, twelve members nominated by a General Assembly of Participants representing the banks and other credit

---

[18] The committee consists of the Ministers of the Treasury (President), Public Works, Agriculture, Industry and Commerce, Foreign Commerce, and Budget. The Governor of the Bank of Italy participates in its meetings.

agencies that hold the bank's stock, and three additional members. The council in turn nominates the Governor and other major officers of the bank, and the nominations are confirmed by a decree of the President of the Republic.

This structure assures that the Governor will be responsive in some measure to Italian banking interests and that he will be kept informed of the problems of concern to interested governmental ministries. A recent EEC study of monetary policy in the Common Market countries found the powers of the central bank especially great in Italy and France.[19] A tradition of vigorous use of those powers was firmly established in Italy by the first postwar Governor, Luigi Einaudi.

The Italian state has had a significant instrument of influence at its disposal in the form of public enterprises constituting a substantial proportion of the investment and employment in some of the most important sectors of the economy. These enterprises have been increasingly weighty elements in the nation's collective bargaining, economic planning, and politics.

Industries that are fully nationalized and subject to the direct administrative control of the state are not the most important of the Italian public enterprises, though this group now includes the state railroads, the post office, telegraph, salt and tobacco monopolies, a banana monopoly, the State Forests Administration, and, since 1963, the electric power industry. The state also has a controlling interest in some other companies, notably Cinecittà, the film industry.

More significant are some rather original forms of public enterprise involving more direct and decisive participation in the day-to-day development of the Italian economy while at the same time minimizing conventional business opposition to socialization and similar emotion-arousing symbols. A large group of important firms remain joint stock companies, with a controlling state interest in their assets but with substantial private participation in their stock holdings as well. These firms are coordinated by the Istituto per la Ricostruzione Industriale (IRI), a state holding company. It first came into existence in 1933 to protect the stockholders of Italy's largest banks, then in dire difficulties because of sizable industrial holdings, many of which were failing or threatening to fail. Having taken over the

---

[19] Communità Economica Europea, *Gli Strumenti della Politica Monetaria nei Paesi della Communità Economica Europea* (Brussels, 1962), p. 20.

assets both of the banks and of the industries, IRI was transformed a few years later into the administrator of these and newly acquired public industrial holdings.

The IRI firms, as of early 1963, represented substantial holdings in shipbuilding, shipping, steel, the metallurgical and engineering industries, radio and television, and banking. Table 2-2 gives estimates of their importance in these fields. IRI firms provide 100 per cent of the country's telephone service and radio and television broadcasting, control Alitalia, the only domestic airline, and have important holdings in the production of auto vehicles, aircraft, industrial machinery, electronic equipment, railway equipment, electric appliances, optical instruments, and other commodities. They also construct and improve highways and freeways.

Table 2-2.[a] Measures of the Importance of IRI Firms in the Economy

Industry	Ratio of IRI to National Employment, 1957	Contribution of IRI to Total Domestic Production	
		End, 1957	End, 1962
	percentages		
Passenger and Passenger-cargo Ships	32.6	14.0 (tonnage)	62.0 (no. of ships)
Dry Cargo Ships	—	—	9.0
Domestic Shipyards	—	—	80.0
Mechanical Engineering	13.6	—	—
Steel Production	51.1	50.0	55.0
Concrete Production	—	—	11.0
Cast Iron Production	—	80.0	90.0
Bank Deposits	28.1	20.0	20.0
Electric Power	27.7	Over 25.0	([b])

[a] The table is based upon data furnished us by IRI and upon the article by Saraceno cited in footnote 20.
[b] The industry was nationalized in 1962–63.

At the end of 1957 the IRI firms had a work force of 251,000, and at the end of 1961, of 271,500.

In the great bulk of their business operations and labor relations policies these companies retain virtually complete autonomy from state control. They have had to rely for their financing principally upon credit operations and upon the issuance of minority shares on the market, although there have been occasional contributions from the Treasury, calculated to do no more than compensate IRI for such special state-imposed tasks as keeping certain unprofitable companies afloat (partly to deal with the unemployment problem) and undertaking schemes for the development of the South.[20]

Holding companies under the level of IRI itself have been set up to coordinate the policies of the various firms in each of the major industrial sectors in which these firms operate: steel, ship construction, engineering, shipping, and telephone service.

Another important state holding company, the Ente Nazionale Idrocarburi (ENI) is organized very much like IRI, but was established only in 1953 and has not been used even in part to salvage ailing companies. It is heavily involved in the refining, transportation, and distribution of petroleum products; in research and production of various other minerals; in the methane, petrochemical, artificial rubber, fertilizer, and atomic energy industries; and in a variety of other enterprises, including motels. It controls nearly 100 per cent of the output of natural gas. It is also active in a number of international enterprises, including oil prospecting and production and pipelines. Until his death in 1962, ENI's guiding spirit was Enrico Mattei, an entrepreneurial genius who demonstrated that a state enterprise authorized to chart its own course and engage in autofinancing could quickly expand the range and scale of its operations and become not so much an instrument of state policy as a major influence upon Italy's economics and politics. In 1961 ENI had 29,711 employees in Italy and an additional 18,093 abroad.[21]

A Ministry of State Shareholdings was created in 1958, ostensibly to define the policy directions of the autonomous state agencies according to the general lines of public economic policy. In practice, however, the Ministry has not set policy or controlled the firms in any meaningful sense, even though one strong-minded Minister, Ferrari-Aggradi, tried to do so. The decisive elements in the IRI-ENI formula are the possibility of direct market financing and the concentration of technical skills. Against these the general language of a statute or the vague directives of a Minister can have little long-

---

[20] For information on IRI see: European Economic Community, *Report of the Economic Situation in the Countries of the Community* (September, 1958); Pasquale Saraceno, "Twenty-five Years of Activity of the Istituto per la Ricostruzione Industriale," *Review of the Economic Conditions in Italy*, XIII (January, 1959), 5–29; Pasquale Saraceno, *L'Istituto per la Ricostruzione Industriale, III, Origini, ordinamenti e attivita svolta* (Rome: Ministry of Commerce and Industry, 1956); IRI, *Esercizio*, 1961.

[21] ENI, *Relazione e Bilancio*, 1961–62, p. 71.

run effect. Market and entrepreneurial opportunities and competitive possibilities are bound to play the decisive roles, and they have done so. Increasingly, moreover, the IRI structure seems to have won the assent and even the approval of the political right, which apparently sees it as both an investment opportunity and a painless means of dealing with some major economic trouble spots.

The inflation of the first two postwar years must also be recognized as influential upon subsequent wage and price decisions. It was not a part of the decision-making structure, but it was an important part of the structure of psychological fears and anticipations that has influenced private and public action in the years since 1948.

In 1946 and 1947 there was a marked disproportion between supplies of goods and demand for them, with prices and rates of money circulation moving upward rapidly in a wage-price spiral. The rate of increase varied widely for different goods, and there were different quotations for goods within individual markets.

An early general price and wage freeze had some temporary effect, but not for long, with a black market spreading quickly. The Bank of Italy's annual report blamed speculation and governmental timidity in taxing liquid funds, which continued to accumulate and spurred inflation.[22] During the period from January, 1946, to December, 1948, the wage index advanced from 1 to 3.4 while the consumers price index was moving to 2 and the cost of living index to 1.7. These diverse movements had the effect of restoring pretty closely the prewar relationship among the three indexes. Consequently, 1948 wages were, on the average, 50 times their prewar level, retail prices 53 times, and the cost of living 48 times.[23]

Beginning in September, 1947, there was a reversal in price movements, due to the combined effect of foreign aid and energetic governmental action. The most telling impact came from the goods UNRRA and the Marshall Plan placed on the market. Elasticity of supply was very low for food, raw materials, and basic industrial goods, in spite of unemployment and unused capacity in some sections of industry; foreign goods therefore helped close the inflationary gap in a direct way. At the same time, the Italian government resorted to monetary measures with good effect. In the fall of 1947 the authorities blocked the excess liquidity in the banks by establish-

---

[22] Banca D'Italia, *Adunanza Generale Ordinaria dei Partecipanti, Anno 1948* (Rome: Tipografia della Banca D'Italia, 1949), p. 101.
[23] *Ibid.*, pp. 103–104.

ing a system of obligatory reserves amounting to 25 per cent of deposits. This rather dramatic action and the improved supply situation evidently did a good deal for business expectations and public confidence. Through the second half of 1947 and all of 1948 the spread between legal and market prices continued to decline until it virtually disappeared by November, 1948. Except for an increase in the prices of bread and "pasta" (noodles) owing to the abolition of direct price controls on these products, stability was the most notable characteristic of 1948 price movements, the cost of living remaining almost unchanged from December, 1947, to December, 1948.

Once embarked upon its energetic attack on inflation, the government relied on fiscal policy as well as monetary policy, though the latter is credited with having been more efficacious. Budget Minister Giuseppe Pella took measures to reduce expenditures and increase revenues in an effort to stop large Treasury drafts on the Bank of Italy. Expressed in 1948 lire, the budget deficit fell from 725,599 million lire in fiscal 1946–47 to 174,132 million lire in fiscal 1949–50.[24] Beginning in the autumn of 1947 there was a reduction in the velocity of currency circulation, and by June, 1948, the Bank of Italy was no longer printing banknotes to meet Treasury requirements.

In Italian politics the rather dramatic and quick end to the postwar inflation is closely associated with the name of Luigi Einaudi, an economist who was Governor of the Bank of Italy from January, 1945, to May, 1947, and then Minister of the Budget. Einaudi's proposals for tight currency controls were widely unpopular at first. Because he was a Liberal, he received political support from the conservative circles, who did not know where to turn in the face of a situation that could not be ignored; and conservative support was essential at that time. With the end of runaway inflation, Einaudi's political prestige boomed, and in May, 1948, he was elected President of the Republic. The sequence of events is suggestive for students of political leadership. Individuals, as parts of organizations, may contribute something to the solution of complex economic problems; but the problems, if they arouse popular fears and hopes, are likely to have even more to do with shaping political careers.

Both the fears of a renewal of a price-wage spiral and the success of monetary controls in dealing with it in the forties have been major

---

[24] *The Development of Italy's Economic System* (Rome: Interministerial Reconstruction Committee, 1952), p. 18.

influences upon Italian economic policy throughout the fifteen years that have passed since the postwar inflation ended. Italian tactics and strategies for avoiding inflationary pressures are distinguished from those adopted elsewhere in Western Europe chiefly by their heavy and almost exclusive reliance upon monetary policy.

Italy's success, especially in the decade of the fifties, in increasing production and productivity very substantially without serious inflation and with only insignificant direct economic controls was made easier by some special economic conditions. These should be noted here, because they also constituted a structure upon which the decision-makers of the 1950's were able to build. The factors that made it easier to control inflation are considered first.

The country began its period of economic rehabilitation with almost no national debt, for the debt had been almost completely wiped out by the inflation of the war years and of 1946–47. Hard as this was on the nation's creditors, it removed an inflationary spur with which many countries had to contend.

Second, it was necessary to build up the financial assets destroyed by inflation. The recorded value of total financial assets (banknotes, deposits, shares, and securities) increased between December, 1947, and December, 1960, from 54 per cent to 170 per cent of GNP. In short, the very low level of financial assets at the start of the period prevented even a large increase from exerting significant pressure on prices.

Third, Italy could make no pretense of being an important military power, and military expenditures were cut drastically. This eliminated the need to pay dearly to import military necessities, especially metals and crude oil, and it released domestic capacity for the production of other goods. Many of these could be exported and so build up foreign reserves; and, unlike military goods, they help satisfy effective demand and so are anti-inflationary.

Fourth, United States aid, which had been vital in bringing the postwar inflation under control, continued to weaken pressure on prices by bringing in raw and semimanufactured materials. It was a diminishing factor, however, declining from 403.7 million dollars in 1948 to 66.9 million in 1958.

Fifth, it was readily possible, by easing travel restrictions, both to increase the income from tourism significantly and to encourage some of the surplus labor to emigrate.

Sixth, the excessive supply of workers and the unions' financial problems kept wages low. Large differences in industrial efficiency among plants, industries, and geographical areas had the same result. Though the effects of these factors upon living standards were of course unfortunate, and often shocking, they did contribute to price stability.

Finally, the low base from which Italy started made it possible to show rapid technical progress, and this was especially true in the fields of petrochemicals, electronics, engineering, and pharmaceuticals. There was a large backlog of demand for consumer goods and of investment opportunities. This may well have been the most significant factor of them all, though in this respect Italy shared an advantage enjoyed by all the European economies.[25]

II

The complex structure just described is "structural" only as a metaphor. All of it really consists of people's decisions to act fairly consistently and predictably, according to rules and roles established for them. Certain other kinds of decisions are less consistent and predictable, and these, in postwar Italy, have been the more dynamic element in the formation of wage-price policy. They have also produced some changes in the decision-making structure itself.

At the end of the decade of the forties a number of special conditions made it easy for Italian businessmen in some key industries to decide to increase output, to modernize their plants, and to make greater use of capital. All of these decisions have been reflected in substantial increases in industrial production and productivity. These conditions, as summarized in the Vanoni Plan, were three in number. First, there was a backlog of technical improvements which could not be adopted until after the war and which spurred productivity when suddenly put into use. Second, there were reserves of plants and equipment in certain fields, notably the engineering industries, which could readily be brought into operation with little expense. Third, the liberalization of imports of the late forties and early fifties made possible the use of a great deal of machinery which

---

[25] For this summary of some economic reasons for the success of monetary polices to promote stability, we have relied very largely upon Paolo Baffi, "Monetary Stability and Economic Development in Italy, 1946–60," *Quarterly Review of the Banca Nazionale del Lavoro*, No. 56 (March, 1961), 3–30, esp. 11–19.

had not been available earlier and which contributed rather suddenly to productivity growth.[26]

Many of the conditions which facilitated the boom were inherently temporary in character and cannot be counted on to continue to help Italy in the future, though continuing strong demand at home and abroad might be sufficient to maintain it.[27]

As a result of temporary and persisting spurs to economic growth, Italy has experienced an advance in production and productivity that has often, like the similar experiences in Germany and Japan, been labeled an "economic miracle." Hildebrand calculated that real GNP grew at an average annual rate of 5.5 per cent or 5.0 per cent per head between 1947 and 1959.[28] Between 1951 and 1961 industrial production increased 12 per cent annually on the average. There was no downturn in any single year, a high of 29.4 per cent in 1949, and lows of 2.9 per cent and 3.1 per cent respectively in 1952 and 1958. The 1958 figure reflects a recession in 1957–58 which had repercussions on a number of the types of decisions with which this study is concerned. Over the period as a whole, however, there has been great effort to modernize existing plant as well as to build new facilities, so as to remedy the capital shortage that the autarchic Fascist years had created.

Labor force statistics, and especially the amount of unemployment, reflect one kind of employer decision but also serve as premises for private and public policies. For various reasons these statistics are especially disputable in Italy,[29] though they have been closely watched because of the severity of the unemployment problem. The Italian labor force has been increasing at an annual rate of about 0.6 per cent.[30] Until very recently unemployment and underemployment

---

[26] Cf. Lutz, *op. cit.*, p. 58. Sponsored by the late Budget Minister Ezio Vanoni, the plan embraced a long-range program for industrial expansion, encouragement of emigration, more rational distribution of the labor supply, and reduction of unemployment.

[27] See *Il Messaggero* (Rome), April 10, 1963, p. 2.

[28] George H. Hildebrand, "Growth and Stability in the Postwar Italian Economy," *American Economic Review*, 51 (May, 1961), 391.

[29] Underemployment, the spreading of available jobs among family and friends, and failure to register at employment exchanges make for underestimation. On the other hand, there is substantial "illegal" registration by employed persons who want various benefits. The Central Institute of Statistics has made periodic surveys of households in recent years but the resulting data on the labor force have differed substantially from the data secured through other sources and from impressionistic evidence.

[30] Hildebrand, *op. cit.*, p. 392.

Table 2-3.[a] Measures of Economic Growth

	Gross National Income (billions of lire, 1954 prices)	General Index of Industrial Production (1953=100)	Value Added[b] (billions of lire, current prices)		Index of Output Per Hour Worked[c]	
			At Factor Cost	At Market Prices	CGIL Computation	Banca d'Italia Computation of Annual Percentage Change in the Index
1951	10,511	89	—	—	—	—
1952	10,719	—	—	—	—	—
1953	11,480	100	—	—	100	—
1954	12,027	109.1	10,501	12,007	106.5	8.2
1955	12,860	119.0	11,490	13,146	116.0	10.6
1956	13,413	127.9	12,302	14,162	123.9	6.7
1957	14,280	137.7	13,276	15,216	130.8	6.0
1958	14,882	142.4	14,217	16,263	139.7	6.8
1959	16,088	157.9	15,148	17,400	153.0	11.1
1960	17,258	182.3	16,638	19,002	164.1	9.4
1961	18,663	202.1	18,178	20,869	173.0	4.7
1962	—	221.6	—	—	—	8.3

[a] ISTAT, except where otherwise indicated.
[b] "Value added," with respect to enterprises, is the value of the goods and services they produce minus the value of raw materials and the value of services furnished by other enterprises. The figures given here indicate value added by both private and public enterprises.
[c] Productivity computations must be regarded with some caution and skepticism because it is not possible to obtain statistics on hours worked that correspond to the official figures on output. The Banca d'Italia computation given here appeared in 24 Ore, June 11, 1963, and applies only to manufacturing industries.

have been very high. In the past three years the drop has been very
marked. Unemployment is consequently a relatively minor factor
today so far as much of the Italian economy is concerned, rather
than the paramount social problem it was during the first fifteen
postwar years. In 1963 there were still serious pockets of unemployment and there was still considerable underemployment, chiefly
among the unskilled and especially in the South. Some skilled
workers were in short supply, with employers in the highly industrialized areas sometimes waiting several months to get them.

Price movements have been complex and confusing in Italy since
the conquest of the 1946–47 inflation. In the fifties price increases
were moderate while at the same time they gave rise to constant
fears they would spurt and to monetary measures to restrain them.
In the sixties the fears have been realized, and additional kinds of
public intervention have resulted. Below this surface level, however,
various prices have been moving at different rates and even in different directions, and diverse explanations, sometimes obvious and
more often speculative, have been offered or accepted.

The average increase in consumer prices between 1947 and 1959
was 3.2 per cent, with relatively large increases only in 1948 (11.4
per cent) and 1951 (9.0 per cent).[31] The 1948 rise was due to the
price decontrol of that year and the 1951 increase to extensive inven-
tory speculation plus a marked spurt in import prices resulting from
the Korean War. As compared with the experience of other countries
in the fifties, the price rise in Italy extended fairly evenly over the
years and was not concentrated in a short period owing to any
specific inflationary impetus. An OEEC study of time periods in
which various European countries have experienced excess demand
shows that in Italy there was no such period of any significance in
the fifties.[32]

The two major reasons for the rises that occurred were both of a
type that made for gradual increases. Each year the government has
allowed an increase in controlled rents, a process that is still going
on. As a result, rents, with a weight of 2.3 among the components
of the consumer price index, sustained by far the largest increase
of any component. A marked surge in the prices of services was the
other chief explanation for the rise in consumer prices. Between 1953
and 1959 services rose 22 per cent while goods were increasing only

[31] Hildebrand, *op. cit.*, p. 391.
[32] William Fellner, *et al.*, *op. cit.*, p. 126.

9 per cent.[33] The pressures and opportunities that explain the decisions to increase these two types of prices disproportionately are
considered below. Between 1948 and 1959 the cost of living index,
intended to reflect the expenditures for goods and services of a
family of "fixed composition," increased by an annual average of
only 1.69 per cent.

Wholesale prices experienced an average decline of 0.4 per cent
between 1947 and 1959. (In only two other OEEC countries, Denmark and the Netherlands, did the CPI increase by a substantially

Table 2-4.ᵃ Employment, by Sector of Economic Activity, 1954-62 (in thousands)

	Agriculture	Industry	Other Activities	Totals
1954	6843	5629	4831	17303
1955	6884	6011	5275	18170
1956	6341	6086	5467	17894
1957	6477	7346	5739	19562
1958	6247	7034	6140	19421
1959	6256	7288	6020	19564
1960	6225	7593	6151	19969
1961	5908	7999	6355	20262
1962	5673	8256	6421	20350
Percentage change, 1954–62	−17.1	+46.7	+32.9	+17.5

ᵃ Table from ISTAT.

Table 2-5.ᵃ Unemployment, 1954-62

	Number (thousands)	Percentage of Labor Force	Percentage of Labor Force Seeking First Job
1954 (May 8)	1669	8.8	4.2
1955 (May 8)	1491	7.6	3.1
1956 (April 21)	1867	9.4	3.5
1957 (May 8)	1662	8.2	3.0
1958 (October 20)	1340	6.5	2.4
1959 (average)	1128	5.5	1.8
1960 (average)	846	4.1	1.4
1961 (average)	674	3.4	1.3
1962 (average)	611	2.8	1.2

ᵃ Table from ISTAT: *Annuario di Statistiche del Lavoro 1959–1961*; Ministeri del Bilancio
e del Tesoro, *Relazioni Generale sulla situazione economica del paese* (1962), published in
Mondo Economico (April 6, 1963).

[33] *Ibid.*, p. 94.

Table 2-6. Indexes of Wholesale Prices, Consumer Prices, and Cost of Living, 1948-62

	Wholesale Price Index	Consumer Prices	Food	Cost of Living
	(1938=1)			
1948	54.43	61.50		48.44
1949	51.69	60.77		49.15
1950	48.97	58.30		48.49
1951	55.81	62.49		53.20
1952	52.70	64.40		55.46
1953	52.50	65.91		56.54
1954	52.93	67.50		58.06
1955	53.20	69.32		59.69
1956	53.80	73.36		62.66
1957	—	—		63.87
1958	—	—		66.93
1959	—	—		66.65
1960	—	—		68.42
1961	—	—		70.42
1962	—	—		74.52
	(1953=100)			
1954	99.1	102.8	103.6	—
1955	100.0	105.2	106.4	—
1956	101.7	108.8	111.2	—
1957	102.7	110.2	111.1	—
1958	100.9	113.3	115.0	—
1959	97.9	112.8	112.3	—
1960	98.8	115.4	113.4	—
1961	99.0	117.8	113.8	—
1962	102.0	123.3	118.8	—
1963				
January	105.5	128.8	125.0	78.23
February	106.4	130.6	127.5	79.67
March	106.2	131.0	127.8	80.12
April	106.3	131.8	128.5	80.65

greater amount than wholesale prices in this period.)[34] The reasons for the decline in Italy were the marked increase in man-hour output of industrial workers (about 10 per cent between 1947 and 1959) and the growing competition domestic industrial products met in the Common Market.

Since 1959 prices have been moving up more rapidly, and in late 1962 and 1963 the rises were sufficiently steep to arouse wide public

[34] *Ibid.*, p. 81.

restiveness and political attention. The consumer price index for
1960 stood at 115.4, for 1961 at 117.8, and for 1962 at 123.3. Even
the wholesale price index reversed its course in 1960 and began to
rise slowly: from 98.8 in 1960 to 102.0 in 1962. The early 1960's
accordingly mark a new era in postwar Italian price history, with
a changed pattern of economic and political pressures.

The prices of some durable goods, on the other hand, have
actually been cut substantially, or have remained fairly constant
over the postwar years. Price cutting has been especially substantial
in the case of refrigerators and washing machines, but it has also
occurred in the automobile industry. Over the decade of the 1950's,
Fiat prices dropped by almost as much as American automobile
prices did during the "Ford revolution."

Export prices have been falling, and this fact probably indicates
that price increases in the export industries have been more moderate than elsewhere. Import prices have been falling more than export
prices, also exercising a moderating influence upon the price structure.[35] It should be noticed, however, that imports constitute a
smaller proportion of GNP than is true of any other OEEC country:
14 per cent. (For the other countries in our study the percentages
range from 45.3 per cent in the Netherlands to 20.1 per cent in the
United Kingdom. For the United States the figure is 4.7 per cent.)

Two general comments about postwar Italian price trends seem
warranted. First, serious inflation has not occurred, though it may
be starting in the early 1960's. Second, price trends have been sufficiently various, ambiguous, and complex as to occasion constant concern about imminent inflation and to offer arguments for almost any
course of governmental action that an economic or political grouping might favor.

Negotiated wage rates have risen by at least 5 per cent yearly
since 1947, with earnings rising faster because of wage drift. Since
the middle of 1961 both minimum rates and earnings have been
climbing more steeply than earlier. Until the early 1960's both wage
rates and earnings in Italy were held well under the rise in productivity, though they exceeded the increases in consumer prices.
Workers therefore experienced a modest increase in real wages and
in living standards. In 1962 and 1963 a number of important collective agreements provided for increases in wage rates that went well

---

[35] *Ibid.*, pp. 115–117.

beyond productivity rises, even allowing for the difficulty of computing the latter and making optimistic assumptions about them.

III

What can we say of the management, worker, and other interests that explain these price and wage decisions? What were the responses of interested private groups to the trends just summarized?

A number of economic and organizational considerations were paramount in shaping price policies. In spite of the favorable factors noted earlier, severe capital shortages constituted the major factor impeding economic growth for the country as a whole in the early postwar years. The individual firm often experienced a serious need for capital in order to increase productivity and efficiency and to compete successfully at home and in foreign markets. One early response was to seek tariff protection, and in the steel and some other industries high tariffs in the first postwar years contributed to monopoly and to the maintenance of high prices.

It was also possible for some industrial groups to avoid domestic competition by using their influence with the banks to exclude potential new entrants from gaining access to sources of credit. Like high tariffs, this tactic served for only a short time, as the necessary close relationships between industrial groups and banks were severed by the end of the decade of the fifties.[36]

In the search for credit the greatest reliance was placed upon autofinancing. With the rapid rises in productivity there is every reason to believe that profits increased considerably,[37] though they had been at a low level in 1950. The use of a substantial portion of profits to finance plant modernization and capital expansion offered important advantages to industrial managers, for it minimized potential restraints on their maneuverability from banks and from governmental monetary policy. Stockholders, some of whom might have preferred higher dividends to self-financed growth, are not in a position to exercise effective sanctions upon management, and in these years heavy unemployment and political divisions within the labor movement prevented the unions from claiming a large share of the fruits of increased productivity in higher earnings for workers.

For the managers self-financing carries even more immediate benefits. It enables them more easily to perpetuate themselves as

---

[36] See Lutz, *op. cit.*, p. 11.
[37] *Ibid.*, p. 312.

a group through cooptation, to fix their own remuneration, and to identify their interests with those of the firm, without any real intervention on the part of stockholders. Its effects upon price and wage policy are thus in part incidental, for managers in a position to acquire capital through pricing rather than recourse to borrowing have persuasive incentives to do so.[38]

Lutz estimates that for the manufacturing industries that are relatively large and most accurately studied the real cost of labor to the employer between 1950 and 1959 rose on the average by about the same proportion as the money cost — about 60 per cent or a little more — and that the productivity increase in these years for the same industries was somewhat under 100 per cent. It should be emphasized, however, that this conclusion applies only to a part of the economy and that it is subject to a considerable margin of error.[39] Autofinancing has continued to serve industrial needs very considerably, though higher costs in the early 1960's have forced greater resort to outside sources of credit. An additional reason for the heavy reliance on autofinancing, especially in the late fifties and early sixties, has been the large demands of public enterprises upon the limited capital market. These have limited the credit available to private industry.

This situation has given management considerable latitude in its pricing policies; but, as the statistics show, industrial prices have not risen inordinately, and there have been substantial cuts in some lines. In part the price restraint and the reductions reflected the ending of high tariff protections. In the main they have been a response to the need to compete in the Common Market and in other foreign markets, and they have been made possible by the impressive increases in productivity and efficiency. A number of industrialists claimed, in talks with us, that they have deliberately lost money on some of their products in order to acquire markets. It is doubtful that price restraint or cuts have often been the result of competition. Monopoly is characteristic of many branches of Italian industry, even though its exact dimensions are not known.

Italian management repeatedly cites the strong and, in the main, quite successful effort to compete as a major reason for the relatively small wage concessions characteristic of the fifties, though this is

---

[38] Cf. Luciano Batti, "Pianificazione e domocrazia," *Tempi Moderni*, 4 (July–September, 1961), 63.

[39] Lutz, *op. cit.*, p. 86.

probably a rationalization, at least in part. Given the pattern of opportunities and pressures just summarized, it was a logical course of action for industrial management. Industry-wide bargaining contributed to the same kind of pricing policy, for the bargaining system means that wage rates must be set in line with the ability to pay of the marginal firms. The firms enjoying the largest productivity increases are therefore further encouraged to cut prices or limit price advances rather than grant larger wage increases, so as not to force the labor costs of their less efficient competitors up too far.[40]

The chief reason for the cost of living increases that occurred was the rise in food prices. These were due partly to occasional poor harvests, as in 1956 and again in the early sixties, but they also stemmed from a remarkably antiquated, complicated, and inefficient distribution mechanism which gives all sorts of middlemen an opportunity to impose charges in local markets. The beneficiaries of this system naturally resisted efforts to change it. Some governmental attempts to do so are considered below.

Just as the general lines of price policy in the fifties were a natural consequence of the opportunities and pressures managers faced in those years, so wage policy can also be explained in terms of the pattern of pressures and possibilities in which industrial managements found themselves. These turn out, on careful examination, to be the predictive considerations. A similar exploration of the pattern of pressures and aspirations of labor organizations, on the other hand, does not have comparable explanatory or predictive power. For reasons to be considered now Italian management has called the turn on wage trends, while labor has usually had to follow its lead.

Explored in terms of the interest groups involved, the Italian system of wage determination shows itself to consist fundamentally of two groups of institutions, each serving important interests. One set of institutions assures a minimum standard of living that will minimize social and political protest while it makes only minimal demands upon industry. A second group of practices gives wide latitude in wage setting to the more efficient firms while exempting the less efficient ones from the need to follow their lead.

Paramount among the institutions that serve to avoid and allay political restiveness among workers is the collective bargaining structure already described. National bargaining to set minimum

---

[40] On this point see Cesare Vannutelli, *op. cit.*, p. 10.

rates is a formula par excellence for accomplishing this end while
requiring nothing beyond it of any firm. At the same time two important ancillary practices have served the same purpose.

One of these is automatic escalation of wages with changes in the
cost of living, a device very likely more widely used in Italy than in
any other country in the world, Denmark being the only possible
exception. In the social tensions of the first postwar years it seemed
politically necessary to eliminate as far as possible grounds for dispute based upon arguments about unequal movements of wages and
living costs by providing for automatic wage adjustments through
a previously established plan. Changes in the technical methods of
computation were negotiated in 1951 and again in 1957, but the
method of computation has not been a major bargaining issue, nor
has the principle of escalation. It is employed not only in industry
but also in all branches of trade, in public employment, in the field
of credit and insurance, and even for agricultural workers.

Given the considerable increases in the volume of output and in
productivity and the cautious use of monetary controls discussed
below, escalation was not inflationary in the fifties, though one minor
exception to that statement offers an instructive lesson in the relationship between the effects of the system and political pressure for
its revision. In the first half of 1956 exceptionally bad weather pushed
up food prices, consolidating a temporary price increase in wages.
This led to a change in the method of calculating the index of retail
prices and of the system for the application of the sliding scale.

The widespread use of escalation has had an impact on the tone
and rhetoric of collective bargaining negotiations. It has made the
discussions more technical and encouraged concentration upon productivity increases and how they should be distributed. A number
of people who have been close to the process have remarked, however, that productivity is far from a wholly objective concept, and
the outcome of bargaining still depends upon who has more power.

In general, the system operates so that earnings above the average
lose part of their purchasing power while those below the average gain in purchasing power. That is, the wage structure tends to be
flattened. There is also some ratchet effect: wages do not fall as
easily as they rise.

While the major effect of the system has certainly been to minimize restiveness due to price increases, it does not help all workers
equally. Many low income workers are excluded from its benefits,

legally or illegally. Inflation may thus make the position of some
low-paid workers even worse, while those who are paid better are
protected.[41] It should be remembered, however, that the unpro-
tected low income workers are often hampered from expressing an
effective political protest. Many are not organized; many are already
firm adherents of the Communist or Christian Democratic parties.
In any case they are not likely to recognize just how the system
works to their disadvantage.

There is also reason to believe that the escalation system may well
become inflationary as price rises substantially larger than those that
took place in the fifties occur. With the onset of more steeply rising
consumer prices in the early sixties unions have begun to complain
that the index is not sensitive enough to price increases, while employers argue that it is inflationary. Under these new conditions the
sliding scale may become a more controversial issue than it has been.

Another Italian institution that helps assure a minimum standard
of living sufficient to avoid serious political protest is the social security system. A very large percentage of the Italian worker's income
comes in the form of social security benefits, including substantial
family allowances (now constituting about 35 per cent of the wage),
and the more conventional types of old age, sickness, and accident
benefits. To keep the family allowances roughly commensurate with
cost of living increases, the wage escalation plan provides that every
fifth "point" by which wages are increased is to be applied to the
family allowances. Other changes in the level of family allowances
have been negotiated collectively from time to time and then given
the force of law by a Ministry of Labor regulation. There are also
end of the year bonuses running sometimes as high as two or three
months' pay. A study by the Statistical Institute of the European
Economic Community in 1960 found that in Italy only 51.28 per cent
of the labor cost for wage earners was paid in direct wages. An additional 18.36 per cent went into bonuses and remunerations for days
not worked, and 30.36 per cent into social security contributions and
other social charges.[42] Since Bismarck, European elites have quite
explicitly looked upon social insurance measures as political insurance for themselves. The extraordinary place of social benefits in

---

[41] Lutz, op. cit., p. 305.

[42] Cesare Vannutelli, "Labour Cost in Italy," Banca Nazionale del Lavoro
Quarterly Review, No. 63 (December, 1962), 13.

the Italian worker's pay envelope leaves little doubt that such benefits are playing their classic role.

By 1954 the system of special benefits had grown enormously
complex, and in that year Confindustria, CISL, and UIL negotiated
a plan for some rationalization of the structure, incorporating most
of the special benefits (bread indemnity, temporary indemnities,
readjustment quotas) into the basic wage structure. The plan, known
as "Conglobamento," also defined more clearly what bargaining
would take place at the interconfederate level and what bargaining at
an industry-wide level. One effect of this agreement was to encourage somewhat more wage variation by industry.

This last result, like the wage differentials by geographical zone
which were also part of the plan, was a recognition of the fact that
workers in radically different social and industrial milieus could not
be satisfied with the same minimum wage rate. The worker in a small
shop in an isolated southern community looked to different reference groups and had different standards from the Fiat employee in
Turin. The provisions for differentials therefore served both of the
functions listed above. They helped assure a minimum living standard and so helped allay restiveness; but they also encouraged some
variations in pay levels in line with gross industrial and zonal differences in industrial efficiency and productivity.

The 1954 agreement provided for thirteen wage zones (there had
been ninety-five previously), with a maximum gap of 30 per cent
in minimum rates. A revision of the system in 1961 provided for six
zones, with a maximum gap of 20 per cent. The actual maximum gap
has been rather greater because small firms in the South have not
always respected the terms of the collective contracts.

For small firms and marginal ones, whose product markets are
local or limited, it is important that labor costs be kept to a minimal level consistent with public order; and for these, as already
noted, national contracts establishing wage minima are highly suitable. For the more advanced sector of the economy, however, low
labor costs are less important than some other objectives: above
all, labor peace and an adequate labor supply so as to gain maximum
maneuverability regarding product mix, markets, wages, and prices.
It is evident that as production becomes more capital intensive,
labor costs become less important to management and the efficient
employment of capital, the acquisition of new markets, and the
avoidance of work stoppages become more important. In addition

to these economic objectives, the more advanced firms have shown that they have a political one: to consolidate and maintain a position of influence in government, as insurance of continued economic maneuverability and perhaps simply for the sake of power as well.

This is essentially the calculus that has faced the more efficient and expanding Italian firms in the period under consideration here. For them the national bargains and the general rules are of little use except as they help maintain stability and quiescence in the less advanced sector of the economy. For them an additional set of institutions are being developed: more flexible, and so fashioned that they can be tailored by each large company to its own requirements.

The basic industrial relations device in the arsenal of the advanced sector is planned wage drift. Using this tactic and some related ones, the large companies have been able, as we shall see in some detail, to use wage policy not only to maintain a high measure of control over their labor costs, but also to maximize labor docility, minimize strikes, and even exert considerable control over the development and political complexion of the labor movement.

The exact dimensions of wage drift cannot be known with much confidence, but there is no doubt that it has been substantial. One study found that the average difference between actual and negotiated wages in 1954 was 26.39 per cent, and by 1961 the gap had grown to 33.27 per cent.[43] Tables 2-7, 2-8, and 2-9 give other pertinent data. For some workers earnings 100 per cent above the minima have not been uncommon, though in general the drift has been much lower for women, for less skilled labor, and in the South. Indeed, as

Table 2-7.[a] Index Numbers of Average Contract Wage Rates for Various Skill Grades (1938 = 1)

	1950	1955	1959	1961
Skilled Workers	41.2	54.9	65.5	71.1
Semiskilled Workers	46.4	59.2	70.1	75.8
Specialized Laborers	49.8	62.7	74.8	80.8
Common Laborers	54.1	68.1	81.2	87.7

[a] Table from ISTAT. In 1950 skill differentials were clearly below normal. The figures for 1955 reflect the changes made in the 1954 Conglobamento agreement. These indexes do no take family allowances into account.

[43] Giuseppe Ammassari and Gianni Scaiola, "La Contrattazione integrativa aziendale nel 1961," *Il Nuovo Osservatore*, 2 (May, 1962), 161. For further information on wage drift in Italy, see Giuseppe Ammassari, *I Salari di Fatto in Italia* (Milan: Guiffre, 1963). This is an excellent study.

Table 2-8.[a] Movement of Contract Wages and Actual Earnings; Measures of Wage Drift

Year	Wage Rates			Actual Wages			Spread Between Annual Rates of Increase of Actual and Contract Wages (Earnings Drift)
	Lire	Index Numbers 1954=100	Annual Percentage Increase	Lire	Index Numbers 1954=100	Annual Percentage Increase	
1954	140.04	100.00	–	177.01	100.00	–	–
1955	146.72	104.77	4.77	187.83	106.11	6.11	1.34
1956	155.29	110.77	5.84	200.33	113.18	6.65	0.81
1957	162.32	115.90	4.52	209.44	118.30	4.54	0.02
1958	170.71	121.89	5.16	219.43	125.97	4.77	−0.39
1959	172.82	123.10	1.23	224.68	126.03	2.39	1.16
1960	180.92	129.18	4.68	235.71	133.16	4.91	0.23
1961	188.44	134.56	4.15	251.15	141.88	6.55	2.40
1962	202.30	144.46	7.31	289.45	163.51	11.12	3.81
Average annual increase			4.95			5.88	

[a] Giuseppe Ammassari and Gianni Scaiola, "I Salari di Fatto nell'Industria Italiana," *Il Nuovo Osservatore*, Vol. 4 (May 1963), p. 409. The data are based upon contract rates reported by ISTAT and earnings data reported by the Ministry of Labor.

already noted, there has been some drift *below* the minima in the South. In Milan the drift found in 138 plants with 183,704 units of labor was on the average 40.15 per cent. In Naples, for 21,447 workers in thirty-five plants the average drift was 26.86 per cent, always with respect to minimum contract wages.

Table 2-9.[a] Drift in Italian Industry on March 31, 1961, in Five Economic Sectors for Seven Skill Levels

Skills	Chemical	Metal Mechanics	Con- struction	Textile	Various	Totals
			percentages			
Skilled Worker	71.15	48.05	41.32	27.24	34.64	48.57
Semiskilled worker	52.92	43.43	26.70	21.35	26.33	35.75
Specialized Laborer	34.82	27.14	19.72	16.58	18.38	25.92
Common Laborer	23.63	20.37	13.36	10.83	12.49	15.86
Women:						
1st Category	21.23	19.76	14.80	12.09	12.64	16.45
2nd Category	15.79	17.30	10.98	8.46	10.92	12.71
3rd Category	10.33	12.92	7.17	5.25	6.34	9.19
Sector averages	37.66	33.51	20.98	13.33	20.12	
National average						26.40

[a] Table from same source as Table 8. The data are based upon a special survey undertaken in 1961 by Ammassari and Scaiola. The skill levels listed in the table are those found in the collective contracts.

Our main concern here is not with averages, however, but with the tactics, strategies, alliances, and counterploys that key managements and unions have used to achieve their wage objectives. While the picture has of course not been identical in all the advanced companies, it is possible to list and analyze the range of maneuvers that has characterized this politics. As Italy's largest company and the one that has experimented most boldly with the range of tactics available to management in this field, Fiat offers a polar rather than a typical example. It exemplifies the opposite extreme from the small, marginal torpid companies content to produce for a limited market in the traditional way and to pay minimum wages or below them: a genre in which Italy abounds. The history of postwar industrial relations at Fiat thus offers a concise survey of the gamut of political techniques that have been used in greater or lesser degree by other efficient firms, and it will suggest that their efficiency has not been limited to the production of goods for the product markets, but has extended as well to the management of men and labor organizations. The present account does not pretend to be a complete case study of Fiat's labor relations, but it does illustrate some of the ties among industrial relations, politics, and organizational goals and tactics.

Throughout the 1950's Fiat, Olivetti, and other major companies paid wages well above the minima required by their contracts. Their wage concessions were certainly higher than would have been necessary to attract the work forces they needed and even more clearly higher than the unions could effectively have demanded.

It must be remembered that until the late 1950's the Italian unions were hardly in a position to force employers to grant wage concessions. Unemployment was very high, the unions could rarely muster rank and file support for strikes except short demonstrations, and union membership was declining. In the case of companies like Fiat, Olivetti, and Montecatini, actual earnings were apparently between 70 and 100 per cent above the basic wage with increases in piece-work rates as the major component of the drift. Italian union leaders today are quite ready to admit the evident fact that these concessions amounted to employer-determined "wage-pull" rather than union-determined "wage push."

The reasons the larger companies chose to pull wages to these levels were basically those cited above. They could easily afford it, and wage concessions could be, and were, used to assure an adequate labor supply at all skill levels, labor docility, and political maneuverability.

At Fiat profits increased from an index of 100 in 1948 to 1,268 in 1957, according to an estimate by the competent economic research organization, IRES;[44] and 57.5 per cent of the money invested in plant between 1953 and 1957 was autofinanced.

The wage increases were not awarded indiscriminately, however, but were so negotiated as to make it clear that they were a managerial concession and that they were granted in return for specific forms of political and organizational conformity. Fiat worked systematically in a not too subtle alliance with CISL and UIL, as a way of opposing CGIL, with its Socialist-Communist ties and its predilection for political strikes. Fiat is reliably reported to have suggested to the unions at times what they should demand. While

---

[44] Carlo Donat Cattin, "La grande impresa a Torino dal 1945 al 1962," *Quaderni di Azione Sociale* (May–June, 1962), p. 9. "IRES" is an abbreviation for Istituto Ricerche Economico-Sociali "Aldo Volente," located in Turin.

granting increases above the national minima to the democratic unions, the company systematically refused to bargain with CGIL. The Montecatini Company, the second largest private concern in Italy, similarly favored CISL, and many others followed the same policy.

There are shop committees in Italian plants, elected by proportional representation from lists of candidates nominated by the various unions. In some cases wage concessions above the minima have been simply announced by the employer, while in others they have been discussed with the shop committees. Vannutelli makes the pertinent observation that the difference between unilateral concession and this kind of negotiation is important chiefly symbolically: "Even if this extra remuneration . . . is in actual fact generally negotiated with the Shop Committee and not spontaneously accorded, this does not impair the balance of the system since the Shop Committee is not a representative trade union agency. Consequently the form is saved and the juridical principal respected, which is important in matters of this kind."[45] There is a discussion of the function of shop committees below, and it helps clarify Vannutelli's remark.

Other tactical uses of wage concessions and related devices have been used by Italian employers. For many years Fiat gave bonuses to employees who did not participate in strikes. In April, 1962, for example, the company awarded a 12,000 lire bonus, with 500 lire deducted for every strike in which the individual participated. Later nonstrike bonuses were awarded in somewhat more subtle form, but they had the same purpose and effect. In the metalmechanics agreement of 1962 the company agreed to discontinue nonstrike bonuses.

Wage increases for "merit" are commonly used in this connection as well. The unions claim that the granting and withholding of merit increases is often based upon the employee's politics, union membership, loyalty, and docility. They further claim, and many management people agree, that employers have clung steadfastly to "merit awards" as a purely managerial prerogative than to any other right.

Fringe benefits have also been used. With the enormous influx of job seekers into Turin from the South in recent years, Fiat has con-

---

[45] Vannutelli, "Topical Aspects and Problems of Italy's Wage Policy," p. 17. For further evidence that "negotiation" of wage supplements with the shop committees was usually purely formal and in fact amounted to unilateral management concession, see *Relazioni della Commissione Parlamentare di Inchiesta sulle Condizioni dei Lavoratori in Italia*, Vols. V, VI, and VIII.

structed a great deal of housing for its workers, and it is widely accepted in Turin that entry and retention in company housing depends upon managerial judgments of the worker's union affiliation, politics, and docility. At Montecatini a great deal of money is spent for social benefits for the employees. Clubs are built for workers in the communities in which there are Montecatini plants, and management professedly hopes these will divert the workers from an interest in politics.[46]

While the discriminating use of wage and related awards has given management considerable influence over the conduct of employees already on the payroll, hiring and firing have also been used. For some time Fiat systematically transferred all known members of FIOM, its CGIL metalworkers union, to a particular plant, which was shortly afterward shut down. To identify possible Communists among job applicants, many firms cast a wide and not especially discriminating net. Applicants may be asked to fill out a detailed questionnaire on their past life histories. If there are Communists in a man's family, he is not hired. If he was an army officer, the company assumes he is safe, as the army also screens. There are no doubt some exceptions, but some such policy is commonly found throughout Italian industry.

Some of the larger companies, and notably Fiat, have not hesitated to use these various tactics in order to strengthen the unions they liked and weaken those of which they disapproved. At Fiat company influences upon the unions' roles and their relative strength has gone even farther, for the company has changed favorites among the unions often enough to make it clear to the most obtuse worker that each union's power to help its members is dependent largely upon management's good will.

In the early postwar years Fiat strongly favored CISL and to some extent UIL, granting them wage concessions beyond their bargaining strength, while refusing to negotiate with CGIL. Both company and union sources admit that this was the case, and at the time the workers realized it, too. Montecatini followed the same policy. The sweetheart arrangement between Fiat and CISL was threatened in 1952, when a large group of CISL members broke away to form an "autonomous" union, LLD, which CISL charged

---

[46] A leading official of Montecatini's personnel office, speaking of these clubs, remarked, "Vanno a giocare a bocce a non nelle cellule del partito." ("They [the workers] go bowling and not to a party cell meeting.")

was company inspired and dominated. This scission ended in 1953, though it was the beginning of tensions which were to have future consequences. In 1955, however, the long company campaign against CGIL had some success, when for the first time CISL and UIL won a majority of the seats in the shop committee elections. Probably the chief reason for the CGIL loss in this election was a threat by the American Ambassador to Italy, Clare Booth Luce, that contracts for American military supplies would not continue to be awarded to Fiat if CGIL held its majority in the shop committee. Much of the additional support for CISL and UIL was therefore forced upon workers anxious to keep their jobs in a period of heavy unemployment.

Giuseppe Rapelli, a Christian Democratic member of Parliament strongly critical of CISL leadership at the time, sounded an ominous note amid the general rejoicing about this victory, pointing out that the company had divided the union movement and put it at its mercy. "That which succeeds today against socialist and communist activists may happen tomorrow to those of other union organizations."[47]

In 1958 the schism within CISL reappeared, a group of CISL members of the Fiat shop committee again organizing an independent union, which CISL claimed was company inspired. CISL refused to sit with members of the "autonomous" union in negotiating sessions, though the company now tried to bargain jointly with the shop committee members representing CISL, UIL, and the independent union. At the same time CISL began to insist that the company include CGIL in joint bargaining sessions with other unions. The new attitude on the part of CISL coincided both with a new toughness in CISL's attitude throughout Italy and with a vehement CISL campaign against the long-standing practice whereby managements had bargained with shop committee members rather than the unions as such, even though this was explicitly prohibited by law. The new, less cooperative attitude on the part of CISL also coincided with a marked decline in its vote in Fiat shop elections. UIL soon became the strongest union at Fiat, with the independent union second, and CISL last, trailing even CGIL. As reported to us by the Fiat personnel department, union membership among the work force was distributed as follows in April, 1962.

UIL	32.6 per cent
LLD	29.5 per cent
CGIL	22.5 per cent

[47] Marco Vais, *Le Commissioni Interne* (Rome: Editori Riuniti, 1958), p. 50.

CISL   15.0 per cent
CISNAL   0.4 per cent

Fiat is apparently still able directly or indirectly to determine which unions will gain strength in its plants and which will lose.

An attitude survey conducted by ACLI[48] at all Fiat plants at Turin, Modena, and Brescia in 1962 adds an interesting commentary to this history. Asked which union management favors, the workers' replies were:

UIL   37.2 per cent
LLD   54.9 per cent
CGIL   1.5 per cent
CISL   15.1 per cent
Other   5.1 per cent

There is not a perfect correlation between the unions the workers support and the ones they think management favors. On the other hand, a belief that management favors a union certainly seems to boost its popularity considerably rather than hurt it.

The course of events during the prolonged and often bitter 1962 negotiations with the metal mechanics unions illustrate and underline the point. The company reached a settlement first with UIL and the independent in June, 1962. CISL refused to join them, partly to challenge the favoritism shown UIL, partly because the company still insisted upon bargaining only with the shop committee and persisted in its use of wage concessions to buy off participation in strikes. Following the early settlement, there were violent demonstrations outside the UIL offices in Turin and a series of strikes over the next several months. The company finally reached an agreement with CISL and CGIL in October, providing for slightly higher wages than in the earlier LLD-UIL settlement; but more important, the company agreed to bargain with the unions rather than the shop committee and also agreed to discontinue its antistrike bonuses. A UIL officer to whom we spoke was overtly uneasy about the UIL gains in Fiat elections, admitting that they were largely the consequence of company favoritism.

In addition to the tactics already noted, a number of other factors help explain Fiat's long history of success in influencing the strength of the unions with which it bargains. One major consideration has been the enormous and continuing influx of immigrants from the South into Turin. These people are not accustomed to factory work,

---

[48] Associazioni Cristiane del Lavoratori Italiani.

Table 2-10.[a] Results of Shop Committee (Commissioni Interni) Elections at Fiat, 1949-61

1949	CGIL	34,272
	CISL	8,753
	UIL	3,827
1950	CGIL	36,555
	CISL	12,449
	UIL	3,513
1953	CGIL	33,125
	CISL	11,219
	UIL	5,622
1954	CGIL	32,885
	CISL	5,446
	UIL	5,650
	LLD	6,927
1955	CGIL	18,860
	CISL	18,718
	UIL	10,971
1958	CGIL	14,440
	CISL	7,360
	UIL	16,139
	LLD	17,750
	Other lists	1,302
1959	CGIL	12,100
	CISL	9,563
	UIL	15,169
	LLD	19,121
	Other lists	1,354
1960	CGIL	13,766
	CISL	10,363
	UIL	17,324
	LLD	20,607
	Other lists	1,212
1961	CGIL	16,390
	CISL	10,503
	UIL	20,019
	LLD	19,273
	Other lists	1,310

[a] Carlo Donat Cattin, "La grande impresa a Torino dal 1945 al 1962," *Quaderni di Azione Sociale* (May–June, 1962), p. 21 (corrected).

are even less accustomed to unions, and are notably sensitive to company cues about the proper industrial relations posture. Allegations of company financial help to the UIL and CISL organizations have already been mentioned.

The company's deft playing upon the political differences among its workers is also noteworthy. It has played an "ideologies game," using various tactics to puncture first the left and later the Christian Democrats. One suspects that this game of ideologies has served more directly to keep the Fiat employees disunited and anxious than to promote either democratic unionism or political moderation. In a country torn by serious political polarization it may be inevitable that a shrewd management should connect political anodes and cathodes to administer periodic shocks to its bargaining adversaries.

Union tactics, schisms, alliances, and pressures of the postwar years have been natural enough responses to the various social structures, economic trends, and management tactics already described. In the first postwar years the emotionally compelling union objectives were the political and ideological ones. These were the years of political strikes and of the splitting off of political currents from CGIL to form new union federations. There was a real chance at that time that the Communists would come to power in Italy through a victory at the polls, and the political parties were inclined to look upon their associated union federations primarily as agents in the political struggle. Heavy unemployment and unions that were economically weak for other reasons already noted contributed to this political and ideological emphasis. It was most overt in the case of the Communists and Socialists, but was prominent as well in the strategies of the Social Democrats and Christian Democrats. The latter were further aided very considerably by the Catholic workers organization, ACLI, devoted to sociability and political education and indoctrination.

CISL was the first of the union federations to begin to place primary emphasis upon economic rather than political objectives. This was at first partly a counterploy to CGIL's political strikes; but with the kind of management support noted earlier, it began to impress northern workers and to result in considerable CISL gains in shop committee elections by the middle fifties. Even earlier, CISL had begun to talk of building local union organizations, though most of these plant unions have existed only on paper or not at all. As late as 1963 a CISL official estimated that there were local organizations in only about one-third the plants and that only about one-third of these function in any way at all.

The drop in the temperature of the cold war after Stalin's death, the wage concessions of the years of the economic miracle, and the subsequent substantial decline in unemployment in Italy have since forced CGIL gradually to soft-pedal political strikes (for which it was getting less and less support) and to follow CISL and UIL in emphasizing bread and butter gains for workers.

Changes have also taken place within the union bureaucracies. In the case of CISL the emergence of a new political and economic climate in Italy has coincided with the entry upon the scene of a new generation of union leaders: younger, less concerned with political doctrine, more militant in their stance against management. These men quite openly scoff at the CISL leadership of the forties and early fifties as "ideologists," and are intent upon reversing the practice of CISL-management connivance that then occurred. They are tough in negotiations, with the result that employers and Confindustria staff people are constantly declaring today, both in sadness and in anger, that CGIL is easier to bargain with than CISL. To compound their problem these employers point out that CISL's ties to the current government, its political respectability, its Christian Democratic connections, and a ten-year history of being favored by some employers as an anti-Communist ploy have made it both more adamant in its demands and more difficult to say "No" to.

For some of the same reasons, CGIL has become more moderate in its tactics. As noted earlier, the possibility of wage concessions and the apparent resistance among workers to political gestures by the union have pointed the way toward an economic orientation. Some developments on the political scene point, somewhat more ambiguously, in the same direction. Pietro Nenni, the Socialist Party leader, has recently broken away from a "'unity of action" pact with the Communist Party, and he supported the Fanfani center-left government. This schism is reflected in the CGIL hierarchy, for CGIL represents both the Communists and the Socialist parties. The Socialists have appointed Brodolini, a trade union moderate now in disfavor with his more doctrinaire former CGIL colleagues, to head a new "labor mass" section of the party. There is evidence that many Socialists in CGIL are re-examining their position and the federation's strategies; and those who favor a change lean toward more conventional trade union objectives. In any case employers are impressed that CGIL usually seems more eager than CISL to reach agreements these days; and, like CISL, it has been forced to learn a more technical language in which to bargain. On the whole, the years of economic prosperity have thus brought the trade union currents closer together, in objectives and in tactics. As will be seen shortly, it has had the opposite effect upon management.

It fits the times and the trends that there has been much less emphasis upon personalities in the union movement in recent years than was the case in the days of ideological in-fighting. While Giulio Pastore of CISL and Giuseppe DiVittorio of CGIL were nationally known figures in the early fifties and symbolized their respective organizations to the general public, the union confederations today are commonly referred to by their initials, with little attention to their officers. There is no Italian counterpart in prestige of Meany, Reuther, Brenner, Leber, or Woodcock.

As another evidence of the trend away from ideology, even in CGIL, top Communist Party officials, including Palmiro Togliatti, have warned CGIL officers in recent years that they are concentrating too much upon trade union objectives and ignoring broader party goals. These warnings have not reversed the trend.

The tactics and developments described above have produced a new series of union-management issues in the last few years and portend major changes both in union-management orientations toward each other and in relationships within each of the camps. Two developments are especially relevant to the understanding of this recent ferment in collective bargaining: the striking decline in unemployment and the influence of capital intensive production and of the Common Market upon the goals and strategies of Italian industry.

Unquestionably the most controversial issue is a movement away from the traditional pattern of national bargaining tightly controlled by Confindustria. In its current and most controversial form, this movement involves the issue of plant level bargaining; but its antecedents are older and more general in nature.

The first important postwar break in the conventional bargaining pattern involved legislation providing that companies controlled by the government, including the important IRI firms, would henceforth bargain collectively through their own organization, Intersind, and not through Confindustria. This separation of the public enterprises from Confindustria was a major political issue in the early and middle fifties and represented a concession to the left. As early as 1947 it had been sought by the Socialist Party and by CGIL, and CISL began to lobby for it in 1953. For a time the issue seriously divided the conservative and liberal wings of the Christian Democratic Party, but the party finally adopted a resolution favoring it, and it was approved by a law of December 22, 1956. Although this legislation was regarded at the time as a victory for the left and a defeat for Confindustria, it seems to have settled the issue rather than aggravated it, which suggests that the issue was largely a symbolic one in the first place. In July, 1960, another bargaining association, ASAP,[49] was established to represent the ENI firms. In spite of the political furor that attended the birth of this new independence in bargaining for the public enterprises, or perhaps because of it, the latter continued for some time to meet with Confindustria bargaining committees to negotiate with unions. Not until the metal mechanics negotiations in 1962 did Intersind bargain separately; but it then went further and concluded an agreement granting some important concessions while Confindustria was still holding out.

In that agreement and in others Intersind has displayed an inclination to lead the way in moving Italian industrial relations in the direction of modern practices, especially on such normative questions as the scope, level, and tone of bargaining. In one IRI firm, Italsider (steel production), for example, a recent contract provided for job evaluation, rare in Italian practice. Intersind's leadership in this respect is conceded by Confindustria, which fears the public enterprises may do it, among other reasons, in order to woo labor's political support for a center-left, antimanagement government.

There were other developments in the fifties suggesting that nationwide bargaining would have to be modified to take account of new pressures. As long as the major objective was to set relatively low subsistence minima for all workers through such devices as zone differentials and escalation, intercategory bargaining predominated. This involved the negotiation of minimal standards for all workers. It was nicely suited both to preserve oligarchic control in the management and union organizations and to permit the wide dissemination of extremist ideologies, for it concentrated negotiation, the choice of goals, and the justification and rationalization of actions within the federal union and management hierarchies. Between Feb-

---

[49] Associazione Sindacale fra le Aziende Petrolchimiche e Collegate a Partecipazione Statale.

ruary, 1945, and December, 1954, forty-one interconfederal agreements were concluded. As time passed there was a growing emphasis upon negotiation by categories, and between 1955 and 1958, 120 national agreements in the principal productive sectors were concluded.

With large and uneven increases in productivity and in profits, the unions grew more and more restive with these undiscriminating contracts, however, for they tended to depress negotiated rates, keeping them close to the level the marginal firms could afford. As one study put it, the category contract "visibly demonstrated its incapacity to secure effective participation of the workers in the productivity increases, yielding profit accumulations in 'islands' of the more progressive companies. . . ."[50] Portions of these accumulations were distributed, as noted earlier, through wage drift and through selective price reductions, at the discretion of the individual managements. Bargaining by categories, or by entire industries, maximized managerial discretion as to production methods and plant organization as well, for it permitted the unions to cover or conceal their failure to deal with these matters.

There were reasons, therefore, why both managements and unions should lag in changing the negotiating system; but there were even stronger reasons why the course of events should bring dissatisfaction with the system in the more advanced industrial sectors. These dissatisfactions involve money, but they probably involve the prestige and status of union bureaucracies even more; in the case of the managements of the larger and more efficient firms, they involve the achievement of vital organizational goals.

That the grant of wage increases over the minima set in contracts is in essence unilateral management decision-making has of course long been clear to the Italian unions, and it has been equally clear that this managerial discretion has often been used to manipulate the workers' economic and political loyalties in some arbitrary ways. With the decline in unemployment, moreover, the suspicion has naturally grown that managerial wage pull may not be moving earnings upward as fast or as equitably as union wage push would do it if there were channels available through which to push.

First CISL and later the others have looked in the direction of decentralized bargaining, and especially plant level bargaining.

---

[50] Translated from Giuseppe Ammassari and Gianni Scaiola, "Il 1960: anno di svolta della contrattazione collettiva," *Il Nuovo Osservatore*, 11 (November 10, 1961), 11.

CISL, which has no Socialist tradition, has been pushing in this direction for about ten years, but has begun to have significant success only recently. Some CGIL officials are still ideologically attached to national bargaining, which conforms more closely to the Marxist view of the proper and inevitable role of labor; but they have been forced to follow CISL in demanding plant bargaining for fear of being outpaced, as they were in the 1954 Conglobamento negotiations. UIL, which has no plant level organizations even on paper, and which has done well in shop committee elections at Fiat and elsewhere in recent years, is not formally committed to plant level bargaining, though it publicly favors sector bargaining.

The "sectors" are, in effect, industries: steel, textiles, and so on; and sector level bargaining has become a halfway house to plant bargaining. Many of the category unions have been making separate contracts with different industries while ostensibly engaging in the category bargaining which Confindustria prefers. The unions, and especially CISL, have also been able recently to win agreements in national contracts that specific issues will be remanded for sector level bargaining and that other specific issues, more limited in number, will be remanded to the plant level.

Confindustria has strongly opposed the movement toward plant level bargaining, arguing that there should be similar pay for similar work, that double bargaining is inefficient, and that the large plants would not concede any more than they already do, while the small employers would pay even less. But there are even clearer *organizational* reasons why Confindustria must oppose negotiations at the plant level. Primarily responsive to the needs of the relatively small firms which comprise the great bulk of its membership, the national employers association must try to avoid any institutional change which increases the pressure on these firms to follow the lead of the more advanced sector in paying higher wages. Even more obviously and more immediately, Confindustria loses one of its chief functions and a major channel for influence if collective bargaining is taken out of its hands and carried on by the managements of the various plants.

Given this balance of forces, there was a long period of frustration for CISL, followed in the last three years by a gradual movement toward plant bargaining on the part of those firms most eager to maintain industrial peace and least dependent upon Confindustria. One study by CISL found that while a total of 564 plant level agreements were concluded in the years 1953 through 1957, there were 591 in the year 1960 alone, and that they were concentrated in the most advanced and efficient sectors of the economy.[51]

In their drive for decentralized negotiations the unions have placed major emphasis upon the argument that it will encourage the matching of wage increases to productivity gains in the particular sector or plant. There is a substantial doubt, however, that the instrument necessarily cuts in quite that way. Many negotiations in 1962 and 1963 resulted in wage concessions that went well beyond productivity increases in the companies concerned. Some skill shortages and the rapid decline in unemployment doubtless had more to do with this result than the forum in which bargaining took place. The 1962 metal mechanics settlement with Intersind provided for a 12 per cent increase in the steel industry, where productivity is very high, and for a 10 per cent increase in ship construction, where it is very low. This hardly exemplifies wage increases to match productivity. Apparently a reason for the very small difference was concern in the unions that large differences would generate intra-union antagonisms.

The unions also hope that plant bargaining will give them a voice in such matters as job evaluation, transfers, and working conditions; but the wage question is paramount.

For the larger and more efficient companies, which have been most willing to concede the principle of plant level bargaining, the calculus of what is to be gained or lost from it is clearly different from what it is for marginal firms. The efficient firms have already been paying wages considerably above the contract minima and may well regard a concession on the principle of plant bargaining as predictably inexpensive. These companies also have least need for the solid front Confindustria offers to supply. On the other hand, they have the most to lose from labor unrest: profitable markets abroad and at home and expensive plant lying idle.

In the bitterly fought negotiations over an agreement with the metal mechanics unions in 1962 and 1963, in which plant bargaining was the most controversial issue, it was the IRI firms which settled first, in July, 1962, agreeing to plant bargaining. After the kinds of maneuvering with its unions described above, Fiat reached a settlement, in October, 1962, also agreeing to negotiate at the plant level, and Olivetti signed an identical agreement on the same day.

---

[51] *Ibid.*, pp. 13–17.

These settlements were milestones, for they institutionalized decentralized bargaining for the first time, and the metal mechanics
agreements are closely watched as trend indicators.

The separate settlements and the concession regarding decentralized bargaining shocked and irritated Confindustria and the smaller
firms for which it chiefly speaks. Confindustria itself did not reach a
settlement until more than four months after Fiat and Olivetti had
done so. Some observers believe Confindustria deliberately delayed
a settlement, as a tactic to create a crisis that would be damaging
to the center-left government. It, too, was forced to agree to a measure of decentralized bargaining, though it is far from a full measure.
The contract provides that negotiations will take place at the sector
(industry) level regarding four types of issues: working hours, skill
classification, pay levels, and hazardous work and occupational disease premiums. Plant level bargaining, to be conducted by the provincial headquarters of the unions and the employer's organizations,
is limited to the fixing of production premiums and piece rates. Production premiums, moreover, may not be set outside limits fixed in
the national contract: from 2 to 5 per cent for plants of between 201
and 1,000 workers, and from 4 to 7 per cent for plants of more than
a thousand workers. From the perspective of Confindustria, however, this concession looks like the nose of a camel peeking into
the tent.

The strain between Fiat and Olivetti on the one hand and Confindustria on the other has been considerable. For many years the
metal mechanics have been regarded as an aggressive union, to be
contained wherever possible. The concessions of the industrial giants
threaten the system of stabilizing institutions described earlier, under which the marginal companies have had to grant only minimal
concessions while wages in the more advanced firms could drift
higher without serving as pattern setters.

Indeed, events of the first three years of the 1960's threaten various
other institutions which had fixed the structure and the power relationships in Italian industrial relations during the 1950's. In the middle of the new ferment are the shop committees.[52] During the few
years the Italian labor movement remained united just after the war
it could reasonably be supposed that these committees would serve

[52] Marco Vais, *op. cit.*, p. 33. See also Maurice F. Neufeld, *Labor Unions
and National Politics in Italian Industrial Plants* (Ithaca, N.Y.: Cornell University Press, 1954).

as the local representatives of the union federation. With the splits in the labor movement, however, and the opportunities for maneuver this development gave employers, the shop committees inevitably became an instrument both of intra-union politics and of management-labor conflict, not to say of international relations. Shop committee elections were closely watched as harbingers of political trends, and all of the involved parties did what they could to influence the results and to give them their own interpretations.

As CGIL dominated the important committees in the early fifties, it is understandable that CISL should view them with some suspicion and begin, in 1953, to plan for its own organization of local unions. Despite its short-lived, if much publicized, victory at Fiat in 1954, CISL has maintained this view, while CGIL has come around to something close to it much more recently, though the CGIL leadership is divided on the point.

Among the reasons has been evidence of employer influence in many of the shop committees. The Parliamentary inquiry into working conditions in Italy, in 1958, found ample evidence that Italian management has not neglected this area in its exploration of devices for influencing the labor scene. "Uncooperative" members of shop committees have been fired, and managements have sometimes dealt only with those members of the "right" political persuasion or those they trusted.[53] As noted above, a group of shop committeemen at Fiat seceded from CISL to form a separate union, which is widely regarded as employer dominated. In other cases managements have in effect predetermined the make-up of the shop committee by fragmenting the seats to the point that it would become obvious how relatively small groups or departments of workers had voted.[54] Letters have been sent to employees promising benefits or threatening reprisals depending on who won.[55] Even apart from these crude bludgeons, CISL has argued that the very dependence of committee members upon management for their livelihood, their proximity to management, and their constant exposure to its premises inevitably mean that shop committees will be relatively acquiescent to management wishes and relatively distant from the union.

The problem of the role of shop committees in bargaining came

---

[53] *Relazioni della Commissione Parlamentare di Inchiesta sulle Condizioni dei Lavoratori in Italia*, Vols. V, VI, VII, 1958.

[54] *Ibid.*, pp. 132–133.

[55] *Ibid.*, pp. 87–88, 286–289.

to a head in 1962–63. An important reason for this has been the insistence of CISL that plant bargaining be conducted directly with representatives of the union rather than with the shop committees or selected portions of them. The 1953 interconfederal agreement on shop committees prohibits them from bargaining collectively, but they typically have done so regarding distribution of wages above the national minima and regarding local methods of payment and conditions of work. This bargaining has frequently been only a formality and has really involved unilateral employer concessions: a state of affairs which has heightened feelings on both sides.

UIL is apparently content to have the committees bargain, and Confindustria strongly favors it. Legislation to recognize their right to bargain is pending. As noted above, the 1962 and 1963 metal mechanics agreements included undertakings on the part of the employers to bargain directly with the unions; and one study suggests that the trend has been in that direction for some time.

Table 2-11.[a] Contracting Agents at Plant Level

	Either Union or Committee	Committee	Not Identified
	percentages		
1953–57[b]	49	51	—
As of April 30, 1958[c]	50	44.5	5.5
1960 agreements	63.3	36.7	—

[a] Table from Ammassari and Scaiola (cited in footnote 51), p. 16. Dr. Ammassari informed us in an interview that the formula "either union or committee" has in fact meant that the union has played the chief role in bargaining.
[b] Data from *Proceedings of Third CISL Congress*, Rome, 1959.
[c] From a study of Dr. G. Ammassari.

It is clear enough that the struggle over the role of shop committees is at its heart a struggle over the amount of influence the unions are to have in wage concessions and the organization of work at the plant and firm level. It is therefore a part of the larger struggle over decentralized bargaining. It is equally clear that the positions of the various union and management groups respecting the proper role of shop committees is a function of their current ability to sway the committees and of their hopes of doing so in the future.

That the recent ferment regarding wage concessions and the forum for bargaining has produced rifts within the ranks of management has already been suggested; but the disarray among employer groups calls for further examination, as it has important implications for future wage and price decision-making and for the role government will play in influencing economic developments.

The large, efficient, and increasingly profitable companies like Fiat, Olivetti, and Montecatini have nothing to lose and much to gain from the fact that Confindustria represents primarily the interests of the smaller and less efficient companies. The minimum rates set in national contracts and paid by marginal firms gives the giant companies a bargaining and public relations argument in their dealings with their own unions, makes their much higher pay levels look all the better, and assures them the cream of the labor market. Nor did Confindustria or the smaller companies have much to fear from the arrangement so long as unemployment was substantial, national or industry-wide bargaining was the rule, and wage concessions above the minima were unilaterally determined or sanctified by discussion with shop committees. Under these conditions pattern setting occurred only in local labor markets and for skilled labor if at all, and the unions had little or no power to discriminate among companies in accordance with their respective abilities to pay.

Decentralized bargaining, in a context of markedly less unemployment and more labor turnover, brings some serious anxieties for the less efficient companies, however. It raises the specter that unions will make increased demands upon them. It also threatens the prestige and functions of the Confindustria bureaucracy. Little wonder that Fiat and Olivetti were resented and sometimes spoken of as "traitors" for having settled separately with the metal mechanics in 1962 and especially for having agreed to plant level bargaining. Though Confindustria has authority under its bylaws to expel a member, it is hardly conceivable that it would throw out one of the industrial giants or would gain anything if it did, resentful of them though many members may be. Dues are proportional to employees, and influence doubtless is roughly so too, even though each member company formally has one vote. As a Montecatini official euphemistically put it to us in an interview, "We are all sons of Confindustria, but Montecatini, because of its experience and merit in social affairs, is surely the first born" (translation).

The still earlier settlement with Intersind and the public enterprises in the same dispute highlighted still another fissure in management's ranks. As nearly as we can judge from many discussions of the public enterprises with representatives of private management, both their actual conduct of labor relations and their past role and function in the economy are fairly widely accepted. Personnel officials in the private firms often point out that the managers of the IRI firms were trained in private industry and share its values, and there is no reason to doubt that they are right in this assumption, by and large. Though Intersind and ASAP have often been more willing than private firms to explore new modes of cooperation with unions, this is apparently viewed with tolerance, the assumption being that it is politically necessary for public enterprises, and the hope being that some of these labor relations experiments might even be worth copying. In the context of current industrial relations problems the IRI and ENI companies are not typically regarded as threats.

When the same subject is mentioned in the context of political trends and future economic planning, however, private industry displays considerable anxiety about IRI and ENI. It is then alleged that some of the top management of IRI, if not of the operating companies themselves, is Socialist in ideology. It is alleged that the rapidly increasing state holdings have been a bulwark of the center-left government. It is pointed out that the IRI and ENI firms have made very substantial demands on the capital market during the last three years, limiting the amount of credit available for private use. This basic ambivalence of private industrial management toward the special kind of public enterprise with which Italy is experimenting is visible again and again, and it seems to turn on whether the focus is upon current, concrete economic problems, or on speculation about future political developments. In any case the early Intersind metal mechanics settlement in 1962, the spectacle of a center-left government, and the greatly increased interest in economic planning that characterized the early sixties have for the time being rather underscored the anxious aspect of private management's outlook toward IRI and ENI, widening the cracks in management's collective bargaining front.

In some measure the two breaks from Confindustria just described run into and extend each other, for the most advanced companies have less reason than the small companies to be anxious about the future political role of the public sector. It will be recalled that IRI and ENI are in part privately owned, and profitable private business has substantial stockholdings in them. It will also be recalled that the mounting foreign sales of Fiat, Montecatini, Olivetti, and other Italian products brings in valuable foreign exchange reserves and inevitably gives their manufacturers some influence in government, apart from the other channels of influence they may enjoy.

The student of wage policy must repeatedly be impressed with the key role of uncertainty in both union and management decisions, and this element is especially important in Italy. Flux in economic trends and indicators; unreliable statistics; a marked undersupply of skilled economists and statisticians, especially on the unions' staffs; clashing anticipations and anxieties about the future; a postwar history of quick changes in alliances and antipathies both within the management and union camps and between them; gross social and economic imbalances; and a strong impact from unpredictable foreign developments mean that all the parties must rely on guesswork in their decision-making to a very considerable degree.

Still another contribution to uncertainty of particular importance in Italy is the way bargaining is conducted. Bargaining is part of the culture here, and Italians engage in it with zest every day as they buy and sell. There is a carry-over of this national folkway into collective bargaining, and it shows itself both in the exuberance with which arguments, counter-arguments, and ploys are bandied about and in the enormous difficulty of inferring what the bargainers mean or where their limits are. All bargaining depends to some degree upon feints; but the shouting at Italian bargaining sessions, the inclination of all involved to ignore what the others are saying, and the scepticism with which offers and demands are greeted magnifies the unpredictability, both of the bargainers and of the outcome. One informant with long experience in union-management bargaining here characterized it as unorganized, volatile, and chaotic.

In the end Italian bargaining, like all bargaining, must depend upon the resources and power to exert sanctions at the disposal of the parties; but it must also help keep the rank-and-file union members satisfied and quiescent. To this end CISL makes some show of learning what its members want, sometimes distributing checklists of possible demands for members to fill in. In general terms rank-and-file "wants" at any particular time are fairly predictable, but specific monetary or other claims are often scaled down at union headquarters as unrealistic. None of the Italian unions submit tentative agreements to a rank-and-file referendum.

Though the need for technical aid in bargaining is now clearer than it ever has been, all the unions suffer from a shortage of skilled statisticians, economists, and industrial engineers. The CISL school at Florence has helped somewhat, with the result that its staff experts on such subjects as job evaluation plans have counseled UIL and CGIL unions as well in a number of important negotiations of the early sixties. CISL complains, however, that a high proportion of the best people it trains are lured away by the higher salaries offered by large companies. In spite of this fact, Italian management in general also lacks the kind of technical help which American management takes for granted. It does not seem to lack legal help, however; and legalism is a favorite keynote of management bargaining.

Negotiators and drafters of collective agreements are always aware that the agreement is a tool of communication and of reassurance as well as a legal document. Italian labor agreements are long, discursive, and repetitive: because it is often advisable to placate a group or mollify a fear by inserting some language that will make people feel better even if it is not wholly necessary or pertinent.

With the continued growth in productivity, the decline in unemployment, and the consequent tendency in the early 1960's for wage concessions to be substantial and even to surpass productivity increases in some cases, the unions face a new political dilemma. This is public anxiety that wage increases are a major reason for the steep price boosts of the last several years. Such public sentiment, they fear, will incline employers to resist wage demands more resolutely than they otherwise would, even when, in the unions' view, they have little financial reason to resist them. They are also afraid that the government will impose direct controls on wages if the inflation is not checked.

As a response to this dilemma CISL has espoused a tactic to which unions in some other countries have also turned when inflation is widely feared: a proposal that a part of new wage gains be placed in savings accounts.

The formula was actually first conceived in 1956, at which time the government was also looking for a way to block wages for fear of inflation. Under the CISL proposal, the savings would remain the worker's property but would be invested in accordance with a national economic program to help underdeveloped areas and otherwise eliminate basic economic imbalances in Italy. The plan has been revived with the sharp wage-price increases of the early sixties, but shows little sign of making headway with employers, government, or even CGIL or UIL. One top UIL official has claimed that the plan would be unfair and unpopular with workers except possibly when inflation is an immediate danger, and that a union which helped administer it would probably be both a bad entrepreneur and a bad union. CISL itself declares it would not accept the plan unless the other unions did so. There is reason to suspect that one of its main values is to suggest to employers that generous wage concessions may be cheaper for them than tough resistance that might bring more complicated pressures into play.

This review of the bases for management and union decisions respecting wages suggests some hypotheses, of which the following are probably the most striking: (1) the level at which bargaining has taken place and the structures and procedures for bargaining have more often been the consequences of economic trends than influences upon those trends; (2) these structures, and the wage decisions themselves, have reflected the diverse pressures upon efficient and marginal companies and have been ingeniously adapted to serve the respective interests of both the efficient and the marginal companies; (3) wage drift and wage pull have been more conspicuous in the postwar Italian economy than wage push, if the latter term is taken to imply the exertion of union pressure that is resisted by management; (4) wage drift has been effectively utilized by the larger and more advanced companies to influence support for particular unions and to induce quiescence in their work forces; (5) the polarization of political opinion in Italy has been effectively utilized by some large companies for the same purposes; and (6) a major function of bargaining itself has been the inducement of quiescence in rank-and-file workers and of a feeling of participation on the part of union officials.

IV

For a short period of time, and for a few commodities at other times, the Italian government has resorted to direct controls. During the severe inflation of 1946 and 1947 ceilings were placed upon prices and wages as described early in this chapter. This action was a response to an abnormal and exaggerated price surge, and it was politically feasible because of public anxiety about the situation and the future. It is not clear that it had a significant impact upon prices paid in view of the extensive black market that developed. In such situations, however, every government has turned to some form of direct control. It is apparently a political necessity whether or not it is the only, or the most effective, economic alternative.

Because direct controls depend upon the compliance of a mass public of buyers and sellers or of employers and wage earners, their effectiveness must always be a function of the incentives of these groups to comply with them or violate them. Given a strong effective demand for goods or labor and a limited supply, the incentive to participate in black markets is correspondingly strong. And it is all the stronger where, as in Italy, suspicion of government and of law is intense and widespread. In the postwar Italian inflation the supply of goods on the commodity markets was far smaller than the effective demand (even though that demand was relatively concentrated in the more prosperous sector of the population). Hence the black market. The labor supply, on the other hand, was large in relation to demand, and unions were weak. Hence there was no problem in maintaining low wages, with or without controls.

When we consider the other direct controls with which Italy has experimented, however, we see different patterns of mass support and therefore different compliance patterns. Easily the most important of these has been the rent control law, under which the rents of many old houses have been held under very low ceilings since the war. Small increases in controlled rents have been allowed each year, but in 1963 about one-quarter of the dwelling units were still under control and still markedly under the market price. As a result of the periodic increases, rents sustained by far the largest increase of any component in the postwar period.

Between 1953 and 1958, for example, Italian rents increased 85 per cent while food was increasing 10 per cent, household and durable goods 9 per cent, and clothing not at all.[56] It should be noticed, however, that in 1949, when other prices were about fifty times their prewar level, rents had reached only five times that level, so that the postwar increases can be understood as a very slow catching up with other prices.

These increases in controlled rents have accordingly had a marked impact upon the cost of living index, accounting for a substantial part of the rise it recorded before 1961. They had an even more important upward influence upon the sliding scale index, which is used to compute wage increases under the automatic escalation agree-

---

[56] Fellner, *op. cit.*, p. 97.

ments, for the sliding scale index takes account only of controlled rents. As the rents of uncontrolled houses remained fairly stationary until 1962, workers living in uncontrolled houses have enjoyed disproportionately large wage gains under the sliding scale clauses.[57]

Direct controls on rents have, then, apparently been effective, but the incentives to comply with them have been stronger than was the case under the general price control law of 1946–47. The key differences were these: (1) Many landlords could not have found tenants at high rentals; a large proportion of the population simply cannot afford to pay much for housing. The number of housing units the prosperous want to rent is limited, while their demand for other goods, even at high prices, is much less limited. (2) A substantial and increasing number of housing units have not been controlled, providing a legal market for those who might otherwise have created a black market. (3) Controlled rents have gradually been increased, diluting the pressure to violate ceilings.

A third kind of direct controls has involved still another public purpose and still another pattern of mass response. An Interministerial Committee on Prices[58] (CIP), established by law number 347 of 1944, was authorized to fix the prices of goods in any phase of the distribution process, including import and export, and also the prices of services and performances. Its authority has gradually been limited. It has actually set maximum rates for public utilities, for a variety of industrial products including solid and liquid fuels, cement, glass, newspapers and periodicals, and pharmaceuticals, and for such farm products as grain, rice, sugar beets, and sugar. The beet prices, fixed in 1959 and 1960, are not only maxima but minima; but this is exceptional.

The committee's legal mandate gives it wide leeway in determining which prices to control and where to set ceilings. It has plainly responded to different pressures and problems in the case of different commodities, and few Italians, even those concerned with its policies, seem to know what its criteria have been. So far as many products are concerned, its regulatory activities have apparently been only nominal, for the belief is common that the committee's staff has relied heavily or entirely upon the cost figures and other data sub-

---

[57] Lutz, op. cit., p. 218.

[58] Commissione Interministeriale per i Prezzi. It includes the Prime Minister, the Ministers of Finance, Treasury, Agriculture and Forests, Transport, Industry and Commerce, Public Works, Labor and Social Welfare, Foreign Commerce, Budget, State Holdings, and three appointive experts.

mitted by manufacturers. Spokesmen for Confindustria claim that some prices CIP "controls" woud be lower without the governmental authorization for ceilings. They also claim that CIP regulations serve a political purpose by permitting the government to allege in Parliament that the prices of medicines, oil, and other products whose prices are politically sensitive are under close surveillance.

In the case of cement the efficient manufacturers have refrained from forcing their small, marginal competitors out of business, which they could easily do through temporary price cuts, because CIP uses the marginal firms' cost figures in establishing its ceilings. The marginal firms thus play a role that is chiefly political rather than economic, making it politically feasible to keep prices above the point at which the "regulatory" agency would otherwise set them.[59]

In the case of oil there apparently is real control, and the industry has lately been demanding that CIP state the basis upon which it sets its prices. Some authorities in this field believe that the ceilings have served to force the parent international oil companies to sell to their Italian affiliates at reduced prices.

In the case of rates charged for utilities and transport the increases of the 1950's should be seen in the same light as the increases in controlled rents: delayed release of the suppressed effects of past inflation.

For the most part CIP's actions are justified on the ground that there are elements of monopoly in the prices it regulates. It has not been looked upon as an instrument for the control of inflation as such. From the point of view of its role in overall price policy, it seems to serve a function commonly performed by antimonopoly agencies in some other countries. It provides reassurance for people concerned about the prices of some vital commodities: especially medicines, newspapers, oil, and public utilities. It seems to have made it easier or "politic" at times for particular sellers to charge prices which might have called forth public protests if they had not been sanctioned by an official agency.[60]

Unlike rents, the products whose prices CIP has regulated do not ordinarily use up a substantial portion of any consumer's income,

---

[59] Luigi Mazzillo, "Un'indagine 'sovversiva,'" Nord e Sud, X (February, 1963), 79.

[60] Cf. Murray Edelman, "Symbols and Political Quiescence," American Political Science Review, 65 (September, 1960), 695–704.

and so consumers do not engage in massive political protest about them if there is a show of governmental surveillance.

The only direct controls upon wages currently in force are minima, not ceilings, and they raise an issue rather than settle it. Law number 741, of July, 1959, authorized the government to extend the collective agreements in force at the beginning of October of that year to all employers and workers of the same category, except where other contracts, including future ones, would provide the workers with greater benefits. A subsequent decision of the Constitutional Court made future extensions of contracts invalid, however. The issue remains a live one.

The impetus for such legislation comes chiefly from the desire to give some protection to unorganized workers in the economically backward areas. The CISL staff opposes this "ergo omnes" approach, evidently fearing it would lessen the incentive of the unorganized to join a union. This position is consistent with CISL's opposition to national contracts that set minimum rates. It also reflects anxiety about Article 39 of the Italian Constitution, which gives unions a "juridical personality" and also authorizes the extension of collective agreements to all workers of the same category. Article 39, however, has never been implemented by legislation and so has no legal effect. In CISL's view it should remain a dead letter for it threatens to impose unwelcome public controls upon unions. CISL prefers a minimum wage law.

UIL favors "ergo omnes," arguing that a minimum wage law is suitable for highly developed countries, but not for Italy, where more sensitive adaptation to local conditions is called for.

For another group of underpaid workers, even more clearly requiring protection than the unorganized employees of marginal firms, the state has acted. A law of March, 1958, tried to do something for outworkers, requiring that they be hired through employment offices, that they be paid piece rates equivalent to those of comparable in-plant workers, and that they receive some types of social insurance benefits, though not family allowances. It is worth noting that these notoriously poorly treated workers of the "grey" labor market received this token public protection only late in the decade of the economic miracle. As wage levels rise and unemployment begins to decline, the contrast between the better paid and the weakest segment of the labor force becomes more conspicuous and the probability grows that the spectacle will generate protective legislation: particularly as more employers can afford to pay legal minima and outworkers are harder to find.

Clearly, resort to direct controls in Italy has been a response to several different types of political claims or pressures, and the various postwar direct control programs have also been quite unlike each other in the measure of compliance they elicited. In no case has the mere fact that a law has been passed brought compliance. Always it has been other incentives, chiefly economic, that have explained people's behavior; in some instances the imposition of direct controls and the publicity attending their administration has served chiefly to reassure a mass public, thereby permitting wider freedom of maneuver for those in a position directly to increase prices.

V

If direct controls served to deal with some special wage-price problems, Italy has relied on indirect controls for the general and continuing regulation of the pace of its postwar economy. If direct controls have depended for their effectiveness upon the incentives of the mass public to comply with them, indirect controls have been more potent precisely because the mass public could not directly influence their effectiveness. In short, the "controls" of which we speak involve not only regulation *of* the public but regulation *by* the public; it is this latter aspect that gives them their political dynamism.

The severe monetary controls with which Luigi Einaudi brought the 1946–47 inflation to a halt set a precedent which has influenced the Bank of Italy and the Interministerial Committee on Credit and Savings ever since. In 1947 the immediate need was to curb liquidity and keep it limited, and this was the objective sought by Giuseppe Pella, Einaudi's successor as Budget Minister, and by Donato Urenichella, Governor of the Bank of Italy, in the subsequent years. Given the extremely high unemployment levels of that period, it was natural enough that the "Pella line" of a hard money policy should be attacked as contributing to the maintenance of unemployment.

Inflation, on the other hand, has remained a constant possibility throughout the postwar years, and the Italian monetary authorities have tailored their acts to the danger. This posture has been politically feasible chiefly because it has been possible to pursue it even while the condition of a large segment of the population continued to improve. For reasons analyzed earlier (especially excess productive capacity in some lines and a strong foreign and domestic demand for Italian goods), production, productivity, and national income increased at very fast rates in spite of monetary controls. If the controls could be thought to hurt anyone, it was the unemployed and those attached to the backward sectors of the economy; but these people did not control enough Parliamentary seats to threaten the center coalition. The votes of these deprived groups went largely to the Communists and the Socialists, who were not in the government.[61] In short, disparity in the distribution of economic progress was matched by polarization between center and left in the popular vote.

A major reason the monetary authorities were so sensitive to the possibility of inflation in the fifties was the serious deficiency of capital from which Italian industry suffered. Because of the need to modernize, to build industrial plant and housing, and meet the demand for Italian goods, there was a "hunger for investible savings," as Hildebrand put it, and this in turn made for high interest rates and a strong demand for bank credit and for imports.[62]

The Bank of Italy has relied chiefly on reserve requirements and controls over the credit activities of the banks to control liquidity. Between the Einaudi reform of 1947 and January, 1962, the reserve rate was maintained at 25 per cent. Einaudi had made vigorous use of the central bank's legal powers to restrain loans by lending banks. In the years of rapid expansion of the economy, moral suasion to exercise restraint in granting credit and in seeking and issuing short term foreign funds sufficed, doubtless because it was clear that compulsion could be used if necessary. The issuance of government bonds was also carefully planned in line with the market's liquidity position.

The Italian money market was until late 1962 almost entirely an interbank exchange and not a market analogous to those in other EEC countries. In consequence the Bank of Italy's controls over the banks' lending operations were the more adequate, and there were no effective open market operations. Nor has there been much re-

---

[61] Cf. Murray Edelman, "Causes of Fluctuations in Popular Support for the Italian Communist Party Since 1946," *Journal of Politics*, 20 (March, 1958), 535–552.

[62] George H. Hildebrand, "Postwar Italy: A Study in Economic Contrasts," *Italian Quarterly*, 1 (Fall, 1957), 60.

course to discount policy. By 1962 the discount rate had been modified only four times since the end of the war, as compared to seventeen times in France and twenty-four times in Germany.[63]

In some other countries with which we are concerned, notably
Britain and the Netherlands, balance of payment deficits have required drastic state intervention in the domestic price and credit
system; but until 1963 Italy did not have this problem, partly because
of careful monetary surveillance, but chiefly because of good fortune
in its foreign markets and exchange arrangements. Foreign trade

Table 2-12.[a] Balance of Payments (billions of lire, current prices)

	Exports			Imports			
	Total Goods and Services	Transfers Abroad	Balance	Total Goods and Services	Transfers from Abroad	Balance	Final Balance
1954	1433	10	1423	1678	210	1468	—45
1955	1620	10	1610	1853	215	1638	—28
1956	1923	12	1911	2173	208	1965	—54
1957	2373	17	2356	2560	226	2334	22
1958	2467	14	2453	2338	234	2104	349
1959	2755	17	2738	2451	185	2266	472
1960	3357	11	3346	3351	214	3137	209
1961	3886	7	3879	3751	215	3536	343
1962	4337	28	4309	4389	—	—	—

ᵃ Table from ISTAT and SVIMEZ.

contributed a great deal to the rapid increase in national income
both because of a generally faster rise in price levels abroad than
in Italy and because changing consumer tastes increased the demand for the very products Italy was able to export.

Until 1958 a trade deficit was partly offset by the invisible transactions that have long been important in Italy: tourism and emi-
grants' remittances. From 1958 to late 1962 there was a surplus in
the goods and services account due to the steep increase in exports.

Besides the controls on bank credit already noted, the chief mone-

[63] For good reviews of postwar monetary policy, see Paolo Baffi, *op. cit.*;
CEE, *Gli Strumenti della Politica Monetaria nei Paesi della Communità Econo-
mica Europea, op. cit.*; Lutz, *op. cit.*, Chap. 14; Francesco Masera, "Recent
Developments in the Italian Balance of Payments," *Review of the Economic
Conditions in Italy*, XVI (November, 1962), 497–509.

tary weapon the authorities have used to influence price levels and the pace of economic activity has been the policy of building up foreign reserves to a relatively high level. In the early years after the postwar inflation Italy was eager to build up its reserves from the very low level they had reached in 1947, and the rapidly accumulated reserves served as a buffer against drains arising from conditions outside the country and outside its control. Another factor that has done a great deal to protect Italy from the effects of adverse economic changes abroad is the low ratio that Italian exports bear to gross national income. In 1960 exports constituted only 16 per cent of gross national income in Italy as against 25 per cent in Germany and 50 per cent in the Netherlands. By the middle fifties reserves had reached a substantial level, but the policy of caution was continued as a general anti-inflation policy.

It should be recalled that this policy of controlling inflation through monetary policy was probably as successful as it was for about fifteen years chiefly because of some special structural factors reviewed early in this chapter, notably the oversupply of labor, the drag upon wages and prices of economic disequilibria and inefficiency in the underdeveloped areas, and unusually rapid technical progress in petrochemicals, engineering, electronics, and some other industries.

In the early years of the sixties monetary policy has had to be used for some new objectives and has had to become more flexible and more vigorous than it had been throughout the fifties. A slowing down of economic activity in 1957–58, followed by increased wage pressure, a narrowing of profit margins, erosion of internal investment funds, and a diminution of the postwar boom in other European countries led to measures to insure against deflation: a liberalization of capital movements and an easing of credit. As noted earlier, the ratio of obligatory reserves was reduced in January, 1962: from 25 per cent to 22.5 per cent. This was one of a number of measures to maintain bank liquidity at a desirable level. The banks have also been allowed to use the proceeds of funds borrowed abroad for internal financing, a reversal of the policy of building up foreign reserves. The new monetary directions coincided with the appointment in 1960 of a new governor of the Bank of Italy, Guido Carli.

As late as November, 1962, the Bank of Italy was still pumping liquidity into the lending banks and helping rechannel their excess liquidity into the capital market, even though businessmen opposed this policy. The governor of the bank was sympathetic to the income redistribution plans of the center-left. The increased wage concessions of 1962 had indeed helped produce such a redistribution. Fifty-seven per cent of the increase in national income in 1961 went into wages, and in 1962 this figure had jumped to 72.5 per cent.[64] Even though prices continued to rise fairly steeply for some time, the Bank of Italy was encouraged to resist business demands and continue a "soft money" policy by the fact that there was still some unemployment, a balance of payments surplus, and a fairly high rate of private savings.

By the late spring of 1963, however, the continuing rise in prices and wages and a marked change in the balance of payments situation had brought the governor of the bank around to a more conservative position. In his annual speech to the assembly of shareholders in the bank on May 31, 1963, Dr. Carli called for a national incomes policy and especially for immediate restraint in granting wage increases. He pointed with some alarm to the recent history of wage increases surpassing productivity gains, to the erosion of business profit margins and financial reserves, to increasing demand flowing from the wage increases, and to growing difficulty in finding credit and in expanding productive facilities. Rising prices had made it harder for Italian products to compete in international markets. Between September 1, 1962, and October 1, 1963, the balance of payments deficit on current account amounted to 225 billion lire.

Dr. Carli laid considerable blame for the worsening situation upon the expanding operations of the government enterprises and ministries and upon their wage concessions.

It was no surprise to anyone that Confindustria spokesmen hailed the new Bank of Italy line as a return to sound doctrine while Budget Minister La Malfa hastened to point out to the public that Dr. Carli had proved the need for economic programming.[65]

In the formulation of monetary policy there is no formal consultation with industry, though business views are indirectly represented by some of the Ministers who serve on the Interministerial Committee on Credit and Savings. Nonetheless Confindustria has at times complained that its monetary and credit proposals have not been

---

[64] Ministro del Bilancio, *Il Bilancio Economico Nazionale* (Rome, 1963), p. 63.

[65] *Il Messaggero*, June 1, 1963; *The Economist*, June 8, 1963, p. 1047.

heeded in spite of repeated interventions.[66] The unions are even further removed from any influence in monetary policy, for they lack formal or informal access to the Bank of Italy, and those who are most influential in formulating policy do not come from the social, economic, or political circles familiar with union and labor problems from the worker's point of view. Some CISL officials have begun recently to recognize that the unions' exclusion from the making of monetary policy excludes them from one of the more potent influences upon real wage levels.

Because monetary policy does not involve dramatic and direct engagement with the economic problems that bother people and affect their votes, it is not a politically adequate device to deal with surging restiveness about prices or income, regardless of its economic potency. The steeply rising consumer prices of 1962–63 posed a serious dilemma for the parties participating in the center-left government, especially as a Parliamentary election was scheduled for April, 1963. The government tried to meet it in the months preceding election day with a series of measures that would bring food prices down quickly and that would be widely regarded as resolute action in the public interest. In February it announced a series of measures to increase imports of food: the abolition, suspension or reduction of tariffs and import quotas on fish, meats, eggs, butter, olive oil, and fruits and vegetables.[67] Through March and April additional imports were encouraged.

Though the increased supplies of goods on the market did depress wholesale prices, they had little effect on retail prices, except for eggs. Their major result was therefore to increase the take of middlemen and not to reduce the embarrassment of the government. Large quantities of imported butter were stored in refrigerators pending the day the market supply would be smaller and the price still higher. It was reported to the cabinet that customs officers at the borders were confiscating or refusing admittance to hundreds of thousands of liters of olive oil because they had not heard about the liberalized customs regulations. Jugoslav, Danish, and Dutch meat, imported at low prices, magically became Italian meat on the butcher's shelves and was offered at the same old Italian prices. A few cities tried to limit the spread between wholesale and retail prices; but an incred-

---

[66] Confindustria, *Relazione All'Assemblea dei Delegati Delle Associazioni Aderenti*, February 28, 1963 (Rome, 1963), p. 152.

[67] *Rome Daily American*, February 20, 1963.

ibly complex and inefficient distribution system succeeded almost everywhere in defeating the government's efforts to control the cost of living.[68] Post-election analyses of the vote attributed a substantial portion of the Christian Democratic losses and the Communist gains to the defection of housewives concerned about mounting living costs.

Prices and wages continued to climb rapidly. Not until the inflationary situation had grown very serious early in 1964 was it politically possible for the shaky center-left coalition to take sufficiently decisive action to have any hope of really restoring stability. By that time unit labor costs had increased 8 per cent in 1962 and a further 10 per cent in 1963. The government action, when it finally came, took the form of increased taxes on some key commodities, especially automobiles, tight credit limitations, and proposed restrictions on hire-purchase sales.

Except for the measures already described relating to the autonomous corporations, the Italian government has not used wage policy in the public sector to try to influence wage levels generally. The effort throughout the postwar period, rather, has been to raise the salaries of public employees and institute other personnel reforms so as to make employment attractive to competent people.

In November, 1954, there were 824,928 public employees, including teachers and university professors but excluding the autonomous corporations. They constituted only 1.7 per cent of the labor force. In July, 1963, DIRSTAT, the union of supervisory officials in the public service, had 31,000 members and Constat, the union of public salaried employees, 880,000, not including teachers or the employees of the autonomous corporations.[69]

Italian public administration is antiquated in its procedures and structure and in need of reorganization. A Parliamentary Commission for Reform of the Public Administration was at work in 1962 and 1963. Among its conclusions especially pertinent to this inquiry was the finding that because of low salaries and slow promotion the government agencies could not attract the professional personnel they needed. University graduates in law, economics, and political science were among those in shortest supply. In the years 1959 through 1961 the Finance Ministry could fill only 27 per cent of the

---

[68] *Il Messaggero*, March 21, 1963, and March 22, 1963.
[69] *Ibid.*, July 28, 1963.

positions it opened to competition; the Ministry of Labor and Public Welfare, 45 per cent; the Treasury Ministry, 75 per cent.[70]

Because the salaries of government employees were extremely low relative to those in comparable private jobs in 1950, they were deliberately increased much faster in the following decade. Between 1950 and 1959, wage rates in the public sector increased 95.6 per cent while those in private industry rose by 49.7 per cent and those in commerce by 48.3 per cent.[71] Public employees received further substantial increases from the center-left government in 1962; and in 1963 their unions were pressing hard for additional raises to bring salaries into line with the still much higher ones in the autonomous corporations, for incorporating various special indemnities into the basic wage structure (conglobamento), and for administrative reforms to encourage careers in public administration.

VI

Fiscal policy has been used in a major way in postwar Italy to encourage economic growth and stimulate investment in the South, and it has been used in a minor way to redistribute income; but it has not been viewed as a significant device for wage or price control.

Budget deficits have occurred in every postwar year. Between 1951–52 and 1958–59 the general trend was toward slightly smaller deficits each year, an end then sought by Treasury policy. In 1959–60 there was a substantial jump in the size of the deficit, chiefly because of larger public expenditures following signs of a business letdown in 1957–58. The deficit has remained at a high level since that time, with expenditures for public investment consistently very high and current government spending also growing. The surplus of public investment over the amount of the deficit has, however, been increasing: evidence that the deficit has been incurred chiefly to create long-term assets.

The 1961 report of the Bank of Italy notes, with apparent equanimity, that, "larger deficits have come to stay," [72] and this tolerant attitude toward deficits is shared, we are assured, by the public in

---

[70] *Ibid.*, May 4, 1963.

[71] Vera Cao Pina, "Interviste," *Il Nuovo Osservatore*, 4 (May, 1963), 435 (data based upon SVIMEZ calculations).

[72] Banca D'Italia, *Abridged Version of the Report for the Year 1961* (Rome: Banca D'Italia, 1962), p. 35.

general and even by management groups. Deficit financing has not been made a political issue in Italy.

In the early sixties the government was committing itself more often to public expenditures to be spread over several years, the chief beneficiaries being agriculture, transport, housing, and schools. In addition, the demands of the state enterprises upon the capital market have been rising. ENI and IRI planned to invest 3,094 billion lire between 1963 and 1966, nearly as much as the two invested in the entire decade between 1953 and 1962.[73] These fiscal policies have their consequences not only in aid to some undernourished sectors of the economy but also, many observers believe, in greater political influence for the public enterprises. During the year 1962 alone the IRI firms increased their investments by 22.3 per cent and ENI by 57.7 per cent.[74]

The tax system has not been used as an anti-inflationary measure, even in 1946–47, when the incentive to do so was greatest. It has been used to stimulate growth, notably in the early fifties, when faster depreciation write-offs were permitted. A tax on all business transactions provides for lump sum rebates for exports, and it is generally thought that this provision has successfully stimulated exports. There have also been substantial tax inducements to the industrialization of southern and insular Italy and to help small- and medium-size industry in general. The incentive to form corporations to avoid the personal income tax has also stimulated growth, for the capital of the corporations has been invested.

The tax system as a whole is quite regressive, though a number of reform laws have been enacted in the postwar period, notably in 1954 and 1962. In 1954 an additional corporation tax was imposed, and efforts were made to make the individual income tax rates more realistic in the hope of reducing evasion, which is very high at all income levels. The 1954 reform of the rate structure had the effect of relieving the lower and upper levels somewhat, but did little for the middle income groups. A law of April, 1962, made the rates graduate more steeply, raising the top rate (on taxable incomes over 500 million lire) from 50 to 65 per cent.

The authority of the Ministry of Labor to mediate labor disputes

---

[73] Report cited in footnote 72, p. 71. See also *The Economist* (May 25, 1963), p. 809.

[74] *Rome Daily American, Annual Business Review*, February 24–25, 1963, p. 5.

has also indirectly influenced wage levels, but hardly to maintain stability. The Ministry may intervene in a dispute on the request of either party, though it is usually the unions that request it. Because the Ministry is strongly preoccupied with maintaining public order and avoiding the street demonstrations common in Italian strikes, its intervention has usually had the effect of placating the unions by granting them more than they might otherwise have won. Its interest in workers' votes pushes the Ministry in the same direction.

Until 1962, high Italian governmental officials made little serious effort to curb price and wage increases through exhortation, as was common in other countries. Governor Guido Carli of the Bank of Italy spoke and wrote occasionally about this threat, but his utterances did not evoke discussion until 1963. Prime Minister Fanfani and Budget Minister La Malfa sometimes urged restraint in public speeches in 1962 and 1963. In the summer of 1963 officials of the Leone government stepped up top level exhortations and warnings regarding the wage-price spiral, even warning of "drastic intervention" if it did not stop.

VII

A number of the economic and political developments traced here converged in the early 1960's to create an interest in national economic programming and the beginnings of an organization for programming. New alliances, new schisms, new strategies, and new goals are appearing in the old power and decision centers: in industry, unions, parties, and the government. Many of the new interest groupings cut across the old associational lines. This makes for a closer community of interest on wage policy, for example, between some unions and some large companies than exists between large companies and the small firms who are their fellow members of Confindustria. It makes for a measure of common interest in economic programming between the liberal wing of the Christian Democratic Party and the Socialist Party, even while it widens the fissures within the Christian Democratic Party.

At the same time it has become clearer and clearer that the existing decision-making structure frustrates the achievement of some important goals. Wage concessions are wiped out by price increases over which the unions have no influence. The penetration of inviting foreign markets is impeded by capital shortages, skill shortages, or other economic imbalances over which even the largest companies have little control. An archaic distribution mechanism nullifies price control programs and hurts the governing parties.

The inevitable result of these developments has been that emerging groups in all the old organizations are groping for a new decision-making structure: a structure comprehensive enough in scope to deal with the intertwined economic, social, and political dilemmas of contemporary Italy. To review the interests for and against economic planning is therefore to summarize the institutional changes with which this chapter has dealt.

Management is divided on the issue. Confindustria opposes it. The typical Confindustria member fears it is a step toward nationalization or iron control of industry by the state, and the association's bureaucracy would lose influence and prestige. At the same time Confindustria appears to recognize that a certain measure of programming is inevitable as a way of dealing with economic imbalances in Italy and of operating within the Common Market, and much of the association's energies go into arguing that any planning be of the "indicative" or advisory sort rather than compulsory. In all management groups the word "programming" is more acceptable than "planning," which has Marxist connotations.

Fiat, Montecantini, Olivetti, and the other industrial giants favor "programmazione," on the other hand. Such companies need a stable environment in which long-term commitments can be made with some confidence that public policy, union power, and other industries' activities will not hurt the firm. Until recently there was little ground for concern because of the economic miracle, the feebleness of union bargaining power, and conservative governments. In all these respects the Italian environment is changing or may soon change. The Common Market especially offers a long-term challenge and opportunity, and also invites joint planning with other member countries. For all these reasons management requires greater ability to make economic and political forecasts, and it also needs technical and entrepreneurial skills and a better developed economic infrastructure. The industrial giants do not really fear a center-left government which would put programming into effect, for they are sure they can control it when they want to. As one well-informed economist and member of the National Economic Planning Commission put it to us, "With two or three phone calls they can veto the appointment of a cabinet minister."

The national economic planning these industrialists favor is the French kind, in which industry has had the major influence. At the same time it suits their purpose to keep Confindustria opposed, for in the negotiations with the Socialists and others who favor a more thorough kind of planning, including sanctions, Confindustria's opposition gives the advanced companies added bargaining power and maneuverability.

The public enterprises, including IRI, ENI, and the agricultural syndicates (Federconsorzi), have long been attached to the idea of planning and do it themselves in their own respective areas of operation. They have unquestionably been among the most effective pressures toward planning. This is true not of those who direct the day to day operations of the various firms, but rather of an important segment of the top management of the public holding companies. One way in which they have most notably planned is in occupying fields which private industry has neglected, such as fertilizers and oil prospecting and refining in the case of ENI. The ability of cabinets and Parliaments to use IRI to help develop the South and improve transportation is also in point.

Among the unions, CISL and UIL are both inclined to favor planning, though with some important caveats. There is much denunciation by union spokesmen of the French form of planning, and one of the more articulate of these has alleged that it incorporates three illusions: that there can be a "third way" between an advisory and a required program, that the traditional incentives to serve the public interest can be efficacious for large companies operating through autofinancing, and that partial and contingent objectives will do.[75] This line highlights a suspicion which is growing in importance among the younger staff leadership of CISL and UIL: that decisive economic policies are made in industrial, banking, and governmental forums from which the unions are excluded, and that only through new decision-making machinery can they hope to gain a voice.[76] The second union reservation, and the one that carries more weight with the rank-and-file members, is fear that planning may mean unwelcome controls upon wage increases.

CGIL is divided on the issue, chiefly because the Communist and Socialist parties do not see eye to eye on it.

---

[75] Franco Simoncini, "La Programmazione degli 'Anni Sessanta,' " *Quaderni del Sindacato*, I (January 31, 1963), 4–9.

[76] Franco Simoncini, *Il Sindacato e la Politica di Piano* (Rome: UIL, 1962).

The Communists have been distant and ambivalent in their attitude, opposing a center-left program from which they are excluded, yet sometimes hoping they may gain some influence in a national plan.

The strongest support for a far-reaching plan that would set imperative objectives and operations comes from an important group of Socialists led by Riccardo Lombardi. These men see planning as a movement with emotional appeal, and apart from their ideological support for it, they expect that it will have political effects beneficial to the Socialist Party. A more conservative group in the PSI shares the position of the Republicans, Social Democrats, and the liberal wing of the Christian Democrats. All these look upon "programmazione" as the only device through which the economy can be reconstructed in a fundamental and rational way and the gross disparities in industrialization, education, and income be overcome. They are "politic" rather than doctrinaire in approach, however, taking it for granted that the details of a planning program must be worked out through political give and take. Representative of this grouping are Saragat, La Malfa, and Fanfani.

The Liberals and conservative Christian Democrats, represented by Malagodi and Scelba, oppose planning on doctrinaire laissez-faire grounds and for much the same reasons that Confindustria opposes it. It is noticeable, however, that there are occasional defections from this group on the part of politicians, journalists, and technicians whose activities bring them close to the large industrial firms.

In spite of the broad range of support for some form of programming since at least the middle fifties, it was politically impossible to take any meaningful steps toward it until 1962. The basic reason for the long years of impasse was the unwillingness of the Socialist Party to break with the Communists and thus make it possible to form a government of the moderate left interested in planning. The Socialists' hesitation was partly due in turn to the unwillingness of the conservative Christian Democrats to support an "opening to the left." The result was that for some fifteen years the approximately 35 per cent of the Italian electorate that voted Socialist or Communist was not represented in the executive branch of the government or in the formulation of policies that had some chance of being enacted. By the same token the liberal planks supported by Social Democrats, Republicans, and Christian Democrats usually came to little. The Vanoni Plan, mentioned earlier, is a case in point.

The impasse was finally broken when Pietro Nenni finally did agree to support a center-left government on key Parliamentary votes, though without participating in the cabinet. The Fanfani government ended with the election of April, 1963, in which the Christian Democratic Party lost strength and the Communists and Liberals gained strength. In the subsequent effort to form another center-left government a majority of the Socialist Party's executive board displayed marked suspicion of the Christian Democrats and hesitated to continue its support, demanding clearer commitments to economic reform and programming. To some extent the Socialists' hesitancy was also due to lingering ties to the Communists, strengthened at least temporarily by the election results. The Communists took advantage of their gains to step up attacks on the center parties, and there was evidence that CGIL strikes and demonstrations in the months following the election were intended at least in part to support this political tactic. At the same time some friction continued between Communists and the more moderate Socialist elements in CGIL.

Clearly, the appeal of the left is still a major factor in Italy, and it will not be easy to find a viable formula for continuing cooperation between center and left. Periodic friction is certain, but there is hardly a stable political alternative to a center-left government. Such a government was formed under Premier Aldo Moro in the fall of 1963 with the active participation of the Socialist Party, even though that party's decision to accept ministerial posts led to the secession of a substantial minority of its more leftist members.

Soon after forming his government in March, 1962, Premier Amintore Fanfani announced the appointment of an Economic Programming Commission [77] to work out the general lines of a program for national economic development. The Budget Minister is chairman of the commission, which includes twelve ministers; the presidents of the peak management, labor, and agricultural organizations; lower level representatives of management and labor; the Governor of the Bank of Italy; political supporters and critics of the current planning proposals; and a working staff under the direction of the commission's vice-chairman and a noted economist, Professor Pasquale Saraceno. The commission thus reflects in its membership and staff all the currents and shadings of opinion regarding planning described above.

---

[77] Commissione Nazionale per la Programmazione Economica.

It is believed that the Premier and La Malfa knew pretty well in what broad directions they hoped to move, and La Malfa had spelled out his general objectives in public speeches and papers. The main goals are to channel industry into those areas, mainly in the South, where labor can be concentrated and trained, to reform the agricultural structure by abolishing share cropping and revising all intermediate forms of farm contract, and to set up autonomous regions as the instruments of future detailed planning, the latter to be coordinated by a central planning authority and then submitted to Parliament.[78]

Professor Saraceno's statement of more immediate goals appeared in a commission document submitted to the Budget Ministry in April, 1963.[79] It identified three categories of problems with which programming should deal. The first concerns imbalances in economic development: poor distribution of the labor supply; malfunctioning and low productivity in the distribution system, in public administration, and in public transport; monopolistic control of some markets and products. The second deals with the need to devote more resources to the improvement of some civic institutions: education, public assistance, research, housing. The third considers the problems arising from urbanization.

The report makes forecasts for the years 1954–68, suggesting that the nonagricultural sector will increase its contribution to national income from 84 to 86 per cent, that the agricultural labor force will drop from 27 to 22 per cent of the total, and that per capita agricultural production will increase about 5.9 per cent annually as against 3.8 per cent in the nonagricultural sector. It foresees a progressive reduction in unemployment and underemployment of 350,000 to 400,000 units a year; and it anticipates an average annual increase in national income of 5 per cent.

It is noteworthy that fifteen of the commissioners chose to attach their independent appraisals or suggestions as appendixes to the report.

Members of the commission and other knowledgeable persons are in agreement that it is too early to know just what function the commission will serve. Its VIP membership and the fact that it represents diverse shades of political opinion suggest that its major function

---

[78] *The Economist* (November 17, 1962), pp. 677–678.

[79] "Lo sviluppo dell'economia italiana negli anni 1964–68 nel rapporto del prof. Saraceno al Ministro del Bilancio," *Il Messaggero*, April 10, 1963.

may be to help win acceptance for plans formulated in governmental ministries rather than to formulate them itself. On the other hand, some members of its staff are among the most authoritative and ardent exponents of programming in the country and can be expected to give technical and policy help to the various political currents with the influence to do something about them.

VIII

Through the decade of the fifties price and wage increases in Italy remained relatively small, and there was no effective pressure upon the government to do more than exercise controls over credit occasionally. Good product markets, expanding output, and high unemployment levels were the real anti-inflationary controls.

In these years Italian ideological ferment and political and economic debate were not enervated by the economic boom, as was happening in Germany. Voters, political parties, and labor unions divided along political and ideological lines, and there was no significant shift in political loyalties or merging of major currents. In their most publicized form, however, the ideological debates of the fifties were largely sterile, for the rhetoric of the right, the center, and the left alike centered around the slogans of past eras rather than the concrete problems of the present. Nineteenth-century monarchy or economic laissez faire, confessional bonds, the relatively infrequent and moderate interventions of government into the economy of the early twentieth century, or the stock slogans of the Second or Third Socialist Internationals molded the content of political debate. Inevitably, these appeals helped keep public opinion polarized rather than making a dialogue possible.

At the same time a more promising, concrete, and technical exploration of the possibility of political alliances and institutional change was beginning underneath the raucous surface. From the start it was clear that a viable majority could be constructed only by finding common interests along that part of the political spectrum between the liberal Christian Democrats and the Socialists. The Vanoni Plan, the build-up of IRI and ENI, the Fund for the South, and Parliamentary inquiries into poverty and other economic and social problems both reflected and helped clarify the areas of possible agreement.

These efforts are continuing, and they were given an important spur by the center-left government of 1962–63. Though the polari-

zation into center and left is fading, it dies hard. This is partly because of the continuing symbolic value of ideologies that represent
attractive nostalgias or future hopes. More important, it dies hard
because there *are* real differences in goals and methods among a
people whose economic situations and backgrounds are so various.
Powerful elements in the Christian Democratic Party resist an opening to the left because they remain attached to the idea of a "free
market" (i.e., a privately controlled market). Their hesitation arouses
serious anxieties among the Socialists, who fear that the formula
"center-left" will in practice mean continuing conservatism with no
real turn toward economic planning. Even if the MSI and Communist Party bureaucrats take tactical advantage of the dialogue,
for a large part of the population it is honest and earnest, and the
issue of economic programming is at its heart.

Improving conditions and living standards have made it even
harder for the most deprived groups to lose their attachment to the
old ideological abstractions. Moving North and finding factory jobs,
they now compare themselves to those who are better off rather
than to their destitute compatriots in Calabria, Sicily, or the slums
of Naples, and the contrast is a powerful incentive to vote Communist.

For these reasons and others the exhortations of high government
officials to exercise moderation in wage and price claims are unlikely
in themselves to be very effective. The efficient firms, torn between
immediate profit and abstract appeals, will take the profits if history
and the experience of other countries is any guide. The unions will
act similarly when they can make the decisive choices, which they
usually cannot. The salaries of public employees still lag, and pressure is strong for some amelioration for them. The less efficient and
marginal companies would be happy enough to heed the call to
virtue in wage policy, but they must continue to pay enough to
attract labor in an increasingly tight market. If they did show
markedly more restraint than the advanced sector, it would accentu-
ate the economic dualism that Italy has been hoping to eliminate.

In pricing the prospects are probably equally dim. For the monopolistic sectors, words have always been weak weapons against the
pull of profits. Lessened demand in international markets will help,
but it is offset by increasing effective demand at home as the wage
bill rises. Given the lack of profit figures, it is hard to say how much
pressure on prices growing labor costs exert, but there probably is

some in some sectors. Though there is still a hunger for investible savings in Italy, rising prices encourage consumption rather than saving, and this in turn pushes prices upward.

Finally, the ideological differences are pertinent. Many Italians have little incentive to be overly zealous about maintaining the existing system, and for a sizable minority there are strong incentives to create discontent.

On the other hand, a twelve-year taste of prosperity in the land long celebrated for its poverty and emigration is a heady potion, and it may be addicting. Industry has been modernizing rapidly. There is reason to hope that the political turmoil will lessen as more people earn higher salaries for a longer period. The Italians have shown impressive ingenuity in monetary policy, in adopting some new norms in industrial relations, and in rigorous exploration of pertinent economic theory and institutional alternatives. If appeals for price and wage restraint represent the conditioned response of politicians to a tighter economy, they may nonetheless foreshadow the application of hardheaded reasoning and pluralistic give and take to severe economic dilemmas.

3

Germany

To explore the making of wage-price policies in the postwar German Federal Republic is to discover the continuing importance of traditional German social structures and attitudes. Neither Nazism nor war nor military occupation erased them, and they help shape economic interplay now, as they did before 1933. Social stratification, with its two faces of elite style setting and pressure for mass conformity, remains.

Among labor groups it is expressed in some old ambitions: for status even more than for money. Old fears persist: of inflation and of unemployment. The divided union movement Hitler converted into a Labor Front has been replaced with a unified labor organization, but it displays some of the weakness that marked it under the Kaiser and in the Weimar years. It is harassed by rank-and-file fears and status seeking, but also by old ideological fissures which "unification" could not hide for long. Among management groups old business practices persist: cooperation and collusion with others in one's own social stratum, in wage bargaining, and in price setting.

The new and dynamic element in the 1950's was not a matter of social or economic structure, but chiefly of economic good fortune. Germany found itself, even after defeat in war, with the productive capacity and the products that the foreign and home markets wanted. If the result was a miracle of prosperity, that made it all the easier for the old ways of life and of business to go on.

I

Although a substantial leveling of social and cultural barriers is said to have taken place in Germany during the Nazi years and the struggle for survival after World War II, the American observer is impressed everywhere with the importance of economic and social stratification when studying the influences on the wage-price picture. More important, he is left with the distinct impression that this stratification is not simply the product of upper-class authoritarianism. Time and again the decisive factor in a given situation appears to be the German worker's satisfaction with the status quo, his enormous concern with security rather than economic or political gain, and his willingness to transfer responsibility.

It is clear that social stratification is not erased overnight in any society. Because of the strong personal controls exercised in Germany by the upper classes long after these functions had been transferred to parliamentary decision in most other Western European countries, it might be expected that they would not have been abolished either by Hitlerism, which elevated many a common man to a decision-making position but hardly taught democracy, or by the subsequent relatively short period of common suffering. It is important to note two points in this connection, however. The first, which promises some change in this respect in the not too distant future, is the age structure of the population.

Because of war losses the ranks of the approximately forty to fifty age group (persons born between 1913 and 1922) are extraordinarily thin in Germany. This means (1) that the country is still run in most respects predominantly by the older generation, whose members carry their ideas of "their place" from the beginning of the twentieth century, and (2) a lack of influential thought from a somewhat younger group which might represent some change in attitudes. The substantially younger age group (under forty) does not represent either strong competition or an adequate challenge. This situation will change very rapidly in the next few years, and it is widely thought that closer contact and better understanding will prevail between labor, management, and the government once the younger group is able to exert its influence.

The second point would tend to work against the gradual relaxation of existing social and cultural barriers in the foreseeable future. It involves the highly stratified educational system, which still carries the scars of willful destruction begun thirty years ago. The rebuilding of the rudiments of a school system (particularly one that could accommodate the refugee children) took many years after the war, and even after this was accomplished one was dealing with teachers who had been trained in the years of educational neglect. The group of the population that suffers most from this development is the 84.4 per cent [1] which does not go beyond the Volksschule (mostly eight, sometimes nine years). Those who get a higher education have greater exposure to foreign educational influences.

In addition to the differences resulting from the quality of education, the fact that the school system generally divides after the fourth grade, separating those who will go on to secondary schools and universities from those who will have only a Volksschule education, has also accentuated social and cultural barriers. When the decision is made, the child is too young to have an opinion or, if he does, to make it felt. If the student made the decision rather than his parents, there might be a greater increase in the number of persons who would select secondary education which would qualify them for higher level jobs. As it is, only 3 per cent [2] of the children from workers' families are currently attending universities, even though education is free.[3]

The generally evident German emphasis on enjoying the newly acquired prosperity to the fullest is as noticeable among the low income groups as among the more affluent, and workers typically want their children to become self-supporting as soon as possible. A child can be apprenticed at the age of fourteen or fifteen and earn a small wage. After three years, he receives the full wages of his trade. Little importance is attached to the fact that he is almost entirely inflexible from there on.

---

[1] Official statistics on the educational level attained are not available. Based on an opinion poll for 1959 of the Allensbacher Institut.

[2] Speech by Lübke which appeared in the *FAZ* of February 25, 1963.

[3] Education in Germany is regulated by the *Länder* rather than the federal government, but the only financial difference among *Länder* is that in some the students must pay for books and tools in secondary schools. Here, however, parents without means can obtain them without charge. There are private secondary schools but no private universities. The latter are generally municipal and *Land* responsibilities. Students pay only token fees to attend a university (currently about DM200 at Frankfurt) and pay for books. Even average students can receive public subsidies which are adequate to allow them to subsist, and the universities run heavily subsidized cafeterias. Subsidies are subject to a means test, and are not granted until the third semester. At the end of the second semester the students are given a test, but if they pass they are assured of assistance for the entire university period.

There are, of course, other reasons: family educational traditions, lack of knowledge about schools and occupational requirements, the parent's pride in his own occupation in which he would like to train his child, the fact that the small self-employed businessman or craftsman still depends on his children to help in and eventually take over his business (even though today his business may be just barely economically viable). All these play a part in educational stratification.

According to the Allensbacher Poll, only 15.6 per cent of all Germans had been graduated from secondary schools in 1959. Of these, 11.8 per cent had been graduated from the Mittelschulen (which qualify students after six years beyond the basic four year Volksschule, and the "mittlere reife" examination for intermediate occupations but not for university); and 3.8 per cent were graduated from the Gymnasium or equivalent (which qualifies them after nine years beyond the Volksschule and the "Abitur" exam for higher occupations and the university). The night university system is poorly developed.

From the point of view of influence in economic policy, the educational picture has several important results:

(1) The well-educated and holders of higher level jobs still come very predominantly from those families in which education, influence, and often conservatism has been a tradition. Because lengthy specialized training and degrees or certificates are needed for all jobs above that of common laborer, it is virtually impossible for those with only a Volksschule education to work their way up except in a specifically defined category.

(2) When a boy from a working class family does go on to the Gymnasium he will, because he is so young, because he is so outnumbered, because of the snobbishness attached to it, but also because the Germans are inclined to conform, very likely lose his identity with labor. Rather than gain a spokesman in government or scholarly circles, the workers are likely to lose a member of their group.

(3) There is widespread willingness to relinquish responsibility to "those who have been taught to think about those things" and to accept a very specific, carefully defined niche in life, by the younger as well as the older generation. This bent is certainly nurtured by the existing school system. It has strongly contributed to a two level society: those who have degrees and authority and, therefore, pre-

sumably know what they are doing ("Die Herren dort oben"), and those ("wir kleinen Leute") who, having shifted the responsibility for thinking and acting are, in turn, willing to accept whatever policy is handed down to them. The respect for "them" and "their" judgment is enormous. This is why moral suasion, when it comes from the right people, is influential and this is why the unions have had to be so careful of public opinion. What "they" say is more likely to be accepted as correct than are the statements of union officials. The psychologically unequal status of labor and management in the public mind becomes an important factor in German industrial relations.

II

The official and complete transfer of sovereignty from the Allied occupation forces to the Federal Republic of Germany did not occur until May, 1955, but West Germany's first elections took place in August, 1949. Its first government was constituted in September, 1949, by the victorious CDU/CSU (Christlich Demokratische Union and its Bavarian branch, the Christlich Soziale Union), with Konrad Adenauer as its head. Neither the political party in control of the government nor its head changed until 1963. The returns in the four elections since the war have resulted in the percentages of votes shown in Table 3-1 for the four parties that have had the greatest political impact.

Table 3-1.[a] Election Returns (excluding Berlin, the deputies of which have no vote)

	CDU/CSU	SPD[b]	FDP[c]	DP[d]
	percentages			
1949	31	29.2	11.9	4.0
1953	45.2	28.8	9.5	3.3
1957	50.2	31.8	7.7	3.4
1961	48.4	36.5	12.1	—

[a] Table from *Statistisches Jahrbuch 1961* (Bonn: Embassy, 1961), p. 137.
[b] Sozial Demokratische Partei Deutschlands.
[c] Freie Demokratische Partei.
[d] Deutsche Partei.

Since political parties need an absolute majority of deputies in order to govern alone, the CDU/CSU has been forced into coalition in every legislative term except 1957–61, and in that term it voluntarily took in a governing partner. The CDU/CSU has governed in coalition with a variety of right-wing parties, but the SPD has never been included.

A political party needs a minimum of 5 per cent of the total votes cast in order to be represented in the Bundestag, and this, along with an apparent desire on the voters' part for a government more stable than that of the Weimar Republic, has limited the number of parties. In 1945 the allies licensed the organization of four parties, feeling that this would cover the various political orientations. The parties that emerged were the CDU/CSU, the SPD, KPD (German Communist Party), and the Liberal-Demokratische Partei Deutschlands, which soon became the FDP. Although other parties were subsequently formed, only the BHE (refugee party) and the right-wing DP (Deutsche Partei) achieved importance. Neither of these is any longer represented in the Bundestag.

Both rightist and leftist extreme parties have been declared unconstitutional and forbidden. The former, the Fascist Sozialistische Reichspartei (which had received noticeable support in some regions but was never represented in the national legislature), was outlawed in October, 1952. The German Communist Party was represented in the 1949 Bundestag, but by the 1953 elections its support had dropped to 2.2 per cent of the votes, thus eliminating it from the Bundestag. In August, 1956, the party was outlawed.

Political stability can also be ascribed to a considerable extent to the CDU/CSU's ability to include a broad electorate among its supporters. It counts both Catholic and Protestant groups among its followers (although it is strongest in predominantly Catholic regions) and draws support from the entire range of voters from big business interests to trade unionists and farmers. It therefore represents a coalition of interests and has often taken the wind out of the Socialists' sails by pushing social legislation just before elections. It is clear that not only the "Christian organized" worker votes CDU/CSU; many other working men who have never been so well off and are afraid of a change, or feel that the SPD is or might be anticlerical, do too.

The only more conservative party of any consequence that has been able to maintain itself through the years (although with occasional upheavals) has been the FDP. It draws its support almost entirely from industrial and conservative upper- and middle-class circles, although two of its deputies in 1961 were white-collar union members. In general, the party prefers a more nationalistic policy than the CDU, both politically and economically (it originally was against the EEC), and is opposed to most social legislation and any sort of redistribution of income.

The Socialist Party (SPD) draws its support from labor, special groups such as war victims and craftsmen, and to some extent small- and medium-sized business, although the latter predominantly vote CDU/CSU.

The SPD adhered for a long time to orthodox Socialist doctrine, but in the middle fifties its leaders realized that its political philosophy had become outdated and that a reform was called for if the party was to grow and participate in the government. Since the Bad Godesberg Program was accepted by the party in 1959, the SPD has undergone major changes and its policies have become far more flexible. It has attempted to create a public image of itself as a "Volkspartei" (people's party) rather than strictly a labor party. There has been only one national election since the Bad Godesberg Program, but in that one the new SPD did well.

Political and economic observers generally feel that the SPD as currently constituted and oriented would make no radical changes in present economic policies if it were to take over the government. This opinion is based, among other things, on its record in the Länder (provinces) where it has been in the government.[4] In early 1963 it was participating in Hesse, Lower Saxony, Hamburg, and Bremen.

The SPD's main contest with the governing parties has been in the social field, where many new programs have been initiated since the war. Economically it has predominantly argued for a fairer distribution of incomes and tighter control of big business. Both of these appeals have found some sympathy among the governing parties, but not enough to precipitate effective action.

Strict party discipline is observed in Germany, and this has been very important with respect to labor influence in parliament. Members of the labor wing of the CDU are outnumbered within their own party bloc and must vote with the majority rather than with the likeminded SPD deputies. Though the SPD commands a substantial share of the vote, its influence is indirect. A strong opposition party makes it necessary for the governing party to adopt some of the SPD's programs for fear of losing votes to the latter. Social legisla-

---

[4] The absence of economic plans in these cases is often mentioned in conversations with people who are not in the SPD.

tion, for instance, has always received particular CDU/CSU attention and blessing in election years. The SPD never sees its bills
adopted without such modifications as are necessary to adapt them
to the orientation of the CDU/CSU and its coalition allies.

Since the Bad Godesberg Program it has also been apparent that
the SPD had been moving to a generally more moderate position
than the unions, though the degree to which party and union policies
are apart is very different from union to union.

Many union members, moreover, look to the labor wing of the
CDU/CSU to represent their interests since they consider themselves part of the Christian-oriented labor movement. This small
but very vocal minority has made it difficult for the DGB (Deutscher
Gewerkschaftsbund, the German Federation of Labor), officially to
support the SPD in election campaigns. With the exception of an
important group of white-collar workers and a few minor special-
interest groups, the DGB represents organized labor in Germany.

The DGB has had to tread carefully where election statements
of any kind are concerned, because its internal problems have been
exploited to the fullest by its opposition. When, before the 1953
elections (the DGB was not established in time for the 1949 elections), it called on its members to vote for "a better Bundestag
because the last one had not adequately considered the interests of
the working population" the appeal evoked such external and internal turmoil that it resulted in a very cautious and retiring union
position prior to the 1957 elections. The 1953 appeal nearly caused
a split in the unified movement laboriously and precariously constituted after World War II, and did, in fact, provide the impetus
for the eventual secession of part of the "Christian" group in 1955,
the latter forming the CGD (Christilicher Gewerkschaftsbund
Deutschlands). This union has never achieved much significance.

By 1961 the climate had changed sufficiently for the DGB to
make some very general statements with respect to the coming elections without being severely attacked. There were even some comments of the opposition and the press to the effect that one could
hardly deny the unions the right to their political opinions. By this
time the "unified labor movement concept," still new in 1953, was
relatively firmly established so that there were no noticeable repercussions from that quarter. It is very likely that in the coming years
the unions will be in a better position to officially align themselves
politically.

Of the 521 deputies in the Bundestag in early 1963 approximately 222 were union members.[5] There were 184 from the DGB and thirty-eight from other unions. The SPD delegation included 179 unionists, the CDU/CSU forty-one, and the FDP two. Because of party discipline these unionists do not constitute a bloc in parliament. Nor do they necessarily constitute a bloc within each party. The unions have not made an effort to see that union members are nominated and have therefore had no influence on the type of union member who is. Quite a few of the 222 have only loose ties with their unions, and only twenty-five are full-time union officials.

The parliamentary activities of the latter group are sometimes resented rather than supported by their union colleagues, who have been known to complain that their union work remains undone.

III

Turning from the political background to economic structural elements, it is well to recognize that the economic chaos of the first postwar years has been a key element in the thinking, fears, and attitudes of the economic decision-makers of the fifties and sixties.

Germany's "unique economic experience" [6] started with complete chaos at the time of its unconditional surrender in May, 1945. The chaos was aggravated by denazification (which often took key men out of an enterprise), partition, dismantling, and the fantastic flow of refugees consisting of ethnic Germans east of the Oder Neisse line who were forced out and those who, fearing the Russians, joined the moving throngs and fled to the West from what is now the Soviet Zone of Germany. Wages and prices were controlled[7] but neither

---

[5] There are serious problems in getting completely accurate figures since only the SPD asks its deputies about union affiliations. The 222 figure was arrived at after careful research by Kurt Hirsche, the DGB liaison man with Parliament.

[6] It is remarkable how many German scholars referred to it that way and added that nothing could be learned from it by other countries.

[7] The wage and price freeze which had existed under the Third Reich was retained by the occupation powers. Neither wages nor prices had been formally frozen until 1936, but a law of 1934 which made all wage increases subject to the approval of the Trustees of Labor had, in effect, frozen wages as of that year. The Trustees of Labor did not approve increases except for small ones in the industries producing war goods.

Between 1934 and 1936 prices had not risen much due to economic conditions. As the supply of money went up and consumer goods decreased toward the end of the war, penalties for price control violations were so severe that serious inflation was prevented. After the collapse of the German government, inflation was engendered in the first place by the fact that the German volume

had any direct relationship to the individual's need for survival.
One could not sustain life on money wages since goods simply did
not get to the market at the controlled prices and could only be
obtained on the black market on a barter basis or for exorbitant
money costs. Therefore, many people stayed officially off the labor
market finding some sort of occupation in which they would be paid
in kind (such as helping on a farm in return for food, rebuilding
someone else's business in return for clothes, fuel, etc.), or they lived
by trading their possessions for the necessities of life.

Postwar economic recovery began with the currency reform of
June, 1948, which was roughly based on a 1:10 exchange but actually
worked out less favorably. Simultaneously, price ceilings were removed from most consumer goods, but industrial raw materials,
some agricultural products, rents, real estate, public utilities, and
transportation continued to be controlled for some time. Included
on the list of prices that would remain controlled were mainly those
goods and services of which the supply was judged to be inelastic
for the near future. Wages were freed a few months later and have
remained free, although purchasing power was controlled from
official quarters by a very conservative fiscal policy.

Germany was transformed overnight. There was production where
previously there had appeared to be no capacity. Goods which had
been hoarded were now put on the market, productivity went up, the
black market dwindled, and there was a resurgence of energy and
faith in the future. The reform had been drastic. It had virtually
wiped out savings and debts. Although it precipitated Germany's
economic recovery, it is still fresh in the minds of all but the youngest
generation and is, along with the years of the early twenties, responsible for the fear that the word "inflation" strikes in the average German. It is highly unlikely that a reform so severe and unpopular
could have been carried out under circumstances much different
from those existing in Germany at the time. A very important aspect
lay in the fact that the Allied military government carried the onus
rather than an elected government working through a parliamentary
system.

---

of money had reached almost RM300,000 million as compared with just under
RM60,000 in 1938. Consumer goods, moreover, were not only scarce but the
when and how of their future availability were very uncertain. Inflation was
aggravated by the presence of occupation soldiers and particularly by the Rus-
sian soldiers, many of whom had not been paid for periods of a year or two
and were not allowed to convert the RM back-pay they received into rubles.

The economic conditions at the time of the currency reform made it virtually impossible to give the new German currency a proper international value. Productive capacity could simply not be judged accurately. To begin with, estimates of industrial war damage were constantly being revised. There are no accurate statistics, but among German economists one now often hears the opinion that, in spite of the extensive destruction, Germany had a somewhat greater industrial production capacity at the end of the war than before. Apparently the industrial plants constructed during the war exceeded those destroyed in capacity. To a much greater extent than originally realized [8] it also proved possible to get relatively high production returns with minor repairs requiring only a small capital investment.

Obsolete equipment was retired, with the result that the rate of retirement per investment unit has been and for some years to come will be much smaller in Germany than in other industrial nations yielding a greater return per investment unit. In rebuilding it was possible both to rationalize production processes and to emphasize those goods which were internationally scarce.

Labor market dislocations also distorted the understanding of Germany's economic picture at the time of the currency reform. The coming together of a skilled labor force and an existing industrial base for the production of capital goods provided a greater industrial potential than could be foreseen at the time. It has been suggested that it was difficult for a long time to get an accurate labor market picture because of an unwillingness to work for controlled wages. In addition, labor was highly immobile at that time because it was exactly in the industrial areas that the greatest destruction had taken place. As a result, there was no housing.[9]

Besides all of the above-mentioned imponderables, the severely

---

[8] In addition to the physical difficulty of estimating damage to equipment, entrepreneurs were hiding what could be used or were exaggerating damage, fearing dismantling.

[9] Official figures for 1949 show that about 10 per cent of the wage and salary earning labor force was unemployed. This does not accurately reflect unemployment of that period, however, because the labor force was so unsettled. Those who had stayed off the labor market during the years of chaos were just drifting back, and large numbers were still coming or returning from the East. Married women, and young first-job hunters most likely did not register as unemployed because they were not eligible for compensation and the large number of people who had small subsistence pensions (invalids, widows, etc.) probably did not either.

damaged transportation system, the shortage of energy, and a disrupted capital market all led to underestimation of Germany's economic potential. In the light of subsequent developments, it all added up to an undervalued currency which many German economists consider *the* reason for Germany's postwar export boom. Low prices are a most important inducement for a prospective buyer.

German businessmen, supported by a friendly government and generally acquiescent labor unions, made the most of the opportunities with which they were presented after the 1948 currency reform, aggressively pursuing international markets. It is a pretty safe statement, nonetheless, that German policies and measures could never have had the same results if simultaneous developments, over which Germany as a nation had no control, had not worked in its favor.

The most important of these developments was the increasing tension between East and West, which not only made it necessary for the United States to help rebuild Germany [10] but also forced other European countries to accept Germany as a partner, thus preventing the political and economic isolation to which a despised Germany might otherwise have been subjected. The international tension eventually erupted in the Korean War, just at the moment when German industries were getting re-established and in need of the boost received from this war. The East-West conflict is also responsible for the constantly growing labor force (supplied with refugees from the Soviet Zone of Germany), when additional labor was sorely needed for industrial expansion.

While Germany reaped the benefits of international tension, it was not burdened (in contrast to its neighboring countries) with the need for defense production. Although by 1957 it had contributed a total of 66.7 billion for occupation costs (in later years designated as defense costs), German investment funds could be used to expand a type of production which would directly further the nation's economy rather than be drained off into equipping an army. Germany did not have to worry about the latter problem until 1956.

Also important, and outside Germany's control, was the fact that as the demand for, and the prices of, the products it manufactured increased, the prices of the raw materials it imported dropped. This

---

[10] Between 1948 and 1954 Marshall Plan aid to Germany totaled approximately $1.3 billion. There were also grants under various other aid programs which came to almost $2 billion between 1952 and 1954 alone. In 1953 and 1954 special assistance for Berlin amounted to approximately $46 million.

coincidence was of major significance in the balance of payments surplus which is, in turn, most frequently credited with having been the decisive element in Germany's economic boom. Surpluses in the balance of payments and consequent financial reserves provided the funds for large scale investment, which in turn promoted rapid growth and full employment.

IV

Within this political and economic framework business and labor officials reacted to opportunities and challenges. Their decisions were also affected, however, by the structure of German management and union organizations, and that structure calls for consideration next.

There are three types of management organizations in Germany: (1) the BDA (Bundesvereinigung der Deutschen Arbeitgeberverbände), which concentrates on social matters, does all the collective bargaining and concerns itself with all labor matters including social security legislation and wages; (2) the BDI (Bundesverband der Deutschen Industrie), which concerns itself strictly with economic policies for the various industries; and (3) the DIHT (Deutscher Industrie-und Handelstag), the German Chamber of Commerce. These three organizations are in turn headed by the Gemeinschaftsausschuss der Deutschen Gewerblichen Wirtschaft, which exists for top level consultation purposes. The management organizations maintain a research institute, the Industrieinstitut.

Of the management organizations in existence the BDI and BDA are the most important for our study. The BDI is probably the more powerful of the two since it concerns itself with fundamental economic decisions. The BDA, however, is the more important for the unions and for wage determination. Both organizations are subdivided into rough national industry groups, of which there are thirty-nine for the BDI and forty for the BDA. These are called Spitzenverbände (top organizations), and they are in turn subdivided into regional groups. For the BDI, regional organization depends largely on the location and concentration of specific industries. An area with many metal products firms will have a regional organization. In areas where there are few such firms these will be members of the nearest regional organizations.

For the BDA the organization is highly complicated at the lower level since it must correspond, for collective bargaining purposes, to that of the unions. Member organizations have sprung up over the years in irregular fashion as the need arose, and they vary in size, competence, and organization.

BDA and BDI may have a personnel union at the lower levels. In any event, a great deal of consultation goes on between them. There are no official statistics concerning the percentage of firms organized. The BDA estimates that it organizes approximately 80 per cent. The BDI would not commit itself.[11]

In the case of the BDI each top industrial organization (Spitzenverband) maintains a secretariat consisting of various divisions according to the needs in the industry. In the Verein Deutscher Maschinenbau-Anstalten in Frankfurt, these divisions cover press, foreign trade, common market, finance and tax, business administration, delivery conditions, general economic problems, advertising and trade fairs, technical assistance, and energy problems. Committees representing member companies and corresponding to the divisions in the Spitzenverband meet with the staff experts from time to time as necessary. The organization's staff may also circularize individual member firms before making decisions or recommendations on an issue.

The organization applies pressure by press conferences, by going through the national BDI to the government, or by directly presenting its case to the Ministry of Economics, Finance, or other pertinent agency.

Besides having the benefit of its various services, which are particularly important to the smaller firms, the advantage of joining the BDI consists in having a voice in the policy-making of the industry, or at least in assuming that one has.

The BDA also gives advice, but on social questions (including workers' education) rather than economic ones. The advantages of membership and motivation for joining are even more evident here than in the BDI. Having the strength of the Verband for collective bargaining purposes is an obvious advantage for the smaller enterprises. For the larger enterprises there is the additional bonus that wages negotiated by the BDA are averages and, therefore, less than they can afford to pay.

---

[11] For a more complete description of the organization of German management see *Structure and Functions of the Top-Level Organizations of West German Trade and Industry* (Bergisch Gladbach: Deutscher Industrieinstitut, 1956).

In the case of labor conflicts which result in strikes or lockouts (there were virtually none of the latter between World War II and the 1963 metalworkers lockout) member firms are compensated. There is a special strike fund. Exact amounts paid out are not made public. Fixed expenses are paid as well as the salaries of white-collar workers (who may belong to another union or may not be organized and seldom strike) and also claims that may be brought by outsiders such as customers or suppliers who suffered damages as a result of the strike or lockout. Management decisions to allow conflicts to result in strikes or lockouts need no BDA approval. They are individually decided by the entrepreneur.

It is not likely, however, that in recent years of operation at full capacity the possibility of financial compensation has been important with respect to the entrepreneur's attitude toward a strike. His business would go to competitors, he would lose his profits, and, in these days of labor shortages, a plant's labor force has been known to disappear during a strike.

The cohesion with which German businessmen operate tends to remain a puzzle to an American observer since, in the end, a BDI Spitzenverband consists of nothing but competitors in the same industry (not to mention the BDA, where cohesion might result from confronting a common enemy). In order to gain an insight here, it is again necessary to resort to considerations which are more sociological than economic.

German business, both big and small, operates, domestically at least, with as little competition as possible.[12] Families have been in the same places for generations and have long been associated in business as well as social activities. Under these conditions, one is not inclined to force a competitor out of business or to embark on a course of action which would generally hurt other entrepreneurs in the area. In addition, there is, even under other conditions, a live and let live attitude which is at times surprising. Thus it is quite

---

[12] A relatively minor exception to this has been noticeable in the past two years in the retailing of appliances where it is said that domestic supplies have exceeded demand because of export difficulties. Thus, many appliance stores in the big cities have "discount" signs on their windows. Competition in the retail field, through a great number of outlets, has been restricted for the immediate future by a one-year prohibition on the construction of nonproductive business facilities. The latter measure was designed to reduce activity in the construction industry in which prices have risen more than any other industry.

apparent that the large department stores and chains adjust their prices to those of the small retailers, rather than vice versa. In part this is due to the effective pressure exercised by the small business group, but it is also a matter of psychology and a different approach to business than exists in the United States.

Cut-throat competition such as goes on in some industries in the United States is not part of the social system. It is simply not done and is considered barbaric. Along with this goes the psychology of getting a large profit per item rather than smaller profits and larger turnover. "Why should a businessman try to undersell another? It means that for the same return he has to work harder, hire more people, perhaps expand and no longer work at full capacity. Just look at the enormous number of business failures in your country. Is it worth it?" Some such comment was made to us time and again. The German businessman, like the German worker, prefers to avoid the taking of risks. Instead of competing he joins, and what results is a highly frustrated anticartel office (Kartelamt) and a consumer who is able to do little about it.

After the war most German unionists were determined to have a unified labor movement rather than the separate unions with differing political orientations that had existed in 1933. For all practical purposes they were successful. What emerged in 1949 as a unified movement was the DGB (Deutsche Gewerkschaftsbund) with sixteen industrial unions as members. Its total membership in 1961 was 6.4 million, comprising about 32 per cent of the labor force. Approximately 40 per cent of the labor force is organized.

A substantial group of white-collar workers established the DAG (Deutsche Angestellten Gewerkschaft) in 1945, however, and in 1961 it had 462,000 members. In 1955 a small, currently insignificant group of "Christian-oriented" trade unionists defected to form the CGD (Christlicher Gewerkschaftsbund Deutschlands), and in 1961 it had about 200,000 members. There are some other relatively small, independent groups, of which the Deutsche Beamtenbund (civil servants), with 500,000 members in 1961, is the most important.

Whether or not a white-collar worker (Angestellter) joins the DAG or one of the DGB industrial unions depends entirely on how successful the particular DGB union in his industry has been in organizing white-collar workers. The latter are proportionately highly organized in the metal and chemical industries but less so in

others. The "white collar" definition includes categories from fore-
men to managing directors.

The DGB claims to organize 600,000 Beamten (civil servants) in
six of its member industrial unions.[13] Included in the Beamten category are such groups as government workers, teachers (including
professors), employees of municipal orchestras, the postal and railway systems, the city and state transportation systems, and publicly
operated gas and power plants.

The federal congress of the DGB meets every three years and
elects the Bundesvorstand (executive). It also votes on major policy
matters and may change the constitution of the DGB. The Bundesvorstand consists of nine persons who carry on the day to day business, plus the presidents of the sixteen industrial unions. The entire
Vorstand meets officially once a month. Between congresses the
Bundesvorstand takes policy directives from the Bundesausschuss,
which meets once every three months and, depending on the size of
the union, consists of two or more Vorstand members of each of the
sixteen unions, all members of the Bundesvorstand, and the chairmen
of the regional unions.

The DGB's de facto organization is such that the actual power lies
with the member industrial unions. DGB headquarters officially
represents the German labor movement and serves as a clearing-
house of ideas. It may suggest guide lines and tries to coordinate
activities. It cannot interfere in collective bargaining, which is the
exclusive prerogative of the sixteen industrial unions. The position
of DGB headquarters is a rather weak one, especially since interunion
friction and personality clashes in recent years have made unity of
action even more difficult than it might have been otherwise. After
years of attempts to present a unified picture to the outside and to
smooth over dissension, strong differences of opinion broke out in
public during the DGB congress in October, 1962.

The differences were centered around two prominent union leaders: Otto Brenner, President of the Metalworkers, who emphasizes
orthodox Socialist ideology, and Georg Leber, President of the Construction Workers Union, who is a reformist and a pragmatist inclined to disassociate ideology from the union movement. Leber is
closer to the present SPD, but in a recent major show of strength with

[13] Railroad, Postal, Teachers, Horticulture, Agriculture and Forestry, Transport, and Art.

Table 3-2.[a] Membership of West German Unions, 1950-61[b]

	1950	1951	1952	1953	1954	1955	1956	1957	1958	1959	1960	1961
						in thousands						
Deutscher Gewerkschaftsbund (DGB)..	5279	5912	6004	6051	6103	6105	6125	6244	6332	6274	6379	6382
Deutsche Beamtenbund (DBB).........	—	234	350	447	468	517	545	599	620	634	650	657
Deutsche Angestelltengewerkschaft (DAG)................	—	344	360	384	406	421	431	437	438	440	450	462
Christlicher Gewerkschaftsbund Deutschlands (CGB).............	—	—	—	—	—	—	—	—	—	112[c]	—	—
Deutsches Beamtenkartell...........	—	—	—	—	—	125	131	132	140	141	142	149
Deutscher Handels- und Industrieangestelltenverband (DHV).........	—	—	—	20	26	32	45	48	52	53	55	58

[a] *Wirtschafts -und Sozialstatistiches Handbuch* (Cologne: Bund-Verlag).
[b] As of September 30, for the Federal Republic including West Berlin.
[c] End of June, estimated.

respect to Germany's proposed emergency legislation Brenner had a strong majority of the unions behind him.

It would be wrong to say, however, that one or the other group is stronger inside or outside the labor movement or even that the labor movement is divided into two distinct camps. In general the Chemical Union, the Textile Workers Union, the Transport Union, and the Union of Food and Restaurant Workers follow Brenner's line of thinking; and the Postal Workers, Railroad Workers, and Miners are more sympathetic to Leber's philosophy. There is much crisscrossing over union lines, however, and the smaller unions do not definitely identify themselves with either group. It is also thought that in a number of instances what is said to be the "union" ideology is very predominantly that of its leader and not necessarily a rank-and-file commitment or a continuing line of action.

Depending on whether a union bargains on a national or regional scale a decision to cancel a collective contract may be made at national headquarters of an industrial union, or it may originate with the collective bargaining committee of the regional union office. In the latter case, the official of the national union Vorstand who is concerned with collective bargaining will usually sit in on the meetings. The problems and plans are then proposed to the Vorstand of the national union. The regional branch office is formally responsible to the national union's headquarters, but occasionally the real influence may lie at the regional level.

At the local level unions have "local administrations" (Ortsverwaltungsstellen, or a similar name). These take care of local union business and supervise the activities of the Vertrauensmänner Koerper in the plant. The latter are groups of men who, on a voluntary basis, take care of the union business in the plant. One Vertrauensman usually represents no more than twenty union members.

Although the DGB executive cannot interfere in collective bargaining, the fact that the DGB Vorstand includes the sixteen presidents of the member industrial unions results in an exchange of ideas and aims. In some instances, such as the move for a shorter workweek, there was close coordination. Usually the DGB is informed of intended collective bargaining moves and kept up to date on developments. The final decisions are made entirely by the member industrial unions, however, and the DGB has little if any influence upon wage policies.

The DGB has for many years had a membership problem. The

statistics show that membership has remained relatively stable, but the percentage of the wage and salary earning labor force which is organized has declined substantially since 1949 and especially since 1951. The reasons for this are discussed below.

The sixteen industrial unions which are joined in the DGB charge dues varying from 1 to 2 per cent of gross earnings. It is an accepted fact that many workers declare earnings which are smaller than the actual ones. Nevertheless the unions do not suffer from a shortage of funds, and have been able to accumulate sizable capital. There have been so few strikes that there has been no financial drain for that reason in spite of the approximately 90 per cent of earnings which most unions are committed to pay in strike benefits.

DGB headquarters has eyed this surplus with mixed feelings as its requests to have its own share increased from 12 per cent of its member unions' incomes have thus far fallen on deaf ears. The DGB bureaucracy has felt that more activities should be centralized instead of being carried out by each individual union, arguing that this would make the programs more effective and might be more economical in the long run.

At the end of World War II, trade union activities in Germany had been interrupted for a long time, first because of the chaos under the Weimar Republic and, after 1933, because unions were completely abolished by Hitler. It is well to remember that Germany's present labor movement was established in October of 1949 and is only about fifteen years old. The Hitler regime had done a complete job of annihilating the unions. It had not satisfied itself with forbidding their existence but had seized all union property and capital and had persecuted, imprisoned, and exiled the union leaders.

Thus the unions emerged from the war with a shortage of leadership and funds, the latter problem being still further aggravated by the currency reform. Communication facilities, one of the prime prerequisites for organization, were completely disrupted. The labor force was grossly dislocated and the future of many of the enterprises (particularly the larger ones) was very much in doubt because of denazification, expropriation, and dismantling. There was the anomaly of enormous unemployment on the one hand and persons leaving the labor force on the other because what little they could earn would not sustain life in the black market economy. There were practically no workers to organize, and those that were working in regular jobs for which they were qualified had little interest in unions because of existing conditions and because of lack of experience in the past. There were no places to meet, no materials to work with, no employers organizations to sign contracts with, and there was nothing to bargain about. Wages were frozen, and many companies paid in kind. Strikes were prohibited in various degrees by the different occupation powers.

The development of a full-fledged union movement was further handicapped by the fact that the three occupation powers applied varying regulations with respect to the organization of labor and were quite differently disposed toward union aims. The British, under the Labor government at the time, allowed unions to organize in any way they wished as early as 1946, sympathized with the unions' aim for the nationalization of key industries such as coal and steel, and initiated the unions' ardent postwar desire for codetermination in their zone. The Americans aided the re-establishment of unions, but favored local and later regional or land organizations rather than a unified labor movement. They successfully opposed all attempts at nationalization of industry. French measures were designed to discourage the development of unions and, once they were established, to keep them from attaining economic power. The Germans do not feel that the French were particularly antilabor; they feared German economic resurgence.

The unions, moreover, had been outside of German developments for many years, and the ranks of their leaders had been thinned. They could not produce the influence or the men to carry much weight in the formulation of Germany's future economic policy. As it was, they were unable to effect socialization, having to be satisfied, after a hard struggle, with codetermination; and they found that their proposals for currency reform were ignored in favor of one of which they disapproved. They clearly gained little advantage from the fact that they were the only major economic group free of the Nazi taint.

Collective bargaining in the Federal Republic of Germany is based on the Tarifvertragsgesetz (law on collective contracts) of 1949 and is carried on between the employer organizations and the trade unions on an industrial and regional basis. Collective bargaining procedure and organization differs from industry to industry. Each of the sixteen industrial unions, in agreement with the competent employers' organizations, has developed its own collective bargaining practices, which in many cases are based on pre-1933 tradition.

Much depends on the peculiarities of the particular industry. Generally, agreements are negotiated between the regional industrial union and the employer organization for that area and industry, and cover the entire industry in a given part of the country.

Although the regional industry-wide agreement covering about 100,000 workers is typical, a number of other bargaining procedures may be followed. Some unions bargain for separate products or occasionally even a single plant. The metalworkers, for instance, bargain separately for steel and have isolated Volkswagen for plant bargaining. The Union of Food and Restaurant Workers particularly emphasizes bargaining for special products, by very small areas, or by plant. On the other extreme are the agreements signed for printing, construction, clothing, private banking, and private insurance, which cover these industries on a national basis.

Collective bargaining in the public services is somewhat complicated, but it needs to be mentioned because there are about 3,000,000 public service workers out of a total labor force of about 21,000,000. Thus one-seventh of the labor force is employed in public services.

Those public servants designated "Beamten," who have civil service status and some special rights, may not strike, and they bargain through a different union from the blue-collar workers (who may strike) and the white-collar workers who do not have "Beamten" status. The latter are called "Angestellten." On the federal level a fairly stable bargaining team composed of the State Secretary of the Interior Ministry and top officials of various other ministries bargains for "management." On the provincial (*Land*) level there is an intergovernmental committee of representatives of all the provinces, chaired by the Finance Minister of one of them.[14] On the local level an organization representing the more important local governments and chaired by the mayor of one of the big cities bargains for the governmental units.[15]

Because the local units of government are sensitive to strike threats in transportation and are often staffed with persons who have had a union background, the public service unions are in general most successful at this level. They accordingly often adopt the tactic of applying pressure at the local level when negotiations at the provincial or federal levels have broken down or threaten to do so. They then

---

[14] Tarifgemeinschaft Deutscher Länder.
[15] Vereinigung Kommunaler Arbeitgeber Verbände.

use the local gains as a precedent, and the higher level units ordinarily have had to follow suit.

Two types of collective contracts are negotiated on a regional basis in Germany. The first is always the "Manteltarifvertrag," which provides for general conditions of work and runs for a period of three to four years. Subsequently, wages, hours of work, and other current matters are negotiated for shorter periods (usually twelve to fourteen months) within the framework of the Manteltarifvertrag. Even these contracts are very general in their descriptions, however. Wages are set by skill (skilled, semiskilled, and unskilled) rather than for specific occupations, and beyond that only such factors as hardship, heavy physical labor, and adverse conditions have played a major part. Attempts to eliminate women as a special lower paid category and to get equal pay for equal work have usually been frustrated by the device of placing women in a lower paid "light work" category.

The Tarifvertragsgesetz of 1949 makes it possible for labor or management, or both, to petition the Land or federal governments (depending on coverage and importance of the agreement) to make a collective agreement legally applicable to all workers and all employers in that industry. The provision for such an "Allgemeinverbindlichkeitserklärung" (AVE) is understandable in the light of the collective bargaining structure. For one thing employers who are not members of a BDA would otherwise not be bound by a collective agreement even if they employed union members. In former days unions feared competition from the unorganized who might accept lower wages. From the organized employers' point of view extension of agreements was desirable in order to force their competitors' lower labor costs up to the level of their own.

The process by which an agreement may be declared generally binding involves an appeal to a committee consisting of three representatives of labor, three of management, and a chairman with no vote who is an official of the Department of Labor. Employers who have signed the agreement must employ at least half the workers in the industry or sector in question, and the appeal must appear to the Minister of Labor to be in the public interest. The practice has tended to keep standard rates at a level marginal producers could afford to pay, while more efficient companies have individually granted further increases.

In recent years extension of contracts has lost importance. Competing employers have had to pay the same wages anyway in order to obtain labor, and the unorganized have also been given the same benefits. Under these conditions organized labor has realized that the AVE is currently more of a handicap than a help and has actually made efforts to keep union negotiated advantages from other workers. The first such "exclusion" attempts were made through "Tarifausschlussklauseln" in contracts which attempted to prevent the unorganized from obtaining a legal right to contract benefits through extension of contracts. These proved to be irrelevant since employers extended wages and benefits to all workers anyway. A small measure of success with an "Ausschlussklausel" was attained by Georg Leber, President of the Construction Workers Union. He succeeded in including a clause in a contract stating that certain negotiated pension rights were to be for union members only. These were increased according to the length of time a member had belonged to the union. The contract, in spite of its apparent innocuousness, caused a national furor, and not only among employers. The fact that Leber succeeded here does not necessarily mean that other unions will be able to follow. There is a general feeling that Leber has been able to get away with a great deal because of clever tactics and substantial personal influence outside the labor movement and also because of the current strength of his industry.

There is no compulsory arbitration or mediation in Germany. Federal government officials did occasionally mediate at first, but later usually left mediation to provincial labor officials. BDA officials claim they prefer private to public mediators because public officials are allegedly interested only in maintaining peace, and their interventions accordingly work to the advantage of the unions.

V

Operating within this social, political, and economic structure, German businessmen and union officials reacted to the conditions of the 1950's and sixties, making a succession of price and wage decisions. The character of these decisions and some reasons they were made as they were are considered next.

The concept and symbol that has dominated the thinking and talking of German businessmen and much of the mass public has been "Marktwirtschaft": a free market economy. It has drawn its political glamour from the remarkable prosperity Germany enjoyed in the fifties, when government intervention in the economy was minimal. That this relative and rhetorical laissez faire came just after the

extremely tight controls of the Nazis and the war years doubtless
made it all the more popular. Its critics and the economists who have
voiced the view that the "economic miracle" was the result of good
fortune rather than Marktwirtschaft have found a meager audience.
In business and politics, as elsewhere, nothing succeeds like success;
and the businessmen and public officials associated with the idea
of Marktwirtschaft have become uniquely powerful people.

The glare of prosperity has made it hard to see the shadows. The
Marktwirtschaft has given organized labor virtually no voice in economic policy formulation; and, although it is ostensibly based on
the principle of unrestricted competition, it has systematically been
used to restrict competition. Prosperity also made it seem unneces-
sary for many years to base private or public decisions upon careful
analyses of their long-run effects. Critics of the Marktwirtschaft have
charged that policies have been responses to the opinions, prejudices,
suspicions, and short-run needs of the economically strong, but the
roaring of the full-speed economy drowned out the charges.

The Korean War gave German industry the boost it needed to get
firmly established. Without it the miracle might not have occurred,
for in 1949–50 both domestic and foreign demand could easily be
met with existing productive capacity. Now a great demand for
the investment goods Germany produces so successfully suddenly
appeared. Other countries soon had labor shortages and backlogs
of orders. Germany was able to step into the vacuum with expertly
engineered products, short delivery dates, and low prices. It had a
large oversupply of labor because in addition to its own unemployed
it could draw on the refugees who continued to flee across the East
Zone border.

The war, together with the other favorable economic factors noticed earlier, kept the economy growing at a brisk rate. Some measures of the rate appear in Table 3-3.

For the period between 1950 and 1961 negotiated hourly wage
rates rose faster than either wholesale prices or living costs, and
average hourly earnings of industrial workers rose faster than negotiated hourly rates. Earnings also surpassed the increase in productivity for the period. The proportion of the national income that went
into wages increased during these years from 59.1 per cent to 62.3
per cent, while the number of employed workers was steadily growing from 14,580,000 to 19,990,000 and the percentage of the labor

force that was unemployed was steadily declining from 9.0 per cent to 0.8 per cent.

While these statistics certainly suggest that German workers improved their standard of living, they tell nothing about the strength of management and union organizations or of the nature and success of their respective policies or strategies. We cannot learn from them how much of the increase in real wages was attributable to wage push by unions or to wage pull by employers; how much can be credited to the drop in unemployment and how much to organizational pressures. For some hints on these matters it is helpful to consider the succession of economic problems the bargaining parties faced, the rhetoric they employed to justify their various claims and actions, and the organizational strengths and weaknesses of each of them.

It was not until 1949 that the unions were able to operate under reasonably normal conditions. Wages had been freed at the end of 1948; the Tarifvertragsgesetz was promulgated in April, 1949, giving collective contracts a legal basis; the Federal Republic, with a constitution guaranteeing freedom of coalition, was established in September; employers were effectively organized in October; and finally the DGB itself was established in October. By that time, however, the unions faced a much more confident and better organized opposition than would have been the case several years earlier, especially since the election in August, 1949, had established the fact that the voters wanted the old capitalistic system in preference to a new socialistic one, and, in the opinion of many union leaders, the currency reform had re-established the old economic order at one blow.

Union wage activities in the years immediately following the lifting of the wage freeze are usually summed up, particularly by foreign observers, as the "period of wage restraint," in which the unions' concentration on the rebuilding of the country allegedly resulted in a conscious policy of self-denial.

An examination of the wage, cost of living, and productivity statistics does not bear out this interpretation. Wages had more than caught up with the cost of living by 1950, when the cost of living index dropped while wages went up. From then on wages kept considerably ahead of the cost of living. Based on 1950 = 100 the index of gross hourly earnings in industry stood at 130 for 1953 whereas the index for the cost of living stood at 108. The wage index also remained well ahead of the productivity index. The latter stood at

Table 3-3.[a] Economic Indicators for Germany

Year	Index of Average Hourly Earnings for Industrial Workers[b] Including Construction	Index of Average Hourly Earnings for Industrial Workers[b] Excluding Construction	Index of Negotiated Hourly Wage Rates for Male Workers in Industry, Trade, and Services (Including Construction)[d]	Cost of Living Index[e,f]	Index of Industrial Producers' Prices[d]	Index of Productivity per Working Hour (Excluding Construction and Energy)[d] Index Numbers	Per Cent of Productivity Increase	Overall Productivity[e,g] Index Numbers	Per Cent of Productivity Increase
1	2	3	4	5	6	7	8	9	10
1950	100	100	100	100	100	100	—	100	—
1951	115	115	110	107.8	119	108	8.0	108	8.0
1952	124	124	116	110.0	121	112	3.7	114	5.6
1953	130	130	121	108.1	118	119	6.3	120	5.3
1954	133	133	123	108.2	116	126	5.9	126	5.0
1955	142	141	130	110.0	119	134	6.3	136	7.9
1956	156	156	141	112.9	129	139	3.7	141	3.7
1957	170	170	151	115.2	124	150	7.9	145	2.8
1958	182	182	160	117.7	125	158	5.3	149	2.8
1959	191	191	167	118.8	124	171	8.2	157	5.4
1960	209	209	178	120.5	126	184	7.6	167	6.4
1961	230	231	193	123.6	128	194	5.4	174	4.2
1962	(k)	(k)	(k)	127.9	(k)	(¹)	—	(¹)	—

[a] Table from Statistische Bundesamt Wiesbaden, except where otherwise indicated.
[b] New series. 1950–59 excl. Saar and Berlin; from 1960 on incl. Saar and Berlin. Take-home pay includes overtime and vacation pay as well as bonuses and certain other benefits. Employers and scholars estimate, however, that these average hourly earnings statistics of the Bundesamt must be augmented by another 25 per cent to arrive at actual labor costs.
[c] Only this column is comparable with the productivity index of column 7..
[d] Excluding Saar and Berlin.
[e] 1950–59 excl. Saar and Berlin. After 1960 incl. Saar but excl. Berlin.
[f] Based on a four-person household with a monthly cost of living expenditure of DM570 from 1958 on. From 1950–56 base on a four-person family household with expenditures of DM300. Each period based on different market basket.
[g] Gross domestic product per employed person in 1954 prices.

Table 3-3. (cont.)

Year	Percentage Increase in Gross National Product[e] At Current Prices	At Constant Prices (1954)	Per Cent of Gross National Product to Wages	Per Cent of National Income (Net National Product at Factor Cost) to Wages[h]	Total Labor Force[h]	Total	Employed Annual Average	Un-employed	Per Cent of Wage and Salary Earners Unemployed (Col. 18:16)	Balance of Trade in Million Dollars[i]	Terms of Trade[j]
	11	12	13	14	15	16	17	18	19	20	21
1950	—	.5	45.4	59.1	(k)	(k)	(k)	(k)	—	−723	100
1951	22.0	10.5	45.0	59.2	22,330	16,015	14,580	1,435	9.0	−30	100
1952	14.3	8.3	44.0	57.9	22,685	16,440	15,055	1,385	8.4	+183	115
1953	7.3	7.5	45.2	59.5	23,075	16,910	15,645	1,265	7.5	+612	126
1954	7.5	7.4	46.0	60.0	23,620	17,505	16,280	1,225	7.0	+660	125
1955	14.0	11.5	45.9	59.6	24,165	18,095	17,160	935	5.2	+316	123
1956	10.2	6.9	46.7	60.4	24,595	18,570	17,805	765	4.1	+700	124
1957	8.8	5.4	47.1	60.6	25,025	19,010	18,345	665	3.5	+1029	126
1958	7.0	3.3	47.7	61.4	25,270	19,255	18,570	685	3.6	+1399	136
1959	8.5	6.7	47.1	60.9	25,345	19,410	18,930	480	2.5	+1278	139
1960	12.0	8.8	47.3	60.9	25,570	19,770	19,530	240	1.2	+1247	140
1961	9.9	5.5	48.4	62.3	25,880	20,150	19,990	160	0.8	+1662	146
1962	8.5	4.1	49.3	63.8	(l)	(l)	(l)	(l)	—	(l)	149

h Excluding Berlin.
i Exports FOB, Imports CIF. As of 1959 government purchases included. Source is *Handbook of Economic Statistics* (Bonn: American Embassy, June, 1956, and December, 1962).
j Index of the average value of exports in percentage of the index of the average value of imports.
k Nothing available on a 1950 base.
l Not yet available.

119 in 1953 based on 1950 = 100.[16] It could always be argued, of course, that these statistics signify restraint because the unions might have gotten much more.

Every influential group in Germany, political and academic, has made it a point to credit the unions with great responsibility of action in the early years of the Federal Republic. There is an equally wide and emphatic consensus, on the other hand, that the unions could not have won larger wage concessions in any case. They might, however, have created more of a disturbance while trying. The suspicion therefore exists that "wage restraint" really meant docility, or, more euphemistically, an accurate appreciation on the part of the unions of what they could get, with or without strikes. Clearly, there was great restraint in striking.

Even though the wage index caught up to and surpassed the cost of living index in 1950, the unions continued until 1954 to justify their wage requests by pointing to rising prices. With workers spending a large proportion of their budgets for food, the upward trend of food prices was certainly conspicuous, and the price argument could therefore be expected to appeal to rank and file sentiment.

When in 1954–55 the unions changed their wage slogan from the price argument to a claim for a larger share of the GNP or an "expansive wage policy," there had been no noticeable change in the wage-price relationship. It was simply that by this time the employers' "inflation" propaganda had borne fruit, and the worker feared the wage-price spiral which, he was constantly told, would not only wipe out all his wage increases but in the end would leave him with less than he already had. It has been consistently true that the unions' choice of slogans to justify wage claims has been based far more directly upon the current fears and hopes of the union membership than upon the objective trend indicators. With their successive slogans, union officials tried to mollify the rank and file, who were usu-

---

[16] One of the points that is very often made in connection with existing wage statistics is that there was an enormous backlog of demand for the German worker as compared to his fellow European worker. This is impossible to prove because of the lack of adequate statistics. Until the currency reform very little could be bought with German wages, but even for the years immediately following the reform there are no international comparisons of hours of work required to buy various items. Certainly wages were higher in most other European countries in the early 1950's (the first years that could be considered "normal") but it is the purchasing power which would be decisive in throwing light on this issue.

ally concerned about the same economic dangers that were worrying the rest of the German public, and especially the danger of inflation.

Wages began a major upward trend in 1955, when it appeared that prosperity had come to stay and the unions, now firmly established, emphasized their right to a larger piece of the pie. As unemployment decreased rapidly and labor shortages became more frequent and finally general, a wage-price spiral began. German prices were still low internationally, and domestic purchasing power was increasing so rapidly that it was easy to pass higher wages on to prices in both markets. The 5 per cent upward revaluation of the DM in the beginning of 1961 was an attempt on the part of the Bundesbank to burst the bubble.

Table 3-4.[a] Wage and Cost of Living Indexes, 1948-56 (1938 = 100)

Year	Cost of Living Index[b]	Gross Hourly Earnings for Industrial Workers (excluding mining)
1948 1st half[c]	143.5	—
2nd half	168.5	129.8
1949	166.5	151.0
1950	156.0	161.9
1951	168.1	185.8
1952	171.6	199.8
1953	168.6	208.9
1954	168.8	214.9
1955	171.6	229.5
1956	176.1	249.9

[a] Table from Statistisches Bundesamt Wiesbaden. The area covered is that of the Bundesrepublik without the Saar or Berlin.
[b] Based on a four-person household with monthly cost of living expenditures of DM300 from 1938 through 1956.
[c] The currency reform took place in June, 1948.

The German economy slowed down (slowly because there was a backlog of orders) and began to experience what most government officials and economists refer to as a breathing spell and businessmen a turning point.

Because of the persistent shortages of labor the leveling off has not had a very pronounced effect on increases in actual earnings.[17] It has resulted, however, in a tougher employer stand vis-à-vis union demands, and, because the unions were usually not willing to strike,

[17] Hourly earnings of industrial workers increased 10 per cent in 1962 compared to 1961.

in a wide gap between original union demands and final settlements. In the early 1960's management complained loudly about very high union wage demands, though for a time these added costs could continue to be absorbed by increased prices and productivity gains. In 1963 this seemed no longer possible, however, and there were constant employer claims that wage increases beyond productivity growth would have dire consequences for the economy, including less investment and unemployment. The unions argue that profits are still large enough to absorb higher wages and that investment need not be self-financed. In spite of the tougher talk, unions have continued to win very substantial increases with very few strikes, even though the increases have been slightly under what they had been in some previous years.

The conditions under which collective bargaining has occurred in Germany since the end of the war have been relatively uncommon. Bargaining has not only taken place in a long period of increasing prosperity, but the rates of economic growth and the increases in productivity have been so substantial that one might conclude that it has not really come to a test of the relative economic strength of the bargaining parties, though there have been revealing tests of their political strength.

For the most part the wage trends of the fifties and early sixties have flowed from the decisions and bargaining of management and unions, with relatively little government intervention, and that chiefly indirect and spotty. That the private parties should work out their own deals has been an article of faith, and there have been frequent disparaging references to government arbitration under the Weimar Republic.

In the Weimar years either party could insist upon arbitration, but both parties were usually dissatisfied with the awards and felt no compulsion to abide by them. As a result there were constant disputes, with large-scale strikes and lockouts. There was simply not enough to go around. Employers could rarely give more than they did, the workers could not live on what they got, and both were tempted to shift the responsibility to the arbitrator ("Staatsschlichter"). This experience has left its mark on present-day thinking and talk, if not always on action. Both labor and management find governmental intervention in the collective bargaining process suspect as an abstract proposition, though each has favored or forced specific interventions on its own behalf.

From what kind of bargaining position did German firms negotiate in the postwar years? The position was a strong one: for an economic reason and a political one. Germany's economic recovery was accompanied by the rapid concentration of wealth and power in the hands of a small group.[18] In the early postwar years it had been thought necessary to allow the entrepreneur as much surplus as possible in order to facilitate self-financing and, as a result, industrial expansion. Government supported this management position, and the unions supported it, too, convinced that only through heavy investment would it be possible to absorb the unemployed and provide a more satisfactory economic base for all. Although recovery measures made it possible for those who had salvaged something from the war to amass enormous fortunes in a very short time and fostered great inequality of incomes, they have not been regretted because of the consistent and rapid economic improvement which eventually gave an unexpected high standard of living to all.

The political reason for management's bargaining strength lay in the wide support throughout Germany's stratified society for the general values represented by the free enterprise system, for the specific program of concentrating capital resources just noted, for the individuals who represented big business, and for their political supporters. Both the economic and the political aspects of this fortunate management position deserve some elaboration, and the two turn out to be aspects of the same thing when they are explored realistically.

The concentration of economic resources and the prestige of those at the top of the economic pyramid have made it easy for businessmen to act in concert and to avoid hurting each other, especially in price and wage policies. As noted earlier, the people in the top jobs in Germany still come very predominantly from a relatively small group in the population. From this group come the top management and top government people as well as the scholars, the newspaper executives, and the economists that negotiate international economic agreements. These people know each other. They travel a great deal

---

[18] The Statistische Bundesamt figures show for 1950 that the bottom 44.6 per cent of the taxpayers received 16 per cent of the income and the top 4 per cent 29.9 per cent of the income. Those of the Deutsches Institut für Wirtschaftsforschung show that in 1955 the bottom 49.1 per cent of the taxpayers had 20 per cent of the income and the top 5.1 per cent had 31 per cent of the total income.

A proportionately large retention of income by corporations rather than its distribution as personal income is characteristic of German business.

and come together often. Economic questions are discussed at formal and informal gatherings, and decisions are influenced without organized pressure having been exerted. To a considerable extent these activities negate the advantages which German economists and government officials attribute to the Marktwirtschaft in contrast to a planned economy, for they create an economy which is not publicly managed but which is privately managed.

The latitude German management has enjoyed in determining prices has both made it easier for employers to grant wage concessions and given unions a case for claiming them. Pricing is well organized in business circles. After years of experience, discussions of price policy are not even necessary in many cases. The group has been through this before; it knows how to react. A favorite procedure for raising prices is the press conference held by one of the leading entrepreneurs in a particular branch of industry. He announces that due to various factors (usually wage demands) his costs have risen to the point where it is impossible to keep prices at their current levels, and that he will reluctantly have to increase them as of a certain date. Within a few days or weeks all the other enterprises in that branch of industry follow suit.

At the BDI we were told that the consumer has not brought much pressure on prices because habit, convenience, social standing, and tradition are much more important in buying and spending patterns in Germany than is price. Whereas this observation is largely true for the traditionally defined upper classes, and also applies to some extent to the lower income older generation (the daily trip to the same local store where one gets all the neighborhood gossip is an institution), it is probably not valid with respect to the vast majority of the consuming public, particularly the lower income younger generation.

Nonetheless, product markets have been so organized as to maximize the power of the manufacturer and seller and minimize that of the buyer. Because German consumers needed everything after the war, they could not be very discriminating and the common absence of labeling has made them even less so. Those products that are trademarked are usually sold under strictly enforced fair trade agreements, which legally prevent price competition. In the early sixties the markets for some goods, especially appliances, were at last becoming saturated, and prices were dropping in these cases.

The solid front German industry displays in its pricing appears in a sense in its wage setting as well, though here the employers' organization, BDA, plays a more overt and conspicuous role. Clark Kerr reported in the middle fifties that "it is generally accepted that they (the employers) are better organized than the workers."[19] In interviews with management representatives there is constant emphasis upon the "voluntary" aspect of membership in the BDA, on its inability to do more than recommend action to its members, and on the allegedly greater ease with which unions can act in concert because, unlike employers, they do not live by competing with each other. In the trade press and in speeches there are admonitions to employers to stick together in the face of union demands and reproof for some who have granted "unrealistic" wage increases.

Solidarity among employers cannot mean the granting of identical increases, of course. It does mean that at the regional and local level the employers' organization for each industry signs the agreement for all its members, setting common minima. It also means some organizational and psychological controls over payments above the contractual rates. Though official action against an individual firm is possible only when it violates a "binding" decision, these are few and limited in scope, dealing chiefly with strike action. The individual employer may be restrained from paying too much above the contractual rates by fear that adverse business consequences might result from creating ill will among fellow members; but labor market conditions in the area, variations in the type and size of enterprises, and the zeal of the Verein's staff are all influential. Employers are legally required to observe the minimum conditions of the collective agreement.

In practice there is substantial drift above the negotiated rates. In their decisions to grant wage concessions above the minima, employers have had to respond to pressures in the labor market and in the product markets, and these concessions therefore represent "wage pull."

The calculation of the extent of wage drift is difficult, and findings must be recognized as approximate. To some extent the drift consists of payments for overtime work, bonuses (an important wage element in Germany), and piece-rate incentive payments. Forty to 60 per cent of the workers are paid on a piece-rate basis, and although their payments for production above the normal hourly quota are

---

[19] Adolf Sturmthal (ed.), *Contemporary Collective Bargaining in Seven Countries* (Ithaca, N.Y.: Cornell University Press, 1957), p. 176.

negotiated, they cannot appear in the statistics of negotiated wages, but do appear, of course, in the statistics of average hourly earnings.

Beyond the obvious statistical discrepancies, differences between wages paid and those negotiated are substantial. They tend to be higher in prosperous industries, for higher skill levels, and where labor shortages are most severe. A thorough statistical investigation of the extent of wage drift has not been done since 1957,[20] but various calculations and analyses, such as Table 3-5 prepared by the Wirtschaftswissenschaftliche Institut der Gewerkschaften, have led prominent union economists to the conclusion (also repeatedly expressed by management, government officials, and scholars) that market forces have been stronger in the process of wage determination than the power of the unions. Also pointing to this conclusion is the fact that, in general, drift has been less when negotiated increases have been higher.[21]

The wage drift problem was aggravated in the late fifties and early sixties by the shortages of labor and competitive employer bidding for the available supply. At least as important, however, has been the fact that the job descriptions still used in collective agreements bear little or no relationship to most present-day jobs. There has been and continues to be a very rapidly increasing number of jobs requiring specialized skills which are not covered by the contract and for which the extra remuneration must be determined in individual negotiations between the employer and the worker performing the task.

That payments above contract rates are completely within the employer's control gives him some important incidental leverage which the unions would prefer that he not have. Wages above the negotiated rates have no legal base. They can be and are cut out, reduced, and withheld from some workers, depending on prevailing conditions and the employer's interests. The situation constitutes a threat to the unions, but it also keeps the organized worker aware that much of his financial security is dependent upon the arbitrary decisions of the company. As wage drift constitutes a significant source of bargaining power for management, it is not surprising that employers

---

[20] By the Statistische Bundesamt Wiesbaden for all industries "Gehalts und Lohnstrukstur Ehrebung. . . . 1957," Heft I, Band 246/1, and, independently, by I. G. Metall for the metal industry.

[21] William Fellner, et al., op. cit., pp. 352–353.

have refused to accept various union proposals to eliminate it. These proposals are considered below.

The bases of German management's strength have been impressive. It has benefited from the German propensity to be submissive to those in positions of authority and influence, from the additional prestige flowing from the economic good fortune of the fifties, from long established habits of cooperation, solidarity, and comity among businessmen, from unemployment and the availability of foreign workers and refugees prior to 1955, from substantial profit margins,

Table 3-5.ᵃ Per Cent of Drift Between Negotiated Wages Rates and Actual Earnings in Selected Industries, 1949, 1955, 1961

| Industry | Year | Type of Worker | | | |
| | | Male | | | Female |
		Skilled	Semiskilled	Unskilled	Semiskilled
Stone and Earth	1949	10	18	13	na
	1955	18	26	18	na
	1961	27	33	24	na
Chemistry	1949	27	32	24	16
	1955	34	37	32	21
	1961	44	49	44	24
Synthetic Fabrics	1949	−03	none	−02	−10
	1955	18	17	10	−06
	1961	22	19	16	none
Iron and Steel	1949	29	51	50	56
	1955	52	68	64	46
	1961	51	69	58	17
Machine Construction	1949	26	31	17	14
	1955	32	44	25	19
	1961	43	43	33	30
Motor Vehicles and Airplanes	1949	26	39	25	26
	1955	39	45	37	32
	1961	52	53	46	48
Electro-technical Equipment	1949	20	25	09	10
	1955	27	33	15	19
	1961	37	40	30	25
Woodworking	1949	01	−02	−09	01
	1955	11	08	−06	01
	1961	24	17	10	04
Leather Products	1949	08	none	−02	−08
	1955	20	08	08	−03
	1961	39	37	24	17

Table 3-5. (cont.)

| | | Type of Worker | | | |
| | | Male | | | Female |
Industry	Year	Skilled	Semiskilled	Unskilled	Semiskilled
Printing	1949	20	30	21	07
	1955	27	26	17	06
	1961	32	31	14	−03
Textile	1949	17	na	−03	na
	1955	34	na	08	na
	1961	28	na	21	na
Clothing	1949	07	08	05	09
	1955	22	23	09	20
	1961	35	25	15	23
Fine Ceramics	1949	26	34	19	22
	1955	32	35	27	23
	1961	33	40	33	12
Breweries	1949	06	12	09	02
	1955	05	10	08	−04
	1961	17	22	23	na
Construction	1949	04	03	−02	na
	1955	03	01	−02	na
	1961	12	10	04	na

[a] Table from Heinz Markmann, "Wandlungen der Industriellen Lohnstruktur in West-deutschland zwischen 1949 und 1961" (Köln: Wirtschaftswissenschaftliches Institut der Gewerkschaften, September 19, 1962, unpublished). The selection of industries was intended to represent a cross section.

and from a bargaining system which made it possible for management to exercise the major influence on the level of take-home pay. Against these immediate and powerful advantages the record of Nazi collaboration before 1945, which once seemed permanently to have weakened German industry, turned out to count for little.

In addition to wage drift there is other statistical evidence that wage increases in Germany have been determined chiefly by the employer's own assessment of his needs and relatively little by wage push exerted by unions. An OECD study concluded that wage determination in Germany has been strikingly sensitive to demand conditions in the product markets, with wage concessions rising quickly as demand pressures increased and falling with even a moderate slackening of the rate of expansion.[22]

Related to this phenomenon has been the tendency for new settle-

[22] *Ibid.*, pp. 352–353.

ments within each of the postwar wage rounds to be uniform, even in different industries and sectors. This has been especially true in periods of high demand. Almost always the settlement in the metal industries has come first, furnishing a cue which other employers followed, even though the unions with which they bargained were typically weaker than the Metalworkers.[23]

The growth situation, then, has been such that wage increases were fairly high without the need for unions to exert marked pressure, quite apart from the question of whether they could have done so if they had tried harder. That they did not try harder, however, was not accidental. It stemmed from basic strains in both the kinds of ties that are most important for every union: with its own rank-and-file members and with the society in which it functions.

The German unions have had to cope in the postwar years with a membership that has often had reason to doubt that its good fortune could be attributed to unions. Worse, the members have been afraid that militant union action would do them more harm than good. Like the rest of the German public, they have been concerned about the danger of inflation, with the result that top union officials have had to convince lower level officials as well as rank-and-file members that they will be better off with higher wages and not lose everything due to inflation, as employers claim they will. Union officials are very much aware of the impact that employer and government warnings have made on the average member and know they cannot find support among their own rank and file for an aggressive wage policy.

A recent opinion poll conducted in Baden-Württemberg by the Frankfurt Divo Institute[24] showed that 65 per cent of the workers questioned thought that higher wages resulted in higher prices rather than lower profits for the entrepreneur, and 26 per cent thought both would be affected. In answer to another question 79 per cent thought that wage increases were useless because they were completely offset by price increases.

It also appears that wage issues are not really of prime concern to the average worker. The Baden-Württemberg poll confirmed what

---

[23] *Ibid.*, pp. 325–326. The Fellner study notes that the pattern was not followed as closely in mining, with its strong fluctuations in demand, or in construction, where the union often took an independent line.

[24] *Sozialpolitische Probleme in der Sicht Baden-Württembergischer Arbeitnehmer* (Frankfurt: Divo Institut, 1963).

many observers have speculated about for years (and German union officials have known): that the German worker is much more interested in security than in higher wages.[25] For the German worker employment and employment security are the issues of the day and they also are the prime concern of the unions.

The unions have also had to tread cautiously because their members fear the return of high unemployment levels. They are aware of the fact that nothing could please the employer organizations more than to have the overfull employment reduced to more "manageable proportions." Labor market shortages have been a serious economic problem in Germany in the past few years,[26] and undoubtedly a slight increase in the number of unemployed (0.5 per cent of the wage and salary earning labor force in October, 1962) would be welcome to all except the workers, who have derived important benefits from the shortage.

In their uncertainty and skepticism about union activities the union members reflect the relatively low status unions hold in German society generally. This lack of prestige in a culture which places great emphasis upon respecting and limiting those at the top has had two significant consequences for the unions. It has led them to allot a large share of their energies to status seeking, and it has kept them constantly subject to criticism as would-be or potential destroyers of the economic miracle and of public order.

The importance of status seeking can be measured by the great support among their members the unions have found for their goal of "codetermination." The more far-reaching form of codetermination exists in the coal and steel industry, where labor has equal representation with management in the *Aufsichtsrat*, a supervisory body

---

[25] *Ibid.*

The survey, conducted among metalworkers, suggests that given a choice the worker would prefer a job with long-range security to one with higher wages. For example, when asked which of two possible jobs they would select — one with a secure old age pension and lower wage, or one with higher wages but with a need for private arrangements for old age — 53 per cent of the workers selected the former, 9 per cent were undecided, and 37 per cent selected the latter. One per cent did not answer.

In another question the workers were given five choices with respect to job preference. Forty-three per cent would select the job offering addition pension benefits, 22 per cent extra pay, 13 per cent additional paid leave, 11 per cent a shorter work-week, and 9 per cent special housing benefits. Two per cent did not answer.

[26] By the end of 1962 there were approximately 730,000 foreign workers in Germany.

that meets every three or four months but is not influential in day-to-day management, and normally one of three members of the Vorstand or board of directors is a labor representative in charge of personnel matters. In all other private industries "codetermination" means only that labor representatives comprise one-third the membership of the *Aufsichtsrat*, and unions are entitled to organize plant councils in enterprises with more than five employees.

Representation for labor in top managerial organs obviously symbolizes status, even though, as will be seen shortly, it has probably hurt the unions' bargaining position more than it has helped it. There is no doubt, however, that the German workers want it, and the unions are currently pushing for its extension. At a time when the unions were acting cautiously "responsible" with respect to wages, they called a one-day general strike in 1951 to put pressure on the government to pass the codetermination law in the coal and steel industry, and the following year they threatened to strike again for codetermination in other industries. Both in writing and in conversation union people constantly mention codetermination as having been their main accomplishment in the postwar period.

Much has been written about the failure of the codetermination laws of 1951, 1952, and 1954 (the last dealing with public enterprises), from which the unions have expected so much. What has happened might have been predicted by any student of organizational theory. Closer identification with management has made the labor representatives on the boards of directors and in the plant councils see problems more clearly from the management perspective.

Especially in the case of Arbeitsdirektoren (labor directors) on the boards of directors of coal and steel plants has it been the experience that appointees become part of management in outlook and in responses to problems. They have not served as a one-way pipeline for union demands and worker interests, as the more naive labor people anticipated they might during the emotional fight for the codetermination law. Here several things have worked against the unions, the most important of which is probably the fact that in formulating the codetermination plan the unions put the "Arbeitsdirektor" in an almost impossible situation. His position is such that one is inclined to think that it was a compromise the unions were forced to accept, until one is told by trade unionists that this was how the unions wanted it.

The labor director is paid by management, and, like other managerial officials, may not reveal what has happened at executive committee meetings. This means that the unions are no better off with respect to knowing anything about their chances in an enterprise than they were before. Because of constant contact with management, their completely different financial status and a human but particularly German tendency to conform, the labor directors have tended to grow away from the group that put them in office and instead to identify with their new colleagues.

The unions suggest that it was difficult at first to find the right people and that the situation will improve with time. They also point to the check they have on the action of the labor director, who must be reappointed by the union members of the *Aufsichtsrat* every five years. It may nonetheless be impossible to find people who can represent labor's interests and yet have the confidence of management under the given set of circumstances. If the labor director protested too much, the other directors would probably find a way to isolate him. The check of reappointment which the unions have is limited by the fact that from public as well as practical considerations it would not be good policy to have a rapid turnover of labor directors when the other directors tend to stay on for long periods of time. At the moment the tendency is to put intellectuals in the jobs because it is thought that a good education is necessary to function effectively as director of a large firm.

For the ordinary worker, and especially the plant council member, the plant councils have also served in some measure to weaken loyalties to the unions. Plant councils are not allowed to bargain, but in practice they have had considerable influence upon plant pay practices and working conditions. Through the ability of council leaders to voice worker dissatisfaction, to negotiate on such matters as rest periods and wash-up periods, and to influence job classifications, merit ratings, bonuses, and incentive pay, they clearly have an impact upon wage drift. Even though the great majority of the plant council chairmen are DGB members, the councils have had the effect of keeping union membership down and making the union less important for the work force. Unions are not organized on a plant basis, and the plant councils have tended to take the place of a local union as far as the worker is concerned. As a result, the councils have developed what union leaders call "Betriebsegoismus," which means that they, and the workers for whom they speak, identify with the plant and its management against the unions on occasion. The phenomenon is reminiscent of the "dual loyalty" some students of American industrial relations have found.[27]

A revealing incident in April, 1956, shows to what extent German workers support and demand status-seeking claims. In Schleswig-Holstein the Metalworkers Union had sought sickness benefits and paid vacations in an effort to gain the kinds of fringe benefits for wage earners that salaried workers already enjoyed. Though a satisfactory settlement on wage and hours issues was reached, the union struck for the fringe benefits. After fourteen weeks the union executive was ready to accept a slightly improved settlement, but the workers voted not to do so, disavowing their officials, and were supported financially by other workers throughout Germany. An OECD study concludes that the strike "showed that workers not only in the region, but in the whole country, were willing to back union action on questions of social status which had no direct relation with wage levels." [28]

The proportional loss of union membership in the last decade is often cited as evidence that the unions "are losing touch." Mitigating circumstances are the increasing percentage of historically hard to organize white-collar workers among the employed, and the large number (over 700,000 in 1962) of foreign workers. The latter, often in Germany for a short time without their families, do not constitute a very organizable group. The lack of close union contact on the plant level, inadequate recruitment measures, and the fact that the worker looks to the plant council rather than to the unions to solve his day-to-day problems have also contributed to declining membership.

The main consideration, however, appears to be that the average worker is satisfied with his lot and sees no need to join a union. He has more money and better living conditions than ever before, is preoccupied with the accumulation of creature comforts, gets considerably higher wages than those negotiated by the unions, and because of the collective bargaining system, wage pull, and contract extensions, gets the fruits of union efforts anyway. He sees little reason to pay union dues.

Prosperity has also affected those that are organized. More concerned with security than with immediate higher wages, they are not

---

[27] For a more detailed description of the codetermination and plant council measures see Verein für Sozialpolitik, *Zur Theorie und Praxis der Mitbestimmung*, Band I (Berlin: Dunker und Humboldt, 1962), p. 556.

[28] Fellner, *et al., op. cit.*, p. 344.

prepared to risk the status quo by strikes. When the worker is willing
to strike at all, he will do it only if he is paid very high strike benefits. The latter vary from union to union but generally approximate
90 per cent of wages. This explains the unions' emphasis upon coming to peaceful settlements, which often has meant a lowering of
demands. In the early sixties, with substantial backlogs of orders and
profits high, employers feared strikes more than the workers, and
it was possible for the unions to obtain substantial concessions with
a minimum of days lost due to strikes.

Strike statistics from the interwar years indicate that the German
worker has not always been so reluctant to strike. Uncertain political conditions, enormous need, greater class consciousness, union
rivalry, and better union control of its membership are often given
as the reasons union activity was so violent under the Weimer Republic in contrast to today. The chaos of those days may well be an
influence on the current reaction of both workers and unions to
strikes. Interesting in this respect are the results of the Divo opinion
poll[29] which indicate that 47 per cent of the workers questioned
thought that strikes were more likely to be disadvantageous for the
worker than advantageous, 28 per cent thought that there were advantages and disadvantages, and only 23 per cent thought that they
were likely to be advantageous. Two per cent did not reply. Nothing
in postwar strike history should give the German workers such a pessimistic view of the eventual outcome of strikes.

In these and other respects, however, the workers reflect the values
of the society of which they are a part, and by the same token the
unions have faced a serious public relations problem. Until now,
labor-management-government relations have taken place in an atmosphere of strong class consciousness and social and economic
rigidity in which the frequent references to "social partnership"
appear to be a conscious or subconscious attempt at compensation
for the lack of it. Informal contact between union people on the
one hand and management or non-SPD government people on the
other was, until recently, virtually unheard of. It was therefore front
page news when *Der Volkswirt* of January 18, 1963, could feature
a picture of Ludwig Rosenberg, newly elected DGB President, drink-
ing cocktails with Mende, leader of the FDP. The *Volkswirt* referred
to Rosenberg's "new style" and spoke of his attempts to take the
unions out of their ghetto.

---

[29] Divo Institut, *op. cit.*

Table 3-6. Strikes and Lockouts, 1919-62, Number of Working Days Lost[a]

Year	Strikes		Sources
	Economic	Political	
Reich territory as of December 31, 1937			
1919	35,132,412	12,934,768	*St. Jb. D.R.* 1926, S.311
1920	17,702,800	36,504,142	*Ibid.*
1921	26,316,390	3,751,504	*Ibid.*
1922	28,894,434	346,306	*Ibid.*
1923	14,583,907	1,048,283	*Ibid.*
1924	36,360,134	(b)	*St. Jb. D.R.* 1930, S.329
1925	17,113,886	(b)	*Ibid.*
1926	1,325,309	(b)	*Ibid.*
1927	6,043,698	(b)	*Ibid.*
1928	20,288,211	(b)	*Ibid.*
1929	4,489,870	(b)	*Ibid.*
1930	3,935,977	(b)	*St. Jb. D.R.* 1932, S.307
1931	2,001,978	(b)	*Ibid.*
1932	1,130,000c	(b)	*St. Jb. D.R.* 1934, S.321
1933	96,460c,d	(b)	*Ibid.*
Entire economy			
1949	270,716		*St. B VI/18/24*
1950	380,121		*Ibid.*
Federal territory (without the Saar and Berlin)			
1951	1,592,892		*Ibid.*
1952	442,877		*Ibid.*
1953	1,488,218		*Ibid.*
1954	1,586,523		*Ibid.*
1955	846,647		*Ibid.*
1956	263,884		*Ibid.*
Federal territory without Berlin			
1957	2,385,965		*Ibid.*
1958	782,123		*Ibid.*
1959	61,825		*Ibid.*
1960	37,723		*Wista* 1963/2
1961	60,907		*Ibid.*
1962	450,948		*Ibid.*

[a] For the years 1919 through 1922 the figures reflect the number of people on strike or locked out multiplied by the length of the strike or lockout; after 1922 they show announced work days lost through strikes or lockouts.

[b] No data available.

[c] Only industrial workers.

[d] *Lt. St. Jb.* 1934: "Since 1933 no labor disputes have taken place."

In talking to people outside the labor movement one often hears references to labor's "inferiority complex." The unions are usually on the defensive, explaining that higher wages will not automatically result in run-away inflation, shorter hours are not a sign of the degeneration of the German worker, and so on.

Because the unions have not been able to produce spokesmen of the stature of Ludwig Erhard, Fritz Berg (President BDI), and Hans Constantin Paulssen (President BDA), the press is not likely to play up union leaders' speeches to the same extent as those of management or government officials, nor does the public attach the same importance or credence to them. Inexperience in public speaking on the part of union leaders, hesitancy about how they will be received by the press, lack of familiarity with the use of modern propaganda methods such as television, radio, and opinion polls, and the absence of a good union press, have all contributed to making organized labor come out a weak second best in the face of an extremely active, carefully prepared, employer-government propaganda campaign.

At the same time that the unions have been showing restraint in striking and have been doing their best to acquire some symbols of status, some of their more articulate leaders have continued to use the rhetoric of pre-World War I social democracy and Marxism. This, too, has alienated Christian Democratic government officials and much of the public, not to say many workers whose only class consciousness consists in an ambition to become middle class themselves. There has thus been anomaly: the older union leaders continuing to voice the radical ideas they had learned in their youth and which they ipso facto associate with trade unionism, while having to act quite moderately in order to hold the support of the workers. This type of ambivalence still characterizes men like Otto Brenner, President of the Metalworkers Union. Some say he does not mean what he says, others that he just cannot carry out his ideas. All have to admit that his bark is much worse than his bite.

One result of the unions' rhetorical line has been a widening breach between the DGB and the Socialist Party. This has been especially noticeable since 1958, the SPD having made the decision to try to enlarge its electorate, as it could never hope to govern if it had to depend strictly on the labor vote.

There may, however, be a change in the union line under a new generation of officials operating in a different economic and political environment, and many expect the new president, Rosenberg, to manifest the change. He is often called a strong man in a weak job but his impact has already been felt. Rosenberg spent the Hitler and war years in England and tends to steer away from having "too much ideology get mixed up with union business." Although Rosenberg is sixty, he is always included when one speaks of "young blood" for the DGB. The advent of this "young blood" with its more pragmatic ideas is watched with mixed feelings by the opposition. It is apparent, particularly when talking to employers, that the older ones were easier to handle. "Those people believed in what they said or did," we were told a number of times. "The young ones are mainly after power and they are shrewder, better trained and more dangerous."

Inadequate technical staffs have also been a problem for the unions. They have had great difficulty attracting competent economists and experts as there are very few people with the necessary qualifications from pro-union groups, and others have feared a stigma in working for the unions or have felt that there is little professional future or esteem attached. The traditional view that union staff personnel should receive low wages has not made the job of getting people easier.

There also is little awareness in union circles of what an economist should do, and the very meager union research staffs are overburdened with day-to-day trivia which not only give the people involved little chance to develop their potential abilities, but also make the job itself unattractive. The field of economics as a whole is underdeveloped in Germany, and it is particularly weak in providing tools for a theoretical approach to labor management relations. There is no field of labor economics.

What the unions publish in the way of press releases, research studies, documentation, and counter argumentation runs a poor second to what is put out by management organizations. The unions have a research office, WWI (Wirtschaftswissenschaftliches Institut der Gewerkschaften), which publishes a monthly called *WWI Mitteilungen,* but its articles are largely technical and have very little propaganda value. Its influence with the unions is also limited. The unions are in addition enormously handicapped by the fact that management also controls the statistics necessary for concrete union arguments. The Statistische Bundesamt is not permitted to collect statistics other than those authorized by the Economic Ministry and

Parliament, and the dominance of management influence in both has precluded the publication of the kinds of statistics labor needs for solid argumentation. In their absence, many of the unions' theses must be built on estimates and assumptions which would be difficult to justify in any society. The absence of profit figures is the greatest handicap. If employers say that they cannot possibly absorb higher wages without higher prices, there is no way to present a substantiated counterargument.

The growing difference between negotiated and actual wages has also had obvious disadvantages for the unions, for it further weakens union influence upon wage levels. It also makes the worker increasingly indifferent to union wage negotiations, for he often bargains for himself for benefits above those established by contract.

The unions have so far not been able to do anything about the threat represented by wage drift. They fear that if they used actual earnings as the base for future negotiations, they might make excessive demands on the less prosperous firms and force them out of business. The textile workers agreement contains a clause stating that negotiated increases must be added to actual wages already paid by an enterprise, but apart from a few other instances covering small groups, this type of arrangement has not been possible.

The Metalworkers tried to get around the wage drift problem by a policy of decentralized bargaining. This intention was quickly thwarted by the BDA, which had the same reasons for not wanting decentralized bargaining that the Metalworkers had for wanting it. Not only did the BDA refuse to bargain on a local basis, but it began to emphasize greater centralization. The Metalworkers were chastised, finding that in all their regional negotiations they were faced with the same central management bargaining committee which had been substituted for the regional bargaining committee. For the BDA this tactic killed two birds with one stone. It prevented the Metalworkers from achieving their aim and it obviated the need for employer solidarity. It avoided "regional weakening" or the establishment of a regional "bad precedent" for the entire industry.

High level union officials and economists realize that another important way in which the unions could try to catch up with wage drift would be to negotiate on the basis of more specific job descriptions. This represents such a major change in the thinking of the old-time union officials, however, that thus far little progress has been made.

Although the unions have claimed since about 1955 that they want redistribution of national income through wage policy, they have come to realize that this is difficult and inevitably very slow. One strategy they have tried in the early sixties is to espouse legislation providing governmental subsidization of savings. The money saved would have to be tied up for a given number of years. For the unions the plan has two main advantages. It would help those with low incomes to accumulate some capital and it would make it possible for the unions to push for higher wages without having to worry about demand inflation.

With employers fearing that Germany's competitive position may be weakening, bargaining was tougher in the early 1960's. For a long time the unions were able to win large wage increases with a minimum of pressure, thanks to a booming economy, a shortage of labor, and the ease with which wage increases could be passed on to prices. If a slackening of international demand for Germany's goods continues and price rises make it harder to sell them, unions are likely to face serious problems on the wage front.

VI

Strong demand for its goods and ample labor to produce them have certainly been the touchstones of Germany's postwar economic good fortune, the chief influences upon its wage and price movements, and the major determinants of management and labor tactics, claims, and talk. The organs of government have only rarely tried to exert a major independent influence upon economic developments. They have rather responded to the social and economic interests of the private groups and have tried to prolong the miracle through warnings, pleas, and occasional indirect interventions of a more forceful kind. The dominant position of business in German society has been reflected both in the continuing CDU dominance of the political scene and in the receptiveness of public administrative agencies to economic interest claims. The voters have kept the CDU in office throughout the postwar period, sometimes in coalition with other conservative and business-oriented parties. The result has been the isolation of labor and the absence of labor-oriented people in important governmental posts.

It is true that in the first flush of defeat, occupation, and scrambling to forget the record of business support for the Nazis, the CDU adopted an economic platform in 1947 that was well to the left of the present SPD Bad Godesberg Program. Known as the Ahlener Program, it called for widespread nationalization and a new economic system. At the time, however, what might have been the most influential conservative voices in the CDU were silenced by fear or imprisonment. As conditions improved, and particularly after the currency reform, party and business leaders were less inclined toward philosophizing, stock taking, autocriticism, analytical thinking, or wrestling with their social consciences. Getting back on one's feet was everyone's prime concern, and this involved the re-establishment of strong special groups. The economic miracle crystallized these tendencies.

In the late forties labor and the SPD had reason to suppose they were becoming part of the "establishment." Talk of nationalization gave way to talk of codetermination, relations were close between Konrad Adenauer and Hans Boeckler, highly regarded first President of the DGB; and there was access to top policy-makers. In view of what followed it may be more to the point that top policy-makers had access to organized labor. Boeckler's death in 1951 and the subsequent years of weaker DGB leadership coincided with the development of strong and confident management organizations and a constantly increasing electoral vote of confidence for CDU policies.

A serious labor dispute in the metalworking industry in the spring of 1963 brought into sharp relief the obstacles German unions face from businessmen cooperating with the CDU and from a membership less than enthusiastic about prolonged strikes. The Metalworkers Union has been the most militant of Germany's labor organizations and the only one to engage in serious strikes for economic goals since the war. It has, in fact, had strikes approximately every three years, and in 1963 a strike was a year overdue by this rough timetable.

There is evidence that the union's rank and file and officials were divided about the advisability of the 1963 strike and that Otto Brenner was seeking a compromise settlement up to the last minute. The evidence is even clearer that employers wanted a power test. They repeatedly rejected counter offers in spite of Brenner's hints to the effect that the unions would be willing to negotiate an increase lower than the 8 per cent officially claimed. Employers demanded a "wage pause" until at least the end of July, although the contracts had expired early in February.

The Christian Democratic Union, worried about a coming election and open strife between Adenauer and his successor-designate, Ludwig Erhard, needed an SPD defeat. The industry accordingly refused at first to grant any wage increase. When the union struck some plants in Baden Württemberg, the industry proceeded to shut down all the plants, solidly supporting a general lockout. The lockout alarmed the German public and hurt both the labor movement and the SPD. It also gave Herr Erhard an opportunity to come forward as mediator at a time when it would help him most politically. The CDU provincial governments refused to mediate themselves, apparently in order that Erhard might get the credit. The strike was more important for its political implications, which underlined labor's basically weak position vis-à-vis management and the government, than for its economic ones.

It is in the executive branch that important economic policies originate and it is here that they are applied. This can mean considerable leeway for subordinate officials. Here, too, labor's interests are far less likely to be recognized than are those of business, because few officials are labor oriented. In each of the ministries concerned with economic policy, a "Referat" and his staff of specialists on various problems are expected to be aware of the feelings and attitudes of the private interests groups concerned, and it is at the Referat level that most government-initiated policy measures are worked out. The Referat consults appropriate people at his own level in other ministries. Once he has prepared his case on a particular proposal and has secured the approval of his superiors, it goes to the Economic Cabinet, chaired by the Deputy Chancellor (Erhard through most of this period) and involving the ministries concerned with economic affairs. Approval by the Economic Cabinet usually means that a policy will be approved by the regular cabinet as a formality, though it occasionally is opposed by the Chancellor or turns out to be politically unrealistic.

In the course of their consideration economic policies are influenced by many economic reports and studies, both from within the government and from economic research institutes. German ministries also have advisory councils of scholars who make recommendations either when asked to do so or at their own initiative. It is not clear, however, that the councils' opinions are influential.

The German civil service consists predominantly of career people, but knowledgeable persons estimate that about one-third of the middle level employees of the Economics Ministry come from private industry. Few employees of the Labor Ministry come from the unions. Indeed, the DGB regarded the Minister of Labor in office since the late fifties as unsympathetic and as especially hostile to Socialist-oriented unions. It claimed that subordinate employees of the Ministry who showed themselves friendly to the DGB were penalized. That this strained relationship between the DGB and the Ministry of Labor should have continued and worsened for more than six years is a revealing commentary upon the arm's-length approach of the Adenauer administration to the labor movement.

The wage and price policies that have flowed from this machinery since the war have consisted chiefly of indirect controls and of exhortations. There have been no governmental ceilings or floors so far as wages are concerned, and no direct public intervention in collective bargaining. Prices were placed under direct controls just after the war, but these ceilings were gradually removed in the early fifties. Because of the Korean War, decontrol of raw materials prices and of public utility rates was postponed until 1952, and these prices were then freed in stages. With some exceptions, rents have remained under controls. The rents on "older housing" are scheduled to be freed between 1963 and 1965 as supply comes into reasonable balance with demand in various localities, but private housing constructed with interest-free or low interest government loans will remain under controls. With some exceptions granted in 1960, transportation remains controlled.

Since the currency reform of 1948 food prices have been free, except for indirect governmental influence through subsidies and market manipulations. The price is supposedly not allowed to drop below the point where the most inefficient quarter-acre farmer can make a profit. This policy is decidedly profitable for the large, efficient farmers, and it is continued because the governing parties are sensitive to pressure from the powerful peasant organizations, from which they draw important support.

The monetary reform of 1948 marked the end of the first postwar years of economic chaos and inflation and the beginning of a new economic and psychological climate of business confidence. In the decade that followed, neither wage-price trends nor balance of payment difficulties required renewed governmental intervention of a drastic kind. Cautious monetary measures, conservative fiscal policies, largely futile gestures toward regulation of monopoly, and occasional appeals for moderation in wage claims and concessions were the indirect devices upon which the government relied. As long as wages and prices continued to increase moderately, profits to grow substantially, and unemployment to decline, there was no effective pressure for government to do more.

The structure for decision-making on monetary matters insures that banking interests will be paramount in day-to-day decisions. The President and Vice-President of the Bundesbank and other members of the ten-man Administrative Council (Direktorium) are appointed by the President of the Federal Republic after being proposed by the Cabinet, which must have consulted the Central Bank Advisory Council (Zentralbankrat). The latter consists of the administrative council and the presidents of the provincial central banks. Each provincial central bank also has a council. At least half the members, according to law, must be chosen from the several branches of banking (Kreditgewerbes) and the others from trade, commerce, agriculture, and salaried and wage labor.[30]

The years following the 1948 reform saw the German economy fluctuate with respect to inflationary danger signals. A six-month boom was followed by fifteenth months of relative stagnation lasting from January, 1949, to March, 1950. Another boom stimulated by the Korean War was succeeded by almost a year of consolidation, and this in turn was followed by a long upward trend in prices that continued into the sixties.

The Bundesbank (before 1957 the "Bank deutscher Länder") has been markedly conservative in its monetary policies throughout the postwar era. During booms it has increased bank reserve requirements, tightened rediscounting policies, otherwise limited credit, and placed restrictions upon imports. In periods of relative stability and consolidation it has been extremely slow to remove these brakes, resisting pressures to stimulate expansion through monetary policy even in the years when unemployment was a serious problem. Currency stability and a balance of payments equilibrium have always been given priority over full employment as objectives.

By 1955 there was concern about the continuing price rise and increasing bank liquidity, and in that year the Bundesbank started open market operations on a large scale in order to curb credit. At frequent intervals through the following years the bank engaged in heavy open market sales of bonds and Treasury bills. It also raised

---

[30] "Beilage zu Monatsberichte der Deutschen Bundesbank," *Bundesgesetzblatt*, Teil I, nr. 33 (July 30, 1957), pp. 745 ff.

minimum reserve ratios slightly in 1957 and more steeply in 1960. The bank also reduced rediscount ceilings on several occasions, and in August, 1957, import duties on most industrial commodities were cut by 25 per cent.[31]

The high liquidity levels which these measures were intended to counteract stemmed chiefly from Germany's marked success in selling its products abroad. The surplus in the balance of payments provided the funds for large-scale investment and was without doubt the major stimulus for the economic boom. Many of the reasons Germany was so successful in the international markets have already been enumerated.

The effectiveness of the Bundesbank's monetary and credit measures was weakened as companies found themselves able to expand and modernize through autofinancing and as high liquidity levels gave the lending banks greater independence. The influence of the Bundesbank was further weakened in 1958 when the German currency became fully convertible. High interest rates have been particularly conducive to an inflow of foreign funds.

Mounting concern about inflation among economists and in the Bundesbank brought the most drastic action in thirteen years in 1961: a 5 per cent revaluation of the mark. As German exports were now 5 per cent more expensive to the foreign buyer, it was harder to raise prices on goods for export, and management was correspondingly less willing to grant wage increases which could not so easily be passed on to prices. The leveling effect of the revaluation on wages was slow to take effect, however, because of a backlog in orders and shortages in the labor market. In any case the revaluation was widely criticized: by some economists who thought it came too late, and by businessmen who thought it should not have come at all.

In the years immediately following the 1961 revaluation, profit margins were lower and some firms were in trouble. Several well-known manufacturing concerns failed in 1962 and 1963. In the second quarter of 1963 the rate of autofinancing stood at 27 per cent, though it had averaged 46 per cent in 1962 and 60 per cent in 1960. The growth rate was also down substantially. In spite of these signs that the era of spectacular boom might be ending, the economy as

---

[31] For a detailed account of monetary and fiscal policy before 1955 see Henry C. Wallich, *Mainsprings of the German Revival* (New Haven, Conn.: Yale University Press, 1955), pp. 63–112.

a whole seemed sound.[32] By the end of 1963 the remedy that had helped German business so much in the fifties was again compensating for some slackening in domestic demand. Foreign trade was flourishing as a result of increased German efforts to export. Nor did the new boom in foreign orders seriously threaten price stability in this disciplined society. Both the unions and the employers remained sensitive to the danger that runaway prices might end the economic miracle.

Conservative fiscal policy has supplemented cautious monetary policy, though objectives other than monetary stability have usually been paramount. During the economic lull and high unemployment of early 1950, for example, tax cuts and a work creation and public housing program were initiated. With the upward trend in prices following June, 1951, the corporation and turnover taxes were increased. As noted elsewhere, the tax laws have been used in the late fifties and sixties to try to spur saving by lower income groups.

In general, the tax system has conformed to the practice of encouraging business and has favored inequality of incomes. Income taxes range between 20 and 53 per cent of taxable income. Corporation profits used for reinvestment receive favored treatment. National revenues are derived to a very considerable extent from indirect taxes which constitute more of a burden on the lower income groups than on the upper. Evasion and avoidance of taxes is also easier for those with high incomes.

Government and management spokesmen claim that Germany's extensive social security system helps redistribute income. As one of the oldest and most complete of such systems in the world, it unquestionably does serve to moderate a lower-class protest, as Bismarck intended it to do when he initiated it. Since World War II the many benefits have been further enlarged and it is widely felt that social security has reached its limits both from the aspect of cost and of what it can be expected to accomplish.

The worker, the employer, and the government all contribute toward social security costs, and many employers also offer social benefits not included in the national system. Some of these are the result of collective bargaining. Since 1950 the cost of social security has increased substantially, and though employers and conservative

---

[32] *New York Times International Edition,* October 11, 1962.

legislators complain about this fact, there is no opposition to the system in principle.

Most fringe benefits are legislated rather than negotiated in Germany. In 1957 fringe benefits meant that 44.4 per cent had to be added to hourly wage rates in order to arrive at labor costs. The costs of these benefits have probably increased since 1957.

Toward the end of the fifties increasing pressure was being brought to bear for government measures to counteract big business concentration, favors, and influences. Demands came from labor and the SPD, but the more politically effective claims came from the "Mittelstand": the small, self-employed people with some property, small- and medium-sized businesses, farmers, and handicraftsmen. As the Mittelstand is well organized in Germany and contributes important support to the CDU and FDP, its demands carry some weight. The Bundestag has a Mittelstands Committee and the Economics Ministry has a Mittelstands Referat. These middle-class people have especially attacked the turnover tax on the various stages of production and trade. Large, vertically organized companies naturally enjoy a price advantage under this arrangement.

Anxieties in the middle class and among labor groups about concentration of economic power have brought a number of governmental gestures toward control of monopoly and competitive price setting. The anticartel and monopoly legislation, which took effect in January, 1958, has been largely unsuccessful, however, for it leaves large loopholes and makes it impossible for the Kartellamt, charged with its administration, to secure the necessary legal proof that there have been violations. More fundamentally, extensive behind-the-scenes cartel activity is relatively easy because of the long history of business combinations in Germany, the existence of so many closely knit business organizations, and long practice in subtle pattern setting and pattern following in pricing.[33]

The law requires that all cartels must register, but as of November, 1962, 218 had done so, as compared with an estimated 2,100 in existence in 1930.

In December, 1960, Parliament enacted another law providing for an inquiry into economic concentration, to be conducted by the Federal Trade Office (Bundesamt für gewerbliche Wirtschaft). Staff friction and lack of business cooperation have delayed the investiga-

---

[33] See Deutscher Bundestag, 4te Wahlperiode, Drucksache IV/617.

tion, and it will apparently produce only the most general kinds of findings.

With the labor shortages of the sixties, the German government has tried some other indirect restraints upon wage increases. Importation of foreign workers has helped somewhat, but this program suffers from inherent limitations. Most of those who come are unskilled, and cannot relieve some major bottlenecks. Furthermore, economic conditions have been improving in the traditional labor exporting countries. In 1962 it was felt that the approximately 700,000 foreign workers in Germany constituted about the maximum obtainable, and labor shortages were still acute in all economic sectors.

Another move to alleviate labor shortages and with them wage push and wage pull was a curtailment of construction. Among Germany's booming industries this has been the one with the largest backlogs and the proportionately highest price and wage increases. By forbidding the construction of nonproductive business enterprises for one year and removing some of the government subsides from private home construction, the government hoped for a leveling off in the industry. It was thought that the measures would contribute toward stabilizing wages and prices and at the same time release workers for other industries. The unusually severe winter of 1962–63, which not only put a stop to all construction for a longer period than in other years but also created additional construction work due to extensive road damage, pretty well counteracted government measures to "normalize" the construction industry.

It has not been possible for the German government to influence wage levels in private industry indirectly through its control over the wages of public employees. The government's attempt to "set a good example" by keeping wages and salaries down among the approximately 3,000,000 public service workers (which constitute one-seventh of the wage and salary earning labor force of about 21,000,000) has been frustrated by labor market shortages and competition from other industries. It has largely come to nothing. At various times the government has postponed wage increases but has then been faced immediately with shortages of blue-collar workers and other non-Beamten categories, and with a morale problem among the Beamten. It has had some success in delaying wage increases for the latter category, however.

Aside from the federal, provincial, and municipal employees, the government has effective control over wages only in transportation, public utilities, and the postal service, for in other industries governmental financial interests are in the minority. At the time the Volkswagen company was fully owned by the government, it offered a neat example of the limits of governmental influence upon wages in a public enterprise. In spite of repeated government admonitions to private industry not to reduce working hours, Volkswagen, which does not bargain through an employers' organization, went ahead with a shorter work-week program. Nordhoff, the very successful head of the company, ignored appeals of high public officials to resist the damands for fewer hours. As it was unthinkable to dismiss so effective an executive for this reason, the government accepted the situation with as much grace as it could.

Where the government's financial interest in an industry is minor, the plants are members of employers' organizations of their respective industries, and the government must abide by the majority decision.

Attempts at wage control through the granting or withholding of government contracts is irrelevant in Germany because virtually no firms depend on such contracts for their existence.

A form of indirect intervention that has drawn more public attention than any of those already discussed is the public appeal to management and labor to exercise moderation in raising wages and prices. Former Economics Minister Ludwig Erhard, hailed in Germany as the architect of the economic miracle, has frequently resorted to moral suasion of this sort. He has argued that higher wages may be inflationary, that they threaten Germany's competitive position, and that they therefore threaten to end the economic boom. The emphasis has always been on the need for "Masshalten" or moderation in wage demands and concessions on the assumption that price increases inevitably follow. With foreign markets weaker, profits tighter, and prices still rising in the early sixties, Erhard intensified his moral suasion campaign in 1962 and has bombarded both labor and management with his "Masshalten" appeals since that time.

Clearly, the moral suasion campaign has not stopped the wage-price spiral. On the other hand, it has been popular even among workers, and this was no doubt one of its objectives. An opinion poll conducted among workers in the Baden-Württemberg metal industry asked, "What do you think of Erhard's Masshalten campaign?" Thirty-eight per cent approved completely, 13 per cent disapproved, 19 per cent did not answer, and the others had reservations or qualifications.[34] Almost certainly, other groups of the population would endorse these appeals even more wholeheartedly.

As concern about rising prices, slower growth, and a worsening trade balance has grown and talk about the need for moderation in wage and price policy has grown with it, there has naturally enough been increased interest in finding an equitable formula for allocating the national income among its various claimants. While other European governments have searched for an incomes policy, there has also been considerable talk in Germany of the desirability of "Versachlichung," or putting wage negotiation on an objective basis. The emphasis here has been rather more specifically upon control of wages than other forms of income, and the moves toward Versachlichung have so far proven abortive.

In 1959 Chancellor Adenauer instructed President Blessing of the Bundesbank to try to establish criteria for a "Versachlichung." The Blessing Memorandum of January, 1960, favored tying wages to productivity increases, and estimated the productivity increase for the following year at 3 to 4 per cent. In February the Research Advisory Council of the Ministry of Economics attacked Blessing's productivity argument, and his case was seriously weakened further when the actual productivity increase in 1960 turned out to be 6.4 per cent. The memorandum has not had any perceptible effect upon wages.

Both the unions and the management groups have favored "Versachlichung" for some time, but only because they attach different conditions to it and expect different outcomes from it. Management believes that governmental and academic "experts" appointed by the administration will support resistance to wage increases. Labor, worried about its unequal power status, hopes to derive strength from an independent board that could get the facts, and it has placed great emphasis upon the need for a board that could gather its own statistics when necessary.

Under these pressures the government somewhat reluctantly acquiesced in the middle of 1962 to the introduction of a bill proposing the establishment of a "Gremium" or committee to analyze economic developments and pinpoint threats to healthy economic

---

[34] Divo Institut, op. cit.

development. The bill was blocked for more than a year by controversies over how appointments to the Gremium should be made and over publication of its reports. Management favored appointment by the Minister of Economics, while the unions preferred that members be chosen by Parliament, where the Socialist Party was influential. Apparently on the assumption that the thrust of recommendations would be toward wage restraint, management favored publication of the committee's analyses and recommendations while unions wanted to prohibit publicity for either.

As finally enacted in August, 1963, the law establishes a Council of Economic Experts whose members may not be connected with the government nor represent trade, employers, or labor organizations. They are appointed by the President of the Federal Republic upon recommendation of the Federal Government. In an annual report, and occasional special reports, the council is to discuss methods of maintaining price stability, a high employment level, a favorable trade balance, and adequate economic growth, all within the framework of a free market economy. It is directed to note undesirable developments and suggest in a general way how they can be prevented, but it is expressly denied authority to recommend specific measures. Both the DGB and the BDA expressed satisfaction with this compromise, which apparently assures that the council will do no serious planning on any controversial issue.

Even before the council was established Minister Erhard felt compelled to publish an Economic Report on February 26, 1963, analyzing developments in 1962 and making forecasts and recommendations for 1963.[35] The press regarded the report as an empty gesture intended to pacify the critics of the wage-price situation without requiring unpopular sacrifices. Labor was irritated because the report proposed limits for wage increases without limiting other incomes and because it had not been consulted in its preparation, though management groups had been.

VII

The interest of the workers in status and of management and government in keeping those with low incomes from rocking the

---

[35] For details see Deutscher Bundestag, 4te Wahlperiode, Drucksache IV/1010, *Bericht über die Wirtschaftsentwicklung im Jahre 1962 und die Aussichten für 1963.*

For a summary see Deutsche Bundesbank, *Auszuege aus Presseartikeln,* Frankfurt/Main, March 5, 1963.

fast-moving boat have been expressed in a variety of laws to give workers a larger stake in the economy and the economic system. Government and management groups have favored a redistribution of capital through voluntary consumption restriction on the part of the worker, and most of the redistribution measures have aimed at giving the worker an incentive to save. The unions have supported this line because they have seen in it a means of achieving noninflationary wage increases.

Among the devices adopted to encourage saving by workers have been tax exemptions on money saved for three years (later seven years) and government subsidies of 20 per cent for money deposited for a five year period, up to a specified number of DM. At the end of 1960 less than 10 per cent of the labor force was taking advantage of the latter program. Fear of inflation seemed to outweigh the government's gift in the workers' eyes. A 1961 law provides that an employer may give his workers up to 312 DM in a calendar year, with important tax benefits to himself and to the employee if the latter obligates himself to save the money for five years.

Another attempt to enlarge the worker's stake in the economy involved the transfer of some important government owned industrial enterprises to private ownership between 1959 and 1961. People with low incomes were allowed to buy the shares at a substantial discount from the current market value. Though the unions and the SPD had fought for this move, they were largely disappointed in the result. Many workers who bought shares of Volkswagen, the most important of the firms involved, promptly sold them at the market price, realizing an immediate profit. The majority of those who did hold on for a time were unable to resist selling during the rapid rise in the market price, from 350 to 1,100. By 1963 most of the Volkswagen shares were again concentrated in relatively few hands.

Both the SPD and the labor wing of the CDU have espoused other proposals to promote capital formation among workers.

VIII

As long as the dynamic of the German economic boom stemmed from a growing demand for goods the economy was well able to produce, there was no serious insistence by any group upon drastic governmental intervention and probably little economic need for it. Moderate controls over credit sufficed to keep price rises in line with trends elsewhere in the Common Market. Even when a tight labor market and some weakening of foreign demand in the sixties contributed to slower growth and faster rising prices, management and labor groups showed little interest in any drastic change in the methods of wage and price setting. The emphasis in Germany has been more clearly upon continuing the old status and power relationships than has been the case elsewhere. Rather than an approach to programming there have been halting steps to set up an advisory council responsive to those already in positions of influence. Rather than an incomes policy, there have been efforts to give workers a stake in defending the Marktwirtschaft by playing upon their appetite for status within it.

High governmental officials have frequently exhorted management and labor groups to show moderation; but in the light of the more rapid rise in prices and wages, one suspects that the effect, and perhaps the purpose, of the exhortation has been more largely political than economic. It has reassured businessmen and union officials that the real decisions are still theirs. More important, it has reassured the German voters that Erhard, Adenauer, and the CDU are on the side of virtue.

The German economy has benefited from much the same influences as produced the Italian economic upsurge in the fifties. Unlike Italy, however, there has been something close to a consensus on broad political and ideological values in Germany. There is little serious interest by any significant group in basic change in economic or political institutions. The national dream has been to get more of what there is to get and to conform to the style and values of "die Herren dort oben." To put it another way, no politically important group in Germany has taken advantage of the economic strains and opportunities of the postwar years to initiate or expand a dialogue on the good society or shown much interest in change toward a different one, while in Italy such interest has been effervescent, to say the least. On the contrary, the German Socialist Party has grown more conservative, for that is where the votes have been. The mood of contentment has been mirrored in academic life as well. We found less interest in Germany than in the other countries we studied in the theoretical foundations of economic programming and less interest in labor economics.

The contentment and the wide conformity to the principles of a free market may not run deep. Certainly, fear of inflation and of depression have been strong, and they have almost certainly limited wage demands more than Erhard's Masshalten appeals. In the light of German history the narrow limits within which pluralistic interplay on economic matters has been contained and the virtual absence of a preliminary searching out of viable institutional alternatives are not reassuring. Whether this speculation is unduly pessimistic or not, it pinpoints a basic difference between the politics of German wage-price policy and that of other countries we have examined.

Incomes policy in the context of overall economic planning has become a dominant political issue in Great Britain. This is a new development, and one that can be understood only against the backdrop of the enormous and rapid political, economic, and social changes which have occurred since the war.

No sooner had the war ended than the Labor Party won the General Election of 1945. During the next six years the Bank of England, the coal mines, the iron and steel industry, and public utilities were put under government ownership and operation. At the same time the bonds of the Empire loosened. India and Ceylon became independent. Burma left the Commonwealth entirely. The mandate over Palestine was given up so that the new state of Israel could be formed.

By 1951 the Conservatives were back in power. Steel and a large part of road haulage were returned to private ownership. By 1955 Anthony Eden had succeeded Winston Churchill as prime minister, but left office in early 1957 as a result of the Suez crisis. Harold Macmillan took over, won an impressive general election on his own in 1959, and found himself increasingly confronted with the complexities of market competition arising out of the growing strength of the Common Market. To remain outside would subject Britain to tariff barriers on the Continent, while joining would seriously strain the ties of the Commonwealth. The painful decision to seek entry was followed by the bitter French veto early in 1963.

Meanwhile changes in Africa, Southeast Asia, the West Indies, and elsewhere moved the once far-flung British Empire further into history. In October, 1963, the Conservative government, already reeling from the Profumo scandal, was forced by the ill health of Mr. Macmillan to find a new Prime Minister. As Sir Alec Douglas Home took over, the odds were heavily in favor of an early election victory for the Labor Party under the leadership of Harold Wilson.

Underlying these political developments were profound structural changes in the economy. New materials, new processes, new productive techniques, and mass markets for consumer goods created in part by artificial stimulation of demand through advertising — all these were giving rise to new industries and retarding some old ones. The National Economic Development Council report on *Growth of the United Kingdom Economy* [1] noted growth rates for the period 1961 to 1966 varying from 7.5 to 13 per cent for such industries as chemicals, electricity, electronics, petroleum, motor cars, heavy electrical machinery and machine tools, in contrast to 3 per cent or less for coal, gas, paper and board, and wool textiles.

Such changes have significant implications for the economy, and for individual employees and employers. They mean new demands for capital investment, public and private. They imply a new pattern of skill requirements, with redundancy of many craft skills, marked increase in demand for others, and the necessity of training for some completely new skills. The labor force is also affected with an extremely rapid increase in the numbers of white-collar and women workers, and in the professions and distribution trades, an exodus from agriculture and coal mining, and very large demands for workers in the new industries, particularly electronics, motor vehicles, and construction. These changes in turn have drastically altered the regional pattern of employment, since the new industries have tended to concentrate in the eastern, southern, southeast, and midland areas of the country, while the traditional but declining industries are located in the northwest of England and in Scotland and Wales.

Another phenomenon which has important implications for economic planning and industrial relations has been the growth of the public sector. Large segments of the British economy are now publicly owned and operated, including postal and telecommunica-

---

[1] National Economic Development Council, *Growth of the United Kingdom Economy to 1966*, February, 1963, p. 5.

tion facilities, coal, electricity, gas, atomic energy, railways, buses, the underground, inland waterways, two national airlines (BOAC and BEA), 10 to 15 per cent of iron and steel, and some oil extracting and processing facilities. In addition, large numbers of people work in the public health and other social services, as well as in traditional public administration. The total number of people engaged in the public sector in 1961 was just under 5,250,000, which is just over one-fifth of the civilian labor force. The public sector accounts for approximately two-fifths of national investment. About one-quarter of the gross national product is spent collectively; of this, social services, that is, housing, education, health, science, public welfare, and so on, account for less than two-fifths, while defense accounts for 27 per cent, interest on the public debt for 9 per cent, and farm subsidies for 6 per cent. In addition, the nationalized industries account for about one-fifth of the national product.

Another structural change which significantly affects industrial relations and economic policy is the growing size of business units. Concentration has been taking place not only in private manufacture, but also in retail distribution and transportation, and in public enterprise. It is a consequence of internal expansion, of mergers and take-overs, and of nationalization. The motives have been a mixture of productive efficiency and the financial advantages of monopolistic control. By mid-1961, 34 per cent of those employed in manufacturing were in the 2 per cent of establishments with 1,000 or more employees. At the end of 1960, the 100 largest businesses in Britain accounted for 54 per cent of the total net assets of all quoted companies, and this figure has risen from 51 per cent since 1957. In the same period the number of quoted companies in manufacturing and distribution fell by about 10 per cent.[2]

The consequences for the British ecnomy of these various developments have not all been favorable. True, technological progress has brought with it a steady rise in living standards. Consumer expenditures in 1962 were nearly a third higher in real terms than ten years earlier. Rising wages and profits, growing public welfare benefits, and new gadgets and ways of life have imparted a general sense of affluence, and from time to time Conservative politicians have found it feasible to remind the electrorate that "You never had it so good."

---

[2] PEP, *Trade Unions in a Changing Society*, XXIX, No. 472 (June 10, 1963), p. 175.

At the same time, however, that electorate has become increasingly conscious of a basic economic malaise. Repeatedly the economic mechanism has faltered, and with every new attempt to patch it up and resume progress the conviction has grown that something has gone amiss, and that a tired and complacent economy is failing to adjust to the requirements of a new era. This conviction has been reflected in increasing social and political unrest, and a corresponding decline in popularity of the Tory regime.

In part the difficulty has taken the form of inflation as wages and prices rose faster than productivity. Earnings have increased on the average more than 6 per cent a year between 1950 and 1960 as compared to an average increase in productivity of a little over 2 per cent, and in retail prices of about 4 per cent.

But inflation does not cause widespread popular unrest in a dynamic economy where living standards are rising. It has given rise to serious concern in Great Britain because of its effect on economic growth; discontent has related much more to the slow increase in investment and in output than to the faster rise in earnings and prices. As the gross national product slowly rose, and with it domestic demand, the proportion of the national product allocated to exports declined. The resulting failure year after year to earn enough on the current account led to chronic balance of payments crises, which were of course aggravated by the rising level of domestic costs and prices. Moreover the development of exports, of costs, and of prices relative to those of Britain's major competitors in world markets was even more adverse.

The elasticity of demand for imports does not seem to have been substantially different in the United Kingdom and in the EEC countries, but the development of exports shows a very strong contrast. After an insignificant rise in the first half of the decade, United Kingdom exports rose only half as fast as imports between 1955 and 1960. In the EEC countries, on the other hand, exports and imports grew in parallel during this period, and in the first half of the decade exports rose substantially faster than imports. Even allowing for the progressive improvement of the terms of trade, the weakness of exports stands out as one of the most striking features of the 1950's. As a result the trade balance moved unfavorably by nearly $1.5 billion from 1950 to 1955 and fell again by a small amount in the following five years, whereas the trade balance of the EEC countries improved by nearly $0.9 billion up to 1955 and by $1.1 billion between 1955 and 1960. Between 1950 and 1960 the United Kingdom's gold and foreign exchange reserves declined by about $200 million, whereas those of the EEC countries rose by over $12 billion.

According to the National Economic Development Council report on *Growth of the United Kingdom Economy*, an important reason for this poor performance as compared with competitors has been the relatively rapid rise in British export prices. This conclusion is documented by Tables 4-1 and 4-2.

In each crisis the Conservative government adopted the same solution. Through restrictive monetary and fiscal measures it checked production in the hope of generating spare capacity, including manpower in the form of unemployment, in order to discourage imports, to make it more difficult for unions to obtain wage increases and for employers to pass on higher wage costs in prices, and to stimulate

Table 4-1.[a] Productivity and Earnings in Manufacturing; Increase, 1953-61 (Per cent per annum)

	United Kingdom	Other Main Exporters[b]
		average
Output per hour	2.7	4.5
Earnings per hour	6.4	5.0
Wage costs per unit of output	3.6	0.5

[a] Table from National Economic Development Council, *Conditions Favorable to Faster Growth*, April, 1963, p. 49.
[b] Weighted according to value of exports of manufactures of each country in 1956. In terms of dollars.

Table 4-2.[a] Exports of Manufactures, 1953-61

	Per Cent Change in Price Index[b]	Per Cent Change in Quantity
United States[c]	20	33
United Kingdom	14	32
Germany	5	191
France	−1	111
Japan	0	290
Italy	−21	345

[a] Table from National Economic Development Council, *Conditions Favourable to Faster Growth*, April, 1963, p. 49.
[b] Unit value indices in terms of dollars. In terms of francs French export prices rose. In terms of marks German export prices hardly changed.
[c] Excluding special category exports which are mainly military aid.

manufacturers to seek export markets for the goods they could not sell at home. But this "stop-go" policy did not improve exports, nor did it stop prices from rising. The degree of unemployment that would have been required to be effective was completely unacceptable politically. What such a policy did do was to inhibit private and public investment and periodically interrupt economic growth. As a consequence, the British growth rate has been far below that of all other industrial countries. In the 1950's it was about half that of the EEC countries; per head of employed population the gross national product grew 2.5 to 3 times faster on the Continent up to 1955 and twice as fast subsequently. And output per man hour in the United Kingdom was between one-half and one-third that in the EEC countries.

Comparisons with the performance of the six countries of the European Economic Community are provided by the tabulation in Table 4-3.

Table 4-3.[a] Comparison of Economic Performance of Great Britain and EEC.

	1950–55 United Kingdom	EEC	1955–60 United Kingdom	EEC
	per cent change			
Gross national product	15	34	13	27
Employment	4.5	5.8	1.7	6.1
Gross national product per head of employed population	10	27	11	20
Industrial production	21	52	14	40
Industrial production per man hour	13	37[b]	16	37[b]
Price index of gross national product	26.5	19.2[c]	16.2	13[c]
Volume index of imports	26	56	26	66
Volume index of exports	6	76	13	63
Imports and exports as percentage of gross national product	38	28	32	30
Change in visible trade balance (million dollars, current rate)	−1,440	888	−48	1,104
Change in official gold and foreign exchange holdings (million dollars, end of period)	−1,287	5,300	1,083	6,850

[a] Table from Organization for Economic Cooperation and Development, *1961–1962 Annual Review of the United Kingdom* (OECD/EDR (61) 1st revision), January 29, 1962, p. 7.

[b] Excluding B.L.E.U.

[c] Excluding France, which had two devaluations during the period. If France is included, the corresponding figures are 25.6 per cent in 1950–55 and 21.4 per cent in 1955–60.

Production recovered rapidly in 1963 after two years of comparatively static output and a particularly severe winter. In the fourth quarter of 1963 gross domestic production is estimated to have been 7 to 7½ per cent above the 1961 level, having increased by about 5½ per cent over the preceding twelve months.

This increase in output, however, has not brought with it a comparable improvement in exports. Between 1961 and 1963 the growth of exports has fallen short of the goals set by the National Economic Development Council. After fluctuating during 1962, exports rose strongly in the earlier part of 1963 but flattened out during the second half. The average annual rate of growth of the volume of exports between 1961 and the last quarter of 1963 was less than 4 per cent per annum. Apparently the United Kingdom's competitive position has improved only slightly during this period.[3]

Overall, unemployment has not been serious; between 1951 and 1961 it averaged less than 1.6 per cent. But the failure to achieve a dynamic rate of growth which would absorb the effects of relative declines in certain industries, plus failure of the efforts to persuade new industries to go to the declining areas, resulted in serious regional pockets of unemployment, as shown in table 4-4.

The areas affected, northern England, Scotland, Wales, and North-

Table 4-4.[a] Registered Unemployed (Percentage Rate of Unemployment)[b] at mid-December

	1958	1961	1962
London and South Eastern	1.4	1.1	1.5
Northern	3.2	3.0	5.0
Eastern and Southern	1.7	1.2	1.8
Scotland	4.4	3.5	4.7
South Western	2.6	1.7	2.2
Wales	4.1	2.8	3.8
Midlands	1.7	1.4	2.0
Great Britain	2.4	1.7	2.5
Yorkshire and Lincolnshire	2.3	1.3	2.1
Northern Ireland	9.0	8.7	7.6
North Western	3.3	1.8	3.0
United Kingdom	2.6	—	2.6

[a] Table from H. M. Treasury, *Economic Report 1962*, supplement to *Economic Trends*, No. 113 (March, 1963), p. 21.
[b] Number registered as unemployed expressed as a percentage of the estimated total number of employees.

[3] National Economic Development Council, *The Growth of the Economy*, London, HSMO, March, 1964, pp. 44–45.

ern Ireland, have long been the centers of concentration for coal, textiles, shipbuilding, heavy engineering, iron and steel, sea fishing, and railroad equipment. This localized problem of unemployment has been widely discussed and has served as a constant reminder to economists, politicians, and trade union leaders of the growing threat unless the rate of growth can be stepped up to provide hundreds of thousands of new jobs over the years ahead.

Economic growth is also seen as the answer to another problem which has been an increasing source of social unrest, that is, the neglect of public services. Galbraith's eloquent demonstration for the United States of "public squalor amidst affluence" as government spending fails to keep pace with growing requirements for education, health services, transport facilities, housing, urban development, public assistance, old age benefits, and so forth, is equally applicable to Great Britain. There has been a spate of special inquiries and reports on each of these areas, and all three parties, Conservative, Liberal, and Labor, are currently promising big increases in public spending.

This kind of public concern has been particularly directed to defects in the educational system. Educational opportunity is looked upon as the key to adjustment to the technological age — not only in terms of providing the necessary skills, but also as a way of overcoming the inertia, complacency, and rigid class structure which are now recognized as obstacles to a dynamic, enterprising economy. Attacks are being made not only on the inadequacy of educational facilities and teaching staff, but also on the snobbery and compartmentalization reflected in the three-tier educational structure of public schools, grammar schools, and other state secondary schools.

The three types of schooling, each with its own peculiar ethos and curriculum, tend to cultivate a three-tier division of young people in terms of psychological outlook and job opportunities; and the tiers are later transplanted into industry in the approximate divisions of top management, administrative-technical-clerical grades and manual workers. . . . It follows that, however much good will may exist on both sides, the communication of views between shop-floor representatives and employer's representatives must often be handicapped by a fundamental lack of common ground. Furthermore, the educational system may engender, not merely misunderstanding, but also bitterness and hostility. About three-quarters of the nation's youth are educated in secondary modern schools, which are regarded by many . . . as facilities for failures.[4]

---

[4] PEP, op. cit., p. 200.

Increased attention is also being given to the waste of human resources incurred in cutting short the schooling of three-fourths
of the nation's manpower at the age of fifteen.

Taken together, all these social and economic problems have
brought about a growing interest in planning — a conscious ordering
of priorities and direction of resources — as the key to economic
growth. On the necessity for planning, the major political parties
do not disagree. The current planning body, the National Economic
Development Council, was established by the Conservatives, but it
has had the strong support of the trade unions which back the
Labor Party.

Within the context of planning, attention has increasingly been
focused on the idea of an "incomes policy." It has become fashionable
to argue that restrictions on incomes, and hence costs, are essential
in an economy which depends on remaining competitive in world
markets and insists upon full employment at home. In the pre-elec-
tion fervor which was already in full swing by the autumn of 1963,
all three parties were committed to an incomes policy. But there were
few concrete proposals, and even less consensus, as to how this
should be accomplished. The efforts of the Conservative government
to control wages, via Selwyn Lloyd's pay pause, and the subsequent
"guiding light" and National Incomes Commission, have proved
largely futile. And hopes of developing an incomes policy within
the framework of the National Economic Development Council re-
ceded as the election approached and it became clearer that no
definitive action could be taken until after the election.

The process of arriving at a wage policy, said the OEEC report
on the problem of rising prices, is "essentially a question which concerns the art of government, conceived of as a process of reconciling
conflicting sectional interests in the common good." [5] It follows that
successful pursuit of this art calls for identification and examination
of the institutions which are involved — trade unions, employer organizations, collective bargaining, conciliation and arbitration, statutory wage fixing, and joint consultation.

THE TRADE UNIONS

Certain structural features of British trade unions have a direct
bearing on the potential willingness and ability of union leaders to

---

[5] Organization for European Economic Co-operation, *The Problem of Rising
Prices*, C(61)12, May, 1961, p. 58.

achieve a moderation of wage claims in line with an agreed national incomes policy. The potentialities for cohesion, coordination, and control within the labor movement hinge on organizational structure, degree of centralization, internal communications, union finances, and political ties and influence.

British trade unions currently have organized about 46 per cent of the total number of employees who contribute to the national insurance scheme. This represents approximately one-half of the male workers and one-quarter of the female employees. While this is a far smaller ratio of organized to unorganized employees than one finds in the Scandinavian countries and in Austria, it is distinctly higher than in the United States, West Germany, France, Italy, and many other industrial countries. Membership in trade unions grew rapidly during the decade of the forties, and in the decade 1948 to 1958 was still expanding faster (52 per cent as compared with 48 per cent) than the working population. However, the trend has reversed in recent years and in 1962 the ratio of trade union members to labor force was well below that of 1948. This reflected declining employment in some of the more highly unionized industries such as coal, textiles, footwear, and railways, and the failure of the unions to keep pace in rapidly expanding fields like chemicals, distributive trades, professional and business services, and insurance.

The influence and strength of the trade union movement is nevertheless greater than sheer numbers would suggest. This is because a substantial portion of the floating population which is between jobs or unemployed may be assumed to be sympathetic to the trade union point of view, because collective agreements cover *all* workers in the relevant grades or industries whether organized or not, and more particularly because in certain industries or occupations the degree of organization is very high, for example, 89 per cent in coal mining, 84 per cent in railroads, 83 per cent of government workers, 75 per cent of transport workers other than on the railroads, and 63 per cent in footwear.

The structural composition of the British trade union movement is difficult to visualize. There are some 635 unions (in 1920 there were 1,384), each with a General Secretary and a governing council. Of these, many are craft unions and a few are industrial, but the majority are "multicraft," including semiskilled workers in a particular industry, for example, engineering, plus crafts in other industries; or "general," including a heterogeneous group of semiskilled and unskilled workers cutting across both horizontal and vertical industry lines; or "occupational," that is, covering noncraft occupations such as clerical work. In the white-collar field the picture is even more complex, with some unions restricted to one industry and some crossing industry or government department lines, and still others, such as teachers, postal workers, and bank employees, vertically organized.

Despite the plethora of unions, nine of the 635 unions account for more than 54 per cent of the members, while 344 of them have less than 1 per cent of the total membership. The fact that many unions have entered into federations must also be taken into account. Unfortunately, it is as difficult to classify the federations with respect to function as it is to discern a neat organizational pattern among the constituent unions. By way of example, the General Federation of Trade Unions unites about eighty unions in a number of industries, but its functions are limited to those of a mutual insurance society. At the other extreme is the powerful Confederation of Shipbuilding and Engineering Unions which conducts all negotiations on wages and working conditions, at national and district levels, with the exception of piecework agreements and prices. By 1959 there were forty-three federations, varying greatly in purpose and authority. In general, individual unions retain their autonomy within the federation and final decisions rest with executives of the various unions.

Trade union leaders in Britain are fully conscious of the problems which confront the movement as the result of the rather chaotic structure found within their ranks. The Trades Union Congress has repeatedly passed resolutions and conducted inquiries into the subject and made recommendations concerning amalgamations, federations, streamlining, and elimination of competition for members. At the same time, TUC officials have disclaimed the necessary authority for enforcing any of the proposed forms of reorganization and little has in fact happened. There have been amalgamations and federations but no major move has occurred in this direction in recent years. There are many obstacles in the path of consolidation aside from the usual problem of vested rights. Dues and benefits differ, strong unions are not inclined to pool resources with weak unions, and policies differ with respect to organization, wage demands, fringe benefits, and other bargaining demands. Craft unions resist amalgamation or reorganization along industrial lines since their influence depends upon their control of the job. The growth of industrial unionism is further discouraged by the fact that the large general unions recruit horizontally across industrial lines as well as vertically within an industry, and by the fact that the white-collar field, which now holds the greatest possibilities for membership expansion, is not well suited to industrial unionism.

The TUC is currently conducting a two-year inquiry into the problem of structure, but General Secretary George Woodcock has publicly acknowledged that progress can only be slow in the face of the autonomy of individual trade union leaders. At the 1963 TUC congress he stated that diversification of structure is a basic characteristic of British trade unions and always will be, and that the General Council could see no hope of persuading the unions to accept a uniform structure, particularly an industrial structure. "We are not disposed to impose it on unions," he said, "and we do not see that it will come by consent."

At the top of the trade union structure in Britain, as the above remarks indicate, stands the Trade Union Congress. Though not all unions are affiliated with the TUC, some are represented through federations and most of the unaffiliated organizations are small, only two have more than 100,000 members (the National and Local Government Officers' Association and the National Union of Teachers), and they are on friendly terms with the TUC. Thus the TUC is a highly representative organization. Its authority over its members, however, is primarily moral rather than legal. The TUC is governed by a General Council comprising thirty-five trade union general secretaries or presidents, representative of nineteen industrial groups. The general secretary and assistant general secretary are appointed by the congress, and the rest of the staff of approximately seventy is appointed by the general secretary. The Council meets monthly but has nothing like the authority that the delegate conference or national executive would have in an individual union. It cannot override the autonomy of the affiliated unions and its decisions are not binding on them. The member unions retain their authority, as well as the bulk of their funds. They resent any interference from the TUC except in certain carefully limited circumstances.

The most important powers of the TUC are contained in Rules 11, 12, and 13 of the Constitution. Rule 11 concerns the obligation of member unions to keep the General Council informed of any negotiations or conflicts with employers or other organizations. Since 1945 the General Council has had authority to intervene if the negotiations seem likely to lead to a work stoppage. Rule 12 concerns TUC powers in disputes between affiliated organizations, and Rule 13 covers the right of the TUC to investigate unions, to issue cease and desist orders, and even to suspend unions until the next Congress.

Channels of communication within the trade union movement are relatively ineffective. At the local level union membership is usually based upon residence rather than place of work. This means that one point of contact between the individual member and his union is the local branch officer. However, local officers are often too busy to familiarize themselves with the problems of individual firms in their area, with the result that their negotiating functions have atrophied at the very time when there is some evidence that plant level bargaining is growing in importance. Because branch officials have so little impact on wages and working conditions, and for reasons of general apathy, attendance at local meetings is very low — being in the neighborhood of 4 to 7 per cent of the membership.

The other contact which the union member has with his union is through the shop steward who is elected in the shop. The steward collects the dues, disseminates information on union activities, and deals directly with the employer on grievances, wage rates, and working conditions. Given the British pattern of union organization there will, of course, be many unions represented in a typical shop. For this reason there will be many shop stewards representing the various unions. In order to achieve some degree of coordination, negotiations with the employer at the shop level are conducted jointly by the stewards, with one of them being elected "convenor." The steward thus finds himself confronted with the dilemma that the rules of his own union (frequently obsolete) may contravene those of the uniform procedure agreed upon with the employer and the other unions. Because he must cooperate with the other shop stewards for purposes of bargaining, the particular steward operates more within the broad context of shop loyalty than of union loyalty. This in turn weakens the hold which his union has on him.

Another point at which contact can be established between members and leaders is at the delegate conferences of the national unions and of the TUC. These serve as sounding boards for rank-and-file opinion and an opportunity for leaders to explain and defend their activities, as well as for communications in the reverse direction in the form of resolutions, minutes, petitions, and votes for officers. These conferences are a vital and significant mechanism for internal coordination. Unfortunately, they are restricted in that only a minority of members can serve as delegates, and also because of the infrequency of such gatherings.

Each union controls its own funds and has offices and a fulltime paid staff. With the growth in size of trade unions — the average size has doubled since 1920 — more and more authority has been delegated to paid officials and executive members with membership participation in policy-making dwindling correspondingly. Cooperation between unions via federations and joint industrial councils has removed bargaining another step from the members. Concentration of authority has not, however, been accompanied by a corresponding degree of influence over members; the membership appears less responsive than before. This is doubtless attributable in part to continued full employment which enhances the worker's feeling of security and reduces his dependence on the union. But it also reflects the unreality of the union's administrative system at the local level.

British unions have been remarkably disinclined to engage in public relations activities. Their passivity in this field appears to stem partly from inadequate finances, partly from a reluctance of officials to delegate authority even to the extent of allowing press officers to speak officially for the union, and partly from an ingrained conviction that the press is hostile to the labor movement. Very few unions, not even the two largest (the Amalgamated Engineering Union and the Transport and General Workers Union) have public relations departments, and not many have even fulltime press officers; many general secretaries and national officials act as their own publicity officers. Even the TUC has but a small publicity department, and there is not even advance coverage for General Council monthly press conferences.

There are about ninety national trade union journals with limited circulation. The Transport and General Workers Record, for instance, sells about 200,000 to its membership of 1,300,000, and the Amalgamated Engineering Union has about 150,000 subscribers in a membership of over a million. The TUC publishes a monthly magazine, Labour, with a circulation of about 15,000 and a fortnightly duplicated Industrial News intended mainly to assist editors

of union journals. As a lot the trade union press has been characterized as uninspiring.[6]

Many of these difficulties spring from inadequate financing. Union
dues vary from 10d to 3/- a week. This represents less than three-
fourths of 1 per cent of basic wage rates as compared with 1.5 per
cent in 1939, and this despite the fact that costs of trade union administration per member have doubled since that time. Financial
limitations result in inadequate staffing at local, national, and TUC
headquarters, inability to recruit, and difficulty in carrying on research and dissemination of information. It is estimated that British
trade unions employ approximately one fulltime official for every
3,250 members, a lower ratio than for any trade movement of comparable size in the world. A recent survey indicated that British
union officials put in a fifty-seven-hour week on the average. Moreover, local officials frequently earn less than the workers they represent. The General Secretary of the TUC earns £2,850, and the
salaries of the general secretaries of the national unions range from
£1,400 to £2,200, as compared to £10,000 for the Chairman of the
National Coal Board, £12,000 for the Chairman of the National
Incomes Commission, and £24,000 for the Chairman of the Transport Commission.

Trade unions exercise a major influence on the Labor Party. All
of the major TUC unions are directly affiliated, though the TUC
itself is not. The unions control five-sixths of the votes at the Labor
Party annual conference. They also control the election of the majority of the Party Executive, eighteen out of twenty-seven, and they
have approximately 100 MPs in the Parliamentary Labor Party. They
provide the bulk of the party finances and, in addition, finance their
own candidates. Trade union members in unions with political funds
pay political levies unless they choose to contract out. Less than
half of the unions affiliated with the TUC have political funds, but
they comprise some two-thirds of total union membership.

The TUC is not affiliated with the Labor Party and remains independent of it. Trade union officials may not serve simultaneously on
the General Council of the TUC and on the Labor Party executive.
In point of fact, this tends to mean that General Secretaries of the
national unions serve on the General Council, and assistant general
secretaries sit on the Labor Party executive. Two TUC representa-

---

[6] Eric Wigham, *What's Wrong with the Unions* (Baltimore: Penguin Books,
Ltd., 1961), p. 177.

tives attend meetings of the Labor Party Home Policy Committee, and two Labor Party representatives attend meetings of the TUC Economic Committee. Occasionally joint committees are set up to deal with a special issue, and there is continuous informal contact leading to very considerable mutual interaction and influence upon policy in both the TUC and the Labor Party. The emergence of economic planning and interest in an incomes policy recently seems to be encouraging an even closer relationship between the Labor Party and the trade unions. In the early spring of 1963 the leaders of the party held a series of fairly well publicized "secret" meetings on economic planning and incomes policy with top trade union officials, trade union research workers, university economists, and businessmen.

The TUC's insistence upon a degree of political independence stems basically from the acceptance by all major parties of the principle of a mixed economy in which the unions want to be free to cooperate with and influence whatever government may be in power. Furthermore, the unions must use some care not to alienate the large fraction of trade unionists (about 30 per cent) who regularly vote Conservative or Liberal. This is a particularly sensitive issue with respect to white-collar workers, who now constitute almost two-fifths of the labor force.

Despite the close working relationship between the TUC and the Labor Party it is clear that the General Council, and particularly the present General Secretary, George Woodcock, are not politically minded. And there is little doubt that the net effect of trade union association with the Labor Party has been to moderate the influence of militants with the party.[7] This has occurred despite the predominance of left-wing unions in both the TUC Congress and the Labor Party conference, and can be explained by the system of block voting and the skillful manipulation of conferences.

Although the TUC and the Labor Party have always been separate and distinct bodies and neither is affiliated to the other, they maintain contact with each other and attempt to coordinate their policies on matters of common interest. The main channel for this is the National Council of Labor, the joint body representing the General Council of the TUC, the National Executive Committee of the La-

[7] William Pickles, "Trade Unions in the Political Climate," in *Industrial Relations, Contemporary Problems and Prospects*, edited by B. C. Roberts (London: Methuen and Co., Ltd., 1962).

bor Party, the Administrative Committee of the Parliamentary Labor
Party and the Executive Council of the Co-operative Union. The
National Council of Labor is a deliberative and coordinating body
without executive powers, its prime function being to consider questions affecting the common interests of the trade union, political
labour and cooperative movements. It meets regularly and its chairman is alternately the chairman of the TUC General Council and
the chairman of the National Executive Committee of the Labor
Party.

The trade unions are fundamentally independent of the party.
While they can influence the party's policy, the party has no analogous means of influencing the policy of the trade union movement.
Nor can the trade unions be bound by any of the party's decisions.
During the period when a Labor government has been in office the
trade unions have been quite independent of the government, just
as at other times. Indeed there have been moments when the Labor
government and the trade union movement failed to agree. Nevertheless, the relationship between them is normally close and cooperative.

MANAGEMENT OPERATIONS

Employer organizations in the United Kingdom are notoriously
reticent and little information is available on them. In form and
function they are at least as complex as trade unions, with the result
that they are difficult to classify as to aim, structure, or degree of
authority. For collective bargaining purposes they are usually organized on an industry basis, defined in relation to a product, a
process, or a type of business or service, and the seat of organizational power is definitely at the industry level. In many industries
there are two types: an employer association designed to deal with
labor matters, and a trade association concerned with technical
matters, supplies, government controls, research, and price-fixing.
Even the latter are relevant to industrial relations in view of their
role in decisions to cover higher wages with higher prices. Moreover, there is no clear division of labor between the two functions,
and in some cases both are combined in a single organization.

Local organizations may be affiliated to regional associations, or
national associations, or both. Many organizations have their own
regional association or branches in different parts of the country
where their main activities are centered; others have sectional bodies

concerned with the manufacture of particular products. National associations may join with others in federations or confederations representing whole or large sections of a single industry, or groups of related industries. A few integrate producers, wholesalers, and retailers, and sometimes exporters and importers. In manufacturing some large firms belong to two, three, or even a dozen or more associations.

Estimates vary as to the number of employer organizations, partly as a result of the difficulty of definition. Roughly there would appear to be between 2,000 and 3,000, covering private employers of 15,000,000 to 16,000,000 workers. Of these, perhaps one-sixth are national in scope. As with the trade unions, there is a large degree of concentration in membership, with the majority of firms being organized in a few large associations and federations. The largest — the Engineering and Allied Employers National Federation — covers over 2,000,000 workers, and the National Federation of Building Trades Employers covers over 1,000,000 workers. Other large organizations are the Master Printers, the Shipping Federation, the British Funiture Trades Confederation, and the major textile associations.

The British Employers' Confederation (BEC) is the employers' counterpart of the TUC for dealing with employment questions affecting industry generally. BEC also provides members with legislative and economic information, and has the function of representing employer views on labor matters to government departments and international organizations. It has represented British employers in the annual conferences of the ILO since the inception of that body.

Membership in the BEC comprises some sixty separate autonomous associations, mostly on an industry basis, which in total represent employers of almost three-fourths of the persons engaged in private enterprise industries and services. Individual companies are represented through their employer organizations since the BEC does not accept individual firms as members. Nationalized industries and public employment are not covered, and employer organizations in boots and shoes, hosiery, furniture, and some food industries remain outside.

The confederation's business is managed by a council of 160 members, which meets under the chairmanship of the president and on which every member organization is represented. Policies are formulated at quarterly meetings of the council. A general purposes committee acts as the executive, and standing committees deal with particular aspects of the work. The most important of these is the Wages and Conditions Committee, which meets quarterly to discuss trends in wage settlements, broad strategy vis-à-vis unions, and the general magnitude of increases to be granted. Although a consensus is sometimes reached, no sanctions are applied other than the pressure of combined opinion. "It is said that, without getting down to actual figures, the employers usually reach a pretty good understanding on the general lines of policy they intend to adopt — but in the end go their own ways." [8]

In addition, there is a wages and conditions information section for servicing members in negotiations; for collecting, collating and diffusing information on claims and settlements, prices, and so on; and for maintaining ad hoc liaison with the nationalized industries. The theory motivating this work — namely, that an employer who is informed as to what the others are doing is less likely to offer "excessive" wages and conditions — led in 1963 to an interesting experiment in the Merseyside area involving a system of consultation and exchange of wages and hours information between local employers. If successful, the project may be extended to other parts of the country.

In contrast to the BEC, the Federation of British Industries, which deals with technical and commercial matters, represents primarily large manufacturing industries, and excludes services, transport, shipping, and construction. Even so, 40 per cent of the membership is said to consist of firms employing less than 100 members. Some 300 trade associations are affiliated plus 7,000 individual firms. The FBI staff numbers about 200, and in addition there is a large overseas department plus a number of representatives abroad.

The National Association of British Manufacturers (NABM), which until recently was known as the National Union of Manufacturers (NUM), is the spokesman for small- and medium-sized firms. It comprises about 5,500 firms and seventy trade associations, most of them with payrolls below 250.

A merger of BEC, FBI, and NABM, or rather their replacement by a new organization, became a distinct possibility in the summer of 1963, when the executive organizations of the three bodies agreed on the desirability of such a move and set up a commission to work out a detailed scheme by the end of the year.

---

[8] *The Times* (London), November 27, 1963.

How important are these management organizations? One answer is that they mean less to employers than trade unions do to workers. It has been said of them: "Employers' associations are only 'second degree' groups — associations of associations — whose existence reinforces but (unlike the union) does not create the bargaining power of their members. They matter more to small employers than big ones and more to employers facing tough unions than to those facing weak ones. But they have seldom in the past been really crucial to anybody.[9]

Employer organizations and trade associations do not provide members with friendly benefits, or educational services, and do not engage directly in party politics or in public relations or propaganda designed to influence public opinion. On the other hand, there is a wide variety of services which they do provide, including apprenticeship and training schemes, insurance schemes for accidents or industrial disease, research on wage rates and earnings, work study, standards of personnel management, legal advice and assistance, cooperative advertising, trade fairs and exhibitions, collection and publication of statistics and trade information, trademark regulations, pooling of credit information, standardization of products, improvement of quality and design, uniform costing and accounting procedures, and occasionally joint purchasing. In addition they are frequently accused of operating restrictive trade agreements, for example exclusive dealing, although these are now presumably covered by the Restrictive Practices Act.

Services of this kind make it advantageous for employers to belong to associations. Members are not required to surrender authority, and the BEC is even less centralized than the TUC. It does not participate in negotiations or in disputes. Its ultimate sanction over its members is expulsion, but this discipline is rarely applied and an expelled member is readily readmitted. The only losses which a member suffers in the meantime are lack of access to the strike funds and loss of services.

The real power in employer associations is wielded at the industry level, not only by the elected officers, but also by prominent businessmen who are members. Thus the General Council or its equivalent elects working committees to deal with particular problems.

---

[9] George Cyriax and Robert Oakeshott, *The Bargainers, a Survey of Modern Trade Unionism* (London: Faber and Faber, 1960), p. 157.

Within these committees there is usually a smaller group which acts, formally or informally, as an "inner cabinet." The leading personalities in these inner circles derive their authority not from their positions in the organizations so much as from their status in industry. And it is often these people who are consulted by Ministers and their departmental subordinates as to policy. The request may be to foster sympathy within the business community for official views and policies, or it may, as in the case of some FBI businessmen, even be to take informal soundings with foreign industrialists prior to negotiations between governments.

The importance of the business leader is greatly enhanced, so far as his influence on the government is concerned, by the fact that the British political system is characterized by an almost complete dominance of the executive in policy-making as well as in day-to-day business affairs. Associated with this is a high degree of party discipline in Parliament and a unified approach to matters of party policy. Because of this, interest groups in search of government support think first of the Ministers and departments rather than the Parliament. Contacts with Ministers tend to be informal. Both trade unions and employer organizations send deputations and memoranda on particular issues (though the TUC feels that it has been largely ignored in recent years), and there is also regular routine direct consultation between Ministers and officeholders in various associations, and between department officials and their opposite numbers on staff associations. Ministers almost always seek the views of interest groups before making changes in law, administrative rules, the nature and extent of benefits, and so forth. There are also frequent opportunities for organizations to submit evidence to ad hoc committees. Furthermore, most departments have a few specialist advisors with formal status who are not civil servants but prominent officeholders in retail trade, professional, or technical associations. Some governmental bodies, like the Cotton Board and the Agricultural Marketing Board, actually have interest group representation within the administrative structure.

WAGE DETERMINATION

Collective Bargaining at the Plant Level

In the United Kingdom wages and hours are typically determined through voluntary negotiations on an industry-wide basis. Within this framework there are variations in negotiating machinery, and in addition, some wages are statutorily fixed. The general pattern is indicated in Table 4-5.

Every major industry except oil refining is covered by a national agreement between an employer's organization and one or more (usually several) unions. This agreement covers basic wages and conditions of employment in the industry. Such a system has been favored by the employers for a number of reasons. It had its origin

Table 4-5 [a]

Per Cent of Total Rise in Pay for a Standard Week Arrived at Through:	1947–50	1951–53	1956–61
Direct negotiation	40	37	38
Sliding scales based on cost of living	6	9	7
Joint Industrial Councils and other standing voluntary councils	25	27	33
Wage Councils and other statutory boards	21	18	19
Arbitration or mediation	8	9	3

[a] Information provided by Professor E. H. Phelps Brown of the London School of Economics.

during the interwar years of underemployment when the paramount fear was wage-cutting by competitors. National bargaining tended to take wages out of competition, and could be rationalized on the ethical principle that those doing similar work should receive similar pay. It also saved time and effort spent negotiating, and was thought to reduce strikes. Interestingly enough, in the period following World War II, when full employment prevailed, national bargaining also had advantages for employers in that it enabled them to bargain above the national agreement in accordance with their own interests without seriously compromising their obligations to the association. Trade unions have also supported the idea of national bargaining because it provided them with a way of mobilizing and maximizing their strength vis-à-vis employers, and because in recent years it has given them flexibility in pushing for extra advantages on the local front.

National bargaining is clearly influenced by certain key industries or pace setters. The engineering industry, for instance, employs 2,000,000 workers directly, and indirectly affects the wage levels of another 1,500,000. Railway negotiations also have an important influence. Coal mining has been regarded as a special case, and the powerful printing industry is too different from other industries to set a pattern. In general, it can be said that engineering and railways have been the most frequent pattern setters, with others like electrical contracting or chemicals assuming prominence in particular years.

The British collective agreement differs in two important ways from the familiar American model. In the first place it is not legally enforceable, and in the second, it is open-ended, that is, it has no fixed term. Wage bargaining has tended to be annual, but since the contracts are without term, the exact timing and strategy are left flexible. There has, in recent years, been a modest trend toward fixed-term agreements covering two-and-a-half to three years or more. Such agreements have been concluded for printing, boots and shoes, tobacco and electrical contracting, electrical supply, gas, police, heating and ventilating, and some segments of the motor car industry. The most important breakthrough in this respect is currently being negotiated. In January of 1963 some forty shipbuilding and engineering unions in the Confederation of Shipbuilding and Engineering Unions (sparked by the Amalgamated Engineering Union, which has 40 per cent of the voting strength) instructed their negotiators to abandon annual pay claims and press for a long-term wage contract covering two or three years. In November, negotiations were still in process. The Engineering Employers Federation, the most powerful employers' body in the country, expressed misgivings about the proposal for long-term contracts based on "guesses about future rates of growth,"[10] and indicated that such contracts would be worthless unless the unions could, through disciplinary action against members, guarantee freedom from sectional and local wage claims during the duration of the contract.

Bargaining at the Plant Level

Despite this commitment to national bargaining, one of the most important features of collective bargaining in Britain in the postwar period has been the development of wage negotiations in the workshop. Much of the size and shape of the pay packet is in actual practice now settled at the plant level, partly within the framework of nationally negotiated agreements and partly independent of them.

---

[10] *The Times* (London), November 27, 1963.

Earnings may be increased over the negotiated level through job and piecework rates, altering the pattern of the wage structure, incentive bonuses, upgrading, merit and overtime rates, promotions and special payments, or, as often happens, rates may be openly set at levels above those specified in the national agreement.

The extent of local bargaining is hard to measure precisely because most of it is neither explicit nor formal. Indeed, there are reasons why both labor and management have preferred not to formalize, or even acknowledge, the fact of extensive plant negotiations. Employers feel that informal practices give them more discretion and constitute less of a restriction on their prerogatives; they do not establish precedent, and are reversible with the turn of the business cycle; they are less likely to lead to strike action or to "whip-sawing" tactics; and they are less offensive to employers' associations whose protection they value and who frown on individual bargaining. On the union side, much of the local bargaining takes place through the shop stewards and is thus outside the formal framework of the trade unions. For this reason the unions have not openly acknowledged or blessed local bargaining.

Thus the arrangement is sufficiently loose and vague to give employers the flexibility they want to meet competition for labor, to satisfy local claims, to set up incentive schemes, and to permit the adjustment of wages and working conditions to the particular needs of the plant and of the area. For workers, too, it has the advantage of permitting them to pool their bargaining strength in national negotiations for the purpose of establishing wage minima, while at the same time exploiting to the full on the plant level local labor shortages which make it possible to raise actual earnings above the national minimum.

Shop stewards exercise a considerable influence over levels of actual earnings. Most national wage bargains leave some scope for variation from the national rate, for example, through upgrading. And even where they do not, local earnings can be increased through special payments for dirty work, exposed conditions, and so on, through "merit" rates, or simply by disregarding nationally negotiated rates; as noted, employers' associations have almost no sanctions short of the ultimate discipline of expulsion, and even this is usually temporary. Shop stewards are also instrumental in what has been called the "conditions drift," via spurious overtime, setting of loose piece rates, and so forth.

Although shop stewards operate nominally as part of trade union structure, their ties to the union are tenuous. The relevant trade union rules and procedures are not adapted to modern industrial structure, and they are too vague to give much guidance and are frequently honored in the breach. Branch trade union officials are too few, too poorly paid and equipped, and too busy to visit particular plants more than infrequently; they seem never to be in the right spot at the right time, and, as noted, few workers attend branch meetings. Also, since there are usually several unions represented in a firm, any one union speaks for only a fraction of the workers.

Workers in the shop regard the steward, rather than their union branch official, as their representative, and tend to consider wage increases as stemming from his efforts. Actually, the industry-wide negotiated rate does influence the local level — by setting a minimum, and, in many cases, by being added to local rates even when these are already above the minimum. But the average worker does not realize this; he never sees the national leaders who are negotiating what he considers to be minima that do not apply to him.

Thus there is a complete break in internal trade union communications. Executive authority flows down to the branch, but the flow of workshop representational and wage bargaining activities goes up to the steward, with almost no connection between the two points. The shop convenor, or joint committee of stewards, may be loosely accredited to a federation of unions, but this means there is no one member organization to which he reports and is responsible.

This problem has led to a spate of proposals for remedial measures, including making the plant bargaining process explicit through full and formalized recognition by employers and trade unions, integrating shop stewards into the trade union structure, putting stewards on a paid basis with adequate protection against their being fired, more adequate supervision by trade union officials, improved training facilities for shop stewards (at the end of April, 1963, plans were announced by the TUC and the BEC for a joint effort to develop the training of shop stewards), and making plant agreements more explicit and specific, requiring them to be written, and perhaps making them legally binding.

The hoped-for advantages of such a development would include enhancing worker status and security in the plant by making workers less vulnerable to arbitrary management, facilitating prompt dispute settlement at the plant level, and providing more flexibility for adjustment to particular plant situations. More specifically in terms of implications for a national wages policy, formalization of wage determination at the plant level might, by strengthening union authority and control over actual earnings, make the unions more responsible collaborators in a national policy of wage moderation, and by improving industrial relations and reducing disputes and unofficial strike action, make it more possible for employers and unions to cooperate in the common interest.

Such a development would also permit a link between pay and productivity that is not possible on an industry-wide basis. In national negotiations, neither employers' federations nor unions are in a position to make concessions on working practices; on the plant level, however, they can make specific "deals." In the case of a national agreement the employer knows that his competitor's wage costs are also being raised, so that he can safely raise his price to cover his higher wage costs. This is not possible at the workshop level where wage increases are more likely to be absorbed either by higher productivity or out of profits. By the same token, workers are more willing in this narrower context to agree to links between pay and productivity.

Conciliation and Arbitration

A large proportion of the important industries have voluntary arrangements for the settlement of disputes through conciliation by boards composed of equal numbers of representatives of employers and workers, and, when they fail to reach agreement, by arbitration at the hands of an umpire acceptable to both sides. It is usually provided that no strike or stoppage may occur while the matter in dispute is under consideration. Differences do, however, arise from time to time on which a settlement through the industry's own machinery cannot be reached. Statutory provision has therefore been made for assistance by the Ministry of Labor under legislative authority derived mainly from the Conciliation Act of 1896 and the Industrial Courts Act of 1919.

If conciliation fails the case may be referred to a special arbitration board consisting of equal numbers of employer and worker representatives nominated by the two sides, with an independent chairman appointed by the Minister. An alternative is for the Minister to refer the case to an ad hoc independent arbitrator or arbitrators, or to send it to the Industrial Court, which is a permanent tribunal set up under the Industrial Courts Act. The act actually provides for panels of independent persons, workers' representatives, and employers' representatives, but in practice the court consists of a fulltime salaried president and two fulltime salaried members representing the employers' and workers' interests respectively.

There is no means under the act of compelling an unwilling party to go to arbitration, nor are awards legally binding. However, the "willingness to resort to arbitration in the last resort, in order to resolve national disputes which cannot be settled by negotiation, is now widespread."[11] As a result the large-scale stoppage, involving the whole or a substantial part of an industry, now rarely occurs. As indicated in the table on page 165, arbitration and mediation awards have played a significant role in determination of wage levels. They accounted for 8 to 9 per cent of total wage increases up to 1953, but the percentage fell to 3 per cent in the period 1956 to 1961. Such figures, however, fail to take account of the indirect influence of mediation on wage negotiations, and the fact that in many industries there was a prior commitment to go to arbitration in event of a failure to agree. Given such a commitment it is arguable that neither party is likely to hold out for conditions which it knows an independent arbitrator will not sustain.

Industrial Councils

Both industrial councils and joint consultation had their origin in a 1916 Whitley Committee report which recommended that the government should encourage employer and trade union groups to form an organization for the purpose of considering "matters affecting the progress and well-being of the trade" from the point of view of all those engaged in it. It was hoped that the joint industrial councils in each industry would consider wages, hours, and conditions of work, formulate measures for regularizing production and employment, encourage research and improve design, consider plans for the improvement of health and of training, collect statistics, and represent the agreed view of both sides to the public and the government. The national councils were to be supplemented by district councils applying national recommendations to local conditions, and by works committees to deal with factory rules, hours, and breaks, individual grievances, training, welfare, and recreation.

---

[11] Allan Flanders, "Collective Bargaining," in *The System of Industrial Relations in Great Britain,* edited by Allan Flanders and H. A. Clegg (Oxford: Basil Blackwell, 1954), p. 292.

Although this grand design was not realized, the long-run influence of Whitleyism has been considerable. At present there are about 120 Joint Industrial Councils (not counting those for civil service, local government services, and the National Health Service), and approximately seventy others which are independent but similar in purpose. These bodies, which vary in size from twelve to 100 members, deal primarily with negotiation of wages and conditions. The government had adopted similar machinery for its own employees (described below). As already noted, almost one-third of total wage increases in recent years have been negotiated through this kind of institution. The whole structure is capped by the National Joint Advisory Council, which consists of seventeen representatives each from the British Employers Confederation, the Trades Union Congress, and the nationalized industries. The council holds quarterly meetings under the chairmanship of the Minister of Labor, and examines and advises on important problems in the field of employment and industrial relations, including automation, practices impeding the full and efficient use of manpower, the recruitment and training of young workers in industry, and establishment of joint consultative machinery in industry.

Wages in Public Sector

Civil servants, workers in nationalized industries, and local government employees are engaged in free collective bargaining very similar to that which occurs in private industry.

In the Civil Service, central pay negotiations take place on the National Whitley Council and negotiations on rates of pay for particular grades are carried out between official representatives of the departments concerned and the appropriate staff associations. The wages of the civil servants and of hospital staff are wholly financed out of central government funds. The official side for general claims is appointed by the Treasury from members of the Civil Service, and Treasury consent must be obtained for any wage settlements entailing higher government expenditure of either a general or a departmental nature. Civil Service has its own arbitration tribunal available at the request of either side; a Treasury officer presents arguments on behalf of the government in its role of employer, and formal Treasury approval is required for giving effect to any arbitration award which involves additional expenditure.

In the National Health Service pay is negotiated on the various

Whitley Councils with the official side including representatives of the Ministry of Health as well as the hospital boards and management committees, executive councils, and local authorities concerned in the claim. Half of the wage costs of the 170,000 employees in the local health services are financed out of central government funds and the rest are met by the local authorities. The Minister of Health has to issue a statutory order giving effect to settlements. The Health Service machinery contains no constitutional provision for arbitration, but it is often the practice to go to arbitration, usually to the Industrial Court, when there is a disagreement over wages.

The wages of the great majority of teachers are negotiated centrally through two Burnham Committees — one dealing with primary and secondary school teachers and the other with establishments for technical and further education. The major share of teachers' salaries is provided out of central government funds and the remainder by local authorities. The Burnham Committees have so far included no central government representatives. Until recently it was considered that the Burnham recommendations could be effected by an order of the Minister of Education or be rejected by him, but that he could not amend them. In 1962, however, a controversy regarding distribution of a recommended award threw open the whole issue. Teachers in Scotland have recourse to arbitration written into their agreement for dealing with disputes; in England and Wales there is no such provision.

In local government services there are National Joint Councils and Committees for nearly all employees who are not covered by the negotiating machinery in the educational and health services. The local authorities are responsible for negotiating and paying the wages of their own administrative, technical, clerical, and general service workers. Differences at the regional level are referred to the National Joint Council. Except in the cases of the police, firemen, and probation workers, there is no provision for arbitration beyond that stage; with most of the major bodies it is the normal practice to use the Industrial Court.

Between 1945 and 1951 the coal, gas, electricity, and iron and steel industries, and much of transport and civil aviation, were brought into the public sector. Most sections of iron and steel and road haulage were later denationalized by the Conservative government, but the rest have remained under public control. Each industry was placed under a separate public corporation and allowed a wide area of freedom from government intervention. For the purposes of wage bargaining the various nationalized boards were statutorily obliged to negotiate with the unions on the form of negotiating machinery to be established and to settle their employees' wages within it. Many existing wage bargaining practices were carried over by the new boards, especially in the railways, in London Transport, and in the coal mines. But nationalization did lead to important changes. In all industries there are now central negotiating bodies to set national, or, in the case of the mines, minimum rates for all wage and most salary earners. Separate joint consultation machinery has been set up, and formal provision made for conciliation and arbitration. Arbitration in coal mining was compulsory and binding until 1961 when the unions decided this arrangement was no longer acceptable. In electricity, the British Road Services, and in civil aviation there is provision for arbitration at the request of either side, and decisions are binding. In gas and most sections of the British Transport Commission there is arbitration at the request of either side, but nothing binding.

Wage determination in the public sector has been based largely on the principle of *comparability*. This criterion has been accepted not only by public administrators, but also by arbitrators and by innumerable investigating bodies.

The basic . . . problem . . . concerning the precise determination of public service wage levels and the fair relations of these levels of earnings in the private sector has in recent years been the subject of several Royal Commissions, government committees (and courts of inquiry). . . . Each reviewed the principles for setting wages in the service under consideration. Their reports naturally differed in many points of emphasis, but each reached the conclusion, or, in some cases, begin with the assumption, that remuneration could and should be in some way associated with rates in similar occupations elsewhere. . . . Comparability has, to some extent, played such a dominant role because it is an application of "fairness." Most of the official committees put forward the long-accepted view that the state has obligations as an employer to uphold the principle of the same pay for the same work. Most union bargainers make a strong appeal for equity, and arbitration courts have been susceptible to this appeal in the past.[12]

The stress on comparability has been partly due to the fact that the usual commercial guideposts on wages do not apply to much of the public service. In the case of civil servants, national health service

---

[12] PEP, *Wage Policies in the Public Sector*, PEP Planning Series No. 467, November, 1962, pp. 374, 379.

employees, workers in local government, and the like, there is no
end product to be sold on the market so that price can serve as an
indicator or allocator. Even in the case of nationalized industry
where the products are sold on the market at a price, the price that
is set by government officials is too arbitrary to serve as a guide to
"economic" wage levels. Nor can wage increases in the public sector
be kept in line with productivity increases, not because public services do not contribute to productivity, but simply because there is
no way to quantify or measure this contribution. Similarly it is not
feasible in the public sector as it is in the private to rely on the confrontation of the bargaining strengths of employer and employee,
since the employer in this case is the state, and the employees, on
the other hand, lack the ultimate weapon of the strike; in short, it
would be an unequal struggle which would not guarantee a "fair"
bargain.

Because the precedent of comparability was so well established as
a criterion for wages in the public sector, it came as a shock when
the Conservative government announced in a 1962 White Paper entitled *Incomes Policy, the Next Step* that it would henceforth move
away from comparability as a criterion in public negotiations because of its inflationary effect, and give priority to "the needs and
resources of the national economy." As it turned out, however, the
government was not able to implement its decision, and after a series of arbitration awards to the contrary it reverted to the comparability principle.

Statutory Wage-Fixing

Approximately 3,500,000 workers are covered by statutory wage
fixing under the Wages Councils Act of 1959, and awards granted
under that legislation have accounted for almost one-fifth of the total
rise in contractual pay in postwar years. The act applies in economic
sectors where government intervention has been considered necessary because bargaining machinery is nonexistent or inadequate,
where trade union organization is weak, and where the nature of
the trade leaves the worker peculiarly exposed to exploitation.

In 1962 there were some sixty industries and trades in which all
or some of the workers were covered by statutory wage-fixing by
Wages Councils. They were for the most part industries in which
small- or medium-sized firms predominate and in which a high proportion of women are employed, for example, baking, dressmaking,
laundries, milk distribution, paper-box manufacture, bespoke tail-

oring, the retail food, tobacco, confectionery, and news-agency trades, and toy manufacturing.

The Wages Councils are appointed by the Minister of Labor. Each council consists of equal numbers of representatives of employers and workers, together with not more than three "independent" members (usually drawn from social workers, university teachers, and lawyers) who represent the public interest. One of the independent members is the chairman. The size of the council varies in accordance with the number and variety of interests in the trade.

The awards of the council must be approved by the Minister; he may accept them, or refer them back, but he cannot amend them. When accepted they are promulgated in statutory instruments called Wage Regulation Orders. The awards are minima, and are not intended to discourage the payment of higher wages or the observance of more favorable conditions if this can be arranged by collective or individual agreement, but the minima are enforceable. The Wages Council system is not intended as a permanent substitute for the normal method of collective bargaining, and a Wages Council may be abolished if the Minister is satisfied that collective bargaining machinery exists and is working satisfactorily. However,

Though they are supposed, in theory, to "wither away," and some of them do, there are strong temptations to cling to statutory forms once they are well entrenched. There is evidence that some unions shelter behind the Councils, secure in the knowledge that their bargaining strength is unaffected by the number of unorganized workers in their trade; and some large employers, it is said, use the Council to undermine the competitive position of their small rivals by pushing up wages beyond the level the smaller firms can afford to pay. In such circumstances, both sides have a vested interest in maintaining the *status quo*, little progress can be made toward strengthening voluntary arrangements, and the taxpayer (in effect) pays for a system that does the organizer's job for him, and subsidizes practices by employers that may lessen competition. It is significant that the Minister has recently been given power (under the Wage Councils Act of 1959) to order an independent inquiry into the affairs of an industry, and even to abolish a Council without waiting for application from the unions and the employers. There is no doubt that the majority of Wage Councils do valuable and essential work, and that the workers in their industries would suffer if they did not exist; but there would seem to be a case for more vigorous action by the Ministry wherever employers and unions are unnecessarily dilatory in conforming to the spirit of the legislation.[13]

---

[13] J. W. Grove, *Government and Industry in Britain* (London: Longmans, 1962), pp. 203–204.

Under the Agricultural Wages Act of 1948 wages are fixed by a national Agricultural Wages Board similar in powers and composition to a Wages Council, though the Minister has no power to reject an award. The Agricultural Wages Board prescribes minimum wages for the country as a whole, but provision is made for local variations which are effective only in the county area for which the order is made, these variations being authorized on the advice of the County Agricultural Wages Committees.

Joint Consultation

There exists some form of joint consultation machinery in most major industries, and this is most fully developed in the larger firms, and above all in the nationalized industries.

The specific form of organization and the subjects of consultation vary from firm to firm, but usually include safety, health, welfare efficiency of the industry, collection of statistics, education, training and apprenticeship, and transport facilities. Sometimes the organization responsible for joint consultation is the Joint Industrial Council mentioned above, which also has negotiating functions quite distinct from its consultative functions. Frequently, however, the machinery for consultation is less formal.

It is fairly generally agreed that joint consultation has not yet had a significant impact upon industrial relations. Responsibility for this lack of success apparently lies with both the bargaining partners. Experience has shown that effective consultation cannot be achieved through machinery alone, and that much depends on the atmosphere in the plant and on the attitudes and goodwill of both management and trade unions. In Britain neither side has been willing to make the effort or to surrender sovereignty to the necessary extent.

One reason may have been the tendency to regard consultation and negotiation as distinct, unrelated processes. Some British observers feel that the sharp distinction between negotiation and consultation, imposed in order to preserve the sanctity of national agreements, may be an obstacle to effective consultation. They argue that consultation has no real value unless workers can participate in decisions, for example, on the impact of technology on wages and conditions, and there there should be a dove-tailing of collective bargaining and consultation at the local level. This would dilute management's exclusive right to decision-taking, but would greatly enhance the value of joint consultation for removing mutual suspicions. Such a move, however, would probably be resisted by both employers and unions. Line management tends to resent the authority of union representatives and the waste of time and effort in going through formal consultation procedures. Frequently, also, it defaults on providing the unions with adequate information on the firm's economic situation. And on the union side hesitancy stems from the relatively weak position in the plant of the union representative, particularly vis-à-vis the shop steward who is frequently regarded as a rival. Thus there is a tendency for the local union representative to be reluctant about exercising his discretion, partly because he fears being considered "soft" by union members if he cooperates by referring issues to regional and national trade union officers. He might agree with management on how to increase output, but not on how to split the gains. This is an issue for bargaining, not for discussion and consultation, and one which unions prefer to fight out on the national level where they can mobilize their full bargaining strength.

Wage Drift

Wages and earnings are only in part determined through formal bargaining, or by statutory wage-fixing. In the United Kingdom, as in most European countries but not in the United States, there is a large gap between negotiated wage rates and payments actually received by workers, usually described as "wage drift."

It is extremely difficult to measure drift. One does not, for instance, know what earnings would have been in its absence, or to what extent some rates consolidate previous drift. Very rough estimates for the United Kingdom indicate that over the decade from 1948 to 1957 drift accounted for 21 per cent of the total rise in earnings, that the proportion for 1959 was about 26 per cent, and that the average annual drift between April, 1956, and October, 1961, was about 2 per cent.

If one thinks of drift in terms of wage policy, it is convenient to distinguish between primary and secondary drift. Primary occurs when certain autonomous forces act to raise earnings of particular groups faster than others, while secondary drift is a response to primary drift resulting from the attempt of employers or workers to restore customary differentials.

Several sources of primary drift have been identified in the United Kingdom. The first is piece rates or other types of payment by result. Approximately one-third of all British workers are paid in this fashion (as contrasted with 27 per cent in the United States and two-thirds in Sweden). Incentive systems tend with the passage of time to yield higher pay per unit of labor input than when first introduced. This is largely because employers find it impossible or inconvenient to adjust the rates for every small improvement in methods, materials, equipment, and organization, but these small changes add up to significant increases in productivity over a period of time.

Second, when particular workers or groups of workers press their special claims at the plant level, employers sometimes find it worthwhile to "buy off" the threat of production by granting increases above the negotiated rates, especially if they can raise prices accordingly.

Finally, and closely related to worker pressure, is the increase which comes about at the initiative of the employer when workers are in short supply. On the assumption that prices can be raised to meet increased costs, the employer sets about to lure workers, either by openly offering wages above the negotiated rates, or more deviously through all kinds of special bonuses, fringe benefits, "loose" piece rates, "contrived" overtime, "contrived" upgrading, and so on.

Secondary drift is distinguishable from primary in that it represents a response to a disturbance of customary differentials. The source of change may be primary drift, a change in scheduled rates, arbitration awards, statutory orders, or negotiated agreements. And the comparison which activates secondary drift may be between different groups within a firm, between firms in an industry or region, or between industries. The attempt to redress matters may be at the initiative of wage earners prompted by a sense of injustice, or trade unions competing with one another for members, leadership, or social status, or of employers in an attempt to retain workers who might otherwise go elsewhere. In any case the effect is that of a chain reaction known as "leap frogging."

The effect of secondary drift is seen clearly in data published by the National Institute of Economic and Social Research on percentage changes in hourly earnings of adult male wage earners in 132 industries for the period 1948-50 to 1957-59. Its report says:

In general, the remarkable feature of the post-war earnings structure is the absence of any significant change in pattern. The ranking of the 132 industries at the beginning and end of the period was very similar. Only 27 moved up or down the ranking by as many as 20 places. More recent changes (from October 1959 to April 1962) in hourly earnings of adult male wage-earners tell very much the same story. Average hourly earnings rose by 18.3 per cent, or one shilling . . . If some allowance is made for the higher level of earnings in October, 1959, compared with 1948/50, the distribution of absolute gains and losses closely resembles the earlier pattern; in about half the 128 industries the change in hourly earnings was within one penny of the average, and in three-quarters, within two pence.[14]

In the context of a wage control policy, drift is obviously impor- tant. But there is a great deal of argument within the United King- dom as to whether it is controllable. Economists dispute whether it is "additive or alternative." Is there a market price for labor that will necessarily prevail one way or the other via drift if not via scheduled increases in rates? Can the rise of scheduled rates be slowed down without increasing drift, or can drift be reduced without generating pressure to raise scheduled rates? There is no consensus on this subject, but the statistical evidence to date seems to suggest that drift is additive. There is little support for the proposition that drift has been greater when scheduled rises were smaller, or conversely, that the general level of pay is impelled toward a given level. Thus there seems to be nothing inherently mechanistic in the relationship between wage rates and earnings which would doom a wage policy. "It seems unlikely that an incomes policy would be nullified by higher drift, or that general action to check drift would only build up pressure to raise scheduled rates."[15] On the one hand, the mar- ket forces which give rise to drift cannot simply be dismissed; they do limit the range of control. On the other hand, the factors deter- mining the size and shape of the drift response are not wholly im- personal market forces; they are partly institutional and in that degree subject to modification and control. Drift depends on employ- ers' expectations in an economic setting determined in part by gov- ernmental economic policy, upon the rules and practices of central organizations which engage in private collective bargaining, and upon wage structures and wage determination practices in the plant.

Overall economic policy of the government has an obvious bear- ing on the problem in that it can influence the pressure of demand for labor. To an important extent the government can control the climate of managerial expectations, or employers' assessments of the feasibility of covering higher labor costs by raising prices. Some

[14] National Institute of Economic and Social Research, *The Wage Structure and Some Implications for Incomes Policy*, London, November, 1962.
[15] E. H. Phelps, "Wage Drift," *Economics* (November, 1962), p. 353.

observers feel that in the last two to three years a profits squeeze —
"profitless prosperity" — has been reducing the proportions of the
inflation problem by making employers more resistant to wage claims
and less confident of their ability to compete for scarce labor by
pushing up labor costs.

Another way in which the government does much, and is being
urged to do more, to reduce the dimensions of drift is through a
selective labor market policy. This is a matter of preventing and
alleviating specific inflationary labor bottlenecks by improving the
coordination between demand and supply for labor of particular
kinds in particular places. For example, the government can increase
geographic mobility of labor by a generous program for travel, moving, and family separation allowances, and adequate workers housing. Occupational mobility can be stimulated by adequate facilities
and financing for training, and better statistical information on which
to base forecasts of demand and supply for particular skills. Where
there are formidable obstacles to labor mobility, capital and employers can be encouraged to move through appropriate relocation
and development programs. Improvements in the efficiency of the
public employment service contribute to all of these approaches.

Against the structural background sketched above it may be instructive briefly to review the various patterns of response by the
government over the postwar years to the continuing problem of
rising costs resulting from a more rapid increase in incomes than
in productivity.

WAR AND POSTWAR WAGE RESTRAINT

During the war the British were forced to consider the problem of
wage controls. The TUC preferred physical controls over the movements of labor to wage intervention by the government. Accordingly,
it rejected proposals for uniform wage adjustments by a special tribunal, and injection into the negotiating machinery of an independent element. It did, however, agree to compulsory arbitration in
exchange for a significant voice in shaping overall economic policy.
The unions retained full authority to make wage claims and negotiate settlements and the government imposed no criteria on arbitrators for the settlement of disputes. In fact, compulsory arbitration
strengthened union bargaining power at certain weak spots by making it possible to bring nonfederated firms into line with collective
agreements.

The wartime policy was facilitated by frequent meetings between Ministers and the TUC General Council. An attempt was made in 1941 to influence trade union opinion through a White Paper (*Price Stabilization and Industrial Policy*), but this was rejected by the TUC as an attempt to secure price stability at the expense of real wages, and as a proposal for "the hoary device of trying to fix wages by regulation." Nevertheless, with the tacit consent of the TUC the government resorted to manipulation of the cost-of-living index as a way of moderating rank-and-file pressure for wage increases. The index, which was based on pre-1914 household budgets brought down to a 1914 basis, bore little relation to current working class expenditures. Moreover, when it failed to show adequate stability, the more heavily weighted items were subsidized in order to increase the downward bias.

Immediately after the war the Labor Party came into power, thus posing a somewhat different problem in wage restraint. The cost-of-living index, as a primary guide to wage policy, was abandoned in 1947, but the urgent need for some kind of pressure against wage increases was universally recognized. War damage was heavy, capital assets had been lost, sources of supply and export markets were disrupted, there was pent-up domestic demand, terms of trade were unfavorable, foreign exchange reserves were depleted as a result of convertibility, and there was a fuel crisis in 1947. On the positive side there was already in existence a framework of controls, including price controls, subsidies, and a modified form of compulsory arbitration.

Two White Papers were issued in 1947 (*Economic Conditions Affecting Relations Between Employers and Workers* and *Economic Survey for 1947*) which had the effect of stiffening the resistance of employers and arbitrators to demands for wage increases. Ministerial contacts with the TUC were maintained through the National Joint Advisory Council and through meetings with the General Council. The Minister of Labor and the Prime Minister appealed for wage restraint. Toward the end of 1947 the Minister of Labor incurred the wrath of the TUC by sending a letter, without prior consultation, which urged both sides of several wage councils to exercise wage restraint. The difference was soon patched up, following a series of meetings with the Minister of Labor and the Prime Minister, following which the TUC issued an *Interim Report on the Economic Situation* to its own affiliates, urging wage moderation.

In February, 1948, the government published a White Paper on *Personal Incomes, Costs and Prices*, recommending that "there be no further increase in the level of personal incomes without a corresponding increase in the volume of production," except, for example, "where it is essential to the national interest to man a particularly undermanned industry." The TUC once again complained about lack of prior consultation and the absence of proposals for comparable sacrifice by other sectors of the economy. Sir Stafford Cripps, then serving as Chancellor of the Exchequer, made a direct appeal on wage restraint in the House of Commons, hinting that otherwise measures might be taken to restrict profits. Finally, the TUC suggested that the criteria for exceptions, under the above formulation, should be broadened to include "substandard" wages, "established" differentials, and productivity increases — in short, virtually all types of wage claims. A vague resolution approving the TUC position was later put through the TUC Congress.

Curiously enough this "policy without a policy" operated fairly effectively for almost two-and-one-half years. There was never any formal wage restraint decision on the part of the TUC Congress or executives of individual unions. There were no guarantees as to prices and profits. There was no criteria to identify "moderation" or "restraint." The program was never explained to union members — some executives did not even inform their members how they voted. There was no standing machinery for consultation between the TUC and union executives, and the ties between the TUC and the employer federations were even more tenuous. Yet no increases were granted to engineers, shipbuilding workers, railway workers, and most salaried employees, and only cost-of-living increases were granted in construction, iron and steel, furniture, and boots and shoes. The wage rate index rose considerably less than the cost of living, and kept within the bounds of the productivity increase.

The key to success during this period apparently lay in the fact that a Special Economic Committee appointed by the TUC had the full support of the General Council, and the General Council in turn was dominated by strong personalities like Ernest Bevin and Sir Stafford Cripps working within the government, and a triumvirate consisting of Arthur Deakin, who was the General Secretary of the Transport and General Workers Union, Sir William Lawther, president of the National Union of Mineworkers, and Thomas Williamson, General Secretary of the National Union of General and Municipal Workers. All three were assured the backing of their executives, and they had among them about one-third of the votes of the annual TUC Congress. In addition, they could count on the support of a number of middle-sized unions for their right-wing policies on such matters as wage restraint, measures to increase productivity, and nationalization.

By the winter of 1950 the wage restraint experiment had broken down. Doubtless a number of factors contributed to the downfall. The pound was devalued in September, 1949, the Korean War came on, and union people saw no evidence that prices and industrial profits were being held down to balance the bargain. It has been suggested, however, that the primary factor in the disintegration of wage restraint was the uneven incidence of wage drift.[16] The essence of this thesis is that under wage restraint workers became increasingly restive about the effect of earnings drift in disturbing differentials between industries and between firms within an industry. As this pressure accumulated, trade union leaders found it increasingly difficult to control their workers and many were in danger of losing their authority. In this view the final breakdown might have been postponed by allowing a partial relaxation of restraint for lagging lower-paid groups. Such a move, however, was opposed by craft and industrial unions more concerned with the interests of better-paid workers, particularly in construction, shipbuilding, engineering, the railways, and mining, where it was almost impossible to increase rates for lower-paid workers without provoking counter demands at the upper end of the scale. Therefore the TUC's Special Economic Committee, unwilling to challenge the autonomy of individual union executives, chose the alternative of a suspension of cost-of-living escalator provisions plus incentive schemes to increase the earnings of the lower-paid workers. But this proposal was stiffly resisted by the unions concerned. The result was an open revolt on the floor of the September, 1950, TUC Congress which culminated in defeat by a majority vote of the General Council's resolution for a wage freeze.

THE 1961 PAY PAUSE AND ITS PREDECESSORS

By 1951 the Conservatives were back in power, and in the decade which followed the influence of trade unions on the government

---

[16] John Corina, "Wage Drift and Wage Policy," *Economics* (Spring, 1963), pp. 284–293.

steadily dwindled. In May of 1952 Chancellor Butler proposed a committee to devise methods of relating wages to national production. His proposal was accepted by the British Employers Confederation and the nationalized industries, but rejected by the Trades Union Congress. In June the Minister of Labor asked for reconsideration by Wage Councils of the dozen statutory proposals for wage increases, but the proposals were resubmitted without change and then approved. Modest claims by workers in public services were rejected by the national commissions concerned, with subsequent reversal and award of substantial increases by arbitration tribunals in the case of the railways and also electrical supply and road transport.

In 1955 there was a balance of payments crisis which led to prolonged public discussion of how to avoid inflation without endangering full employment. In November, 1955, a White Paper was issued on the *Economic Implications of Full Employment,* and later the Prime Minister held a series of meetings with representatives of the employers' organizations, the TUC, and the nationalized industries. On May 25, 1957, former Chancellor Macmillan declared that "another round of wage increases could not be repeated without disaster," and launched an appeal for a "price plateau." The nationalized industries were asked to adopt a policy of wage restraint, and were encouraged to think that they would receive support from the government in resisting wage claims. Employers responded by endorsing a recommendation by the BEC, FBI, NUM, and the Association of British Chambers of Commerce for wage and price restraint.

Despite employer acceptance of the government's proposal, it was rejected by the TUC Congress in September, 1956. In the words of Frank Cousins, the new and militant General Secretary of the Transport and General Workers Union: "[The] Congress . . . rejects proposals to recover control by wage restraint, and by using the nationalized industries as a drag-anchor for the drifting national economy."

The Suez crisis in 1957 brought higher transportation and distribution costs, petrol rationing, and rising bread prices because of earlier cuts in subsidies. These increases in the cost of living sparked large wage demands. Major national shipbuilding and engineering strikes in the spring of 1957 were finally settled by appointment of Courts of Inquiry which warned of inflationary consequences of wage increases, but recommended 6.5 per cent increases. This was widely interpreted by the employers as a "surrender" by the government and a "betrayal" of their interests.

At the end of October the Chancellor of the Exchequer, Mr. Thorneycroft, announced that instructions had been given to the civil service that whenever possible increased costs should be offset by economies, and that the government would not advance any more money for the railway deficit in 1958 than in 1957, and suggested that employers, conciliators, and arbitrators should bear in mind the danger of wage increases unrelated to production. His statement that the squeeze was "intended to make it harder both to earn profits and to get wage increases" was amplified the next day by the Minister of Labor, Mr. Macleod, who said "we will not finance inflationary awards however these awards are secured, whether through negotiation or through arbitration."

In February, 1958, the Cohen Council on Prices, Productivity and Incomes, in its first report, recommended moderation in wage claims. Accordingly the Minister of Health refused to sanction increased salaries agreed to by the health service authorities, and the Railway Staff National Tribunal refused to recommend wage increases. Nevertheless, the government allowed the Transport Commission to make an offer of 3 per cent to cover the cost of living.

In March, 1960, the government accepted the Cameron-Guillebaud report on railway wages recommending a general rise of 8 per cent with additional increases for skilled workers and salaried employees up to a further 10 per cent. More important, for long-run purposes, the report accepted rates paid in other industries as a relevant standard of comparison, and this has been a major factor in subsequent negotiations.

In 1961 the Conservative government tried a new tack. It sought simultaneously to hold down increases in the public sector which was under the ostensible control of the government, and to appeal to the parties for restraint in the private sector. Chancellor of the Exchequer, Selwyn Lloyd, announced in the House of Commons, on July 25, 1961, "a pay pause until productivity has caught up and there is room for further advances. . . . In those areas where Government has direct responsibility, we shall act in accordance with this policy. The Government asks that the same lines should be followed elsewhere both in the private sector and in those parts of the public sector outside the immediate control of the Govern-

ment." [17] The announcement was made without prior discussion with
the TUC, but in August the Chancellor outlined in letters to the
TUC's General Council plans for a wage freeze. These the General
Council rejected on grounds that it would damage the machinery
of collective bargaining and undermine trade union confidence in
arbitration. During further exchanges in November, 1961, and January, 1962, the General Council pointed out that announcement
of the pay pause had coincided with recessionary tendencies in the
economy and was accentuating them. The Chancellor replied that
the pay pause was a short-term expedient to be replaced as soon
as practicable by a national incomes policy based on periodic assessments of the country's economic prospects and circumstances, and
conducted in such a way that not only those immediately concerned
with particular negotiations, but also the community as a whole,
could judge what rate of increase in income would be practicable
and safe. He indicated that he proposed to consult both industry
and the trade unions in an effort to reach such a policy. Thus following the immediate pay pause there would be an interim policy to
be followed, in turn, by a full long-term policy on incomes.

The TUC reply did not deny the need for a wage policy, but it
did point up sharp differences with the Chancellor in a statement
which said:

It is of course a condition of reasonable price stability that increases in
income should keep in step with the growth of real output. On the other
hand experience shows that the restriction of production in an attempt to
prevent the growth of incomes is self-defeating. It is possible that a con-
certed move to a higher level of economic activity could generate an
increase in incomes which could not be matched immediately by an increase in the resources available for personal consumption. In such circumstances pressure might have to be relieved not only by higher taxation
but even by temporarily limiting increases in incomes or preventing part
of these for a time from being spent.[18]

The TUC also argued that the Chancellor was asking the trade
unions to accept restraint at a time when it was quite unlikely they
could obtain the consent of their members. Without the willing
cooperation of working people any agreement on the part of union
executives or the General Council would be valueless. The trade
unions thought that the climate of opinion resulting from the gov-

---

[17] Parliamentary Debates, Hansard, July 25, 1961.
[18] Trades Union Congress, *Report of 94th Annual Trades Union Congress,
1962,* 1963, p. 244.

ernment's arbitrary introduction of the policy and dogmatic maintenance of the pay pause had destroyed any chance they might have
of agreeing. Moreover, a pay pause would only result in an accumulation of claims which would have to be paid later.

Ignoring trade union protests, the government proceeded to ban
wage increases for government employees, for the nationalized industries, and for wages affected by Wages Council decisions, and
to appeal to private industry for wage restraint. In April the "pay
pause" was supplanted by a "guiding light" of 2 to 2.5 per cent as
the upper limit for wage increases including wage drift, as enunciated in a White Paper on *Incomes Policy, the Next Step.*

Within a very short period the pay pause and guiding light created
serious industrial unrest and political tensions. Moreover they were
rapidly eroded by increases granted by the nationalized industries,
Wages Councils, and arbitration tribunals, as well as by private
industry. In April, 1963, under the influence of the NEDC target of
3.2 per cent annual increase in productivity, the guiding light was
changed from 2.5 to 3 to 3.5 per cent. "The pay pause was undoubtedly a partial success, in the sense that for about 8 months
wages rose less than they otherwise would have done (although the
retail price index rose over the period by 5 points). But this was at
the cost of concentrating a large number of wage increases on the
date of the end of the pause, and of further alienating the unions.
The guiding light was a total failure, partly because the unions were
put on their mettle to defeat it, partly because the Government made
no effective attempt to enforce it. . . ." [19]

THE NATIONAL INCOMES COMMISSION

Because of the resentment and industrial unrest generated by the
inequities and ineffectiveness of the pay pause and guiding light,
the government was under considerable pressure to find a new
approach. Accordingly a top-level working group composed of ministers and departmental officials, with the active participation of the
Prime Minister, developed the idea of a National Incomes Commission to review wage settlements. The proposal was tried out on the
TUC and was promptly rejected as an "obstacle to a national incomes
policy." The General Secretary, Mr. Woodcock, argued that the
"public interest" could only be defined by the government itself

[19] Michael Stewart and Rex Winsbury, *An Incomes Policy for Labour*, Fabian
Tract 350 (October, 1963), p. 12.

working with labor and management, and that the effort to pass the buck to an "independent" body with no authority to define or enforce public policy could only damage collective bargaining by stiffening union resistance, introducing uncertainty into negotiations, and undermining the independence of arbitration.

In early June, 1962, the government decided to proceed with NIC as an independent body charged with looking into pay claims of special importance and publishing its recommendations and reasons for them in the hope of mobilizing public opinion, or, in the words of Macmillan, bringing excessive claims "to the bar of public opinion." The structure and function of NIC reflect the improvisation which characterized its conception. Because the TUC refused to participate, it had to be nonstatutory and nonrepresentative, that is, "independent." To dissociate it from the pay pause, it had to be a permanent institution. And to distinguish it from other arbitration tribunals and Courts of Inquiry, it had to be given the assignment of looking into agreements retroactively as well as into pending agreements.

The commission is composed of a chairman and three members. It may consider the following types of case:

1. Claims on pay or conditions under negotiation where both parties agree to refer; the government may in cases of special importance ask them to refer;

2. The government may refer any matters relating to pay or conditions where the costs are met wholly or in part from the Exchequer, but not including nationalized industries or cases that could be referred to arbitration;

3. The government may, without consent of the parties, ask for retrospective examination of any case in the private sector which might damage the national interest; it cannot alter the settlement, but can draw attention to "mistakes" and make proposals for improvement.

The commission is also authorized to report from time to time on the need for fiscal or other action to prevent undue growth in total profits as a result of incomes restraint.

Three cases had been referred to the commission by the summer of 1963. The first reference was in the private sector, a restrospective examination of a settlement under which 90,000 Scottish building workers and plumbers were to go on a forty-hour week starting in

October. Motives involved included fear of repercussions in British construction and also in other industries like engineering, the desire to attract more industry to Scotland because of unemployment there, and fear of harm to British exports. On April 22, 1963 the commission reported that the granting of a forty-hour week in the Scottish building industry was really a concealed wage increase of 9 per cent, as a result of overtime, and that accordingly there should be no more wage increases for three years. It recommended that the English building industry should ignore the Scottish agreement and grant instead a wage increase related to the long-term 3 to 3.5 per cent rate of increase projected by the National Economic Development Council for national production; this was the new guiding light.

The second NIC reference, on December 28, 1962, was the claim of university teachers for increases of 25 to 30 per cent. Since the report was expected to take several months, an interim award of 10 per cent was made by the University Grants Committee.

The third reference, in April, 1963, concerned three agreements in electrical contracting, heating, ventilating and domestic engineering, and exhibition contracting, two of them for a period of three years and all providing, at varying dates, for introduction of the forty-hour week. In its written evidence to the commission, the government concluded that in each case the rate of increase in hourly rates of pay had been greater than the rate of increase in national productivity and also greater than the rate at which productivity is expected to rise over the next few years.

In its report, issued on July 23, 1963, the commission found that the electrical contracting agreement was not against the national interest in view of the union's pledge to eliminate time-wasting on sites; it said that the benefits of the heating and ventilating agreement should have been spread over four years rather than three, and bluntly declared the exhibition contracting agreement to be against the national interest because it provided increases substantially higher than the revised guiding light of 3 to 3.5 per cent. A major section of the report was devoted to profits. The commission, noting that it was unable to obtain information on profits from the employers concerned, concluded that there is an urgent case for a survey of pricing, profit margins, and dividends in the construction industry. It also stressed the importance of profits in the context of a national incomes policy, and argued that both sides in a particular industry should be prepared to forego the full fruits of an above-average increase in productivity, the excess to be enjoyed by the community at large in the form of lower prices.

In all cases the TUC advised its affiliates not to appear before the commission, and the advice was followed. On the other hand, the initial reaction of the British Employers Confederation was to welcome the establishment of NIC. In the Scottish building case the National Federation of Building Trades Employers asked for a speedy finding "to help the Federation to resist a 40-hour week this year in the building industry in England and Wales." [20] But by the time the third case came along, the National Association of Exhibition Contractors joined the unions in refusing to give evidence. According to newspaper reports, the association took this position because, first, the retrospective character of the commission's examination could have no practical effect, and second, the association would simply be subjecting itself to inquistion without any hope of benefit.[21]

There was other evidence that employers were not entirely ready to accept interference from the National Incomes Commission. After the first report on the Scottish building industry was released, the National Federation of Building Trades Employers acknowledged the value of advice from a body "of the standing of the Commission," but opined that "it remained the responsibility of employers and unions to settle claims before them." [22] And in the electrical industry case the National Federated Electrical Association defended the agreement as being in the national interest "because it gives the basis of better labour relations in the industry and therefore will lead to efficiency and productivity." [23] At the same time it gently reminded the commission that "it had been noted from various Government pronouncements from time to time that the revision of working hours was a matter between employers and unions."

The basic difficulty with NIC appears to be confusion as to the precise nature of its functions. There is a fair degree of consensus that in the context of a national policy of keeping overall wage increases within certain agreed limits, there must be a mechanism for defining and refining *exceptions*. But it has never been clear

[20] *The Times* (London), March 1, 1963.
[21] *Manchester Guardian*, May 31, 1963, p. 4, col. 8.
[22] *Ibid.*, April 23, 1963, p. 5, col. 3.
[23] *Ibid.*, April 30, 1963, p. 4, col. 4.

whether the commission was supposed to administer a given policy on exceptions, or to develop a policy of its own. If, as some feel, the purpose was to set up an independent body which could by its findings rally public opinion in favor of a specific wages policy already enunciated by the government, it is clear that until the government has developed and implemented such a policy, the commission cannot hope to carry out its assigned task. If, on the other hand, the hope was that the commission would itself evolve a policy on exceptions which it could then publicize or "sell" to the public, then the trade union objections are pertinent. One of these objections is that the commission's terms of reference comprise a set of vague and mutually inconsistent criteria. In addition, the unions feel that the commission, as set up, is not an appropriate body for evolving and enforcing an effective policy on exceptions. It has no staff of experts, and no authority vis-à-vis employers or unions. Because it is nonrepresentative, its findings do not carry weight, and it is in no way integrated with the government which alone has the responsibility and the power to define and implement the "public interest."

THE NATIONAL ECONOMIC DEVELOPMENT COUNCIL

For a number of reasons public attention in the West has in recent years focused on economic growth. In substantial part this was because of the rivalry with the Communist world and the threats of a show-down between conflicting economic systems. But there were other factors. The development of the Coal and Steel Community and the Common Market demonstrated clearly what planning and cooperation could do for the economies of several Western European countries. Germany and Japan furnished spectacular examples of economic strength through growth, while the United States, with a slow growth rate and high unemployment, floundered.

Concern with economic growth, particularly in countries like the United Kingdom where growth has been relatively slow, has in turn led to interest in economic planning. In the United Kingdom the planning idea is far from new. A number of earlier attempts in the same direction proved abortive, including: the creation in 1947 by Sir Stafford Cripps of a Central Economic Planning Staff and a tripartite Economic Planning Board, which faded away to little more than a discussion group within the Treasury; the National Production Advisory Council on Industry, which now does little more than hold quarterly meetings for the purpose of hearing reports by government officials; the Cohen Council (COPPAI), which never achieved more than an academic advisory status considerably removed from the center of power; and even the Treasury's annual Economic Survey, which was originally intended to provide a blueprint for industry and labor.

By 1960 a number of influences were converging to create a climate in Britain which favored having the government set a target for long-term economic growth, or, at the very least, an agreed forecast of an attainable rate with a precise description of its probable impact on various industrial sectors. In November, 1960, the Federation of British Industries emphasized that economic growth should have first priority, subsequently organized a conference on the subject at Brighton, and set in motion a number of study groups. Simultaneously both the Liberal and Labor parties were pushing the idea of long-range economic planning, and a number of pertinent reports were published. These included a National Institute of Economic and Social Research study on rates of growth over the past century in various industrialized nations (August, 1961), a PEP report on national economic planning in France (August, 1961), a White Paper known as the Plowden Report suggesting longer-range planning in the public sector (July, 1961), the fourth report of COPPAI (July, 1961) on a ten-year program for planned investment, and forward assessments of manpower needs and resources as a guide to planning of production, prices, profits, and earnings.

In July, 1961, the Chancellor expressed his dissatisfaction with existing joint consultative bodies and his hope of improving the machinery for consultation and for forecasting in order to produce commonly held ideas on how economic growth could be combined with a sound balance of payments position. He therefore proposed a "joint examination of the economic prospects of the country, stretching five or more years into the future," for the purpose of trying to establish the "essential conditions for realizing potential growth." In February, 1962, following a prolonged exchange of views with employer groups and trade unions, the National Economic Development Council was announced.

Two fundamental policy problems had to be resolved in the establishment of the council. Should it operate within the framework of the Treasury, the traditional source of financial planning in Britain, or should it be independent of it? If that problem were resolved in favor of independence from the Treasury, there would remain the further problem of whether it should be completely independent of the government or whether it should represent a genuinely tripartite machinery which would include management, labor, and the government. Those who argued in favor of placing the body within the orbit of the Treasury pointed out that to be effective the new body should not be divorced from the center of power, that domestic stability and growth were not independent objectives divorced from balance of payments considerations, and that economic policy should rest with responsible government ministers. Those who favored independence from the Treasury frankly admitted their fears that Treasury conservatism would inhibit the selection of a dynamic target for rate of growth. They hoped to invest the new body with the requisite authority by providing it with an expert staff, a national figure as director, and enough participation of industrial and labor groups at all stages of planning to ensure dynamism and momentum.

In the end it was decided that the council should operate outside the Treasury, but should include representatives of the government as well as of management and of trade unions. The problem of providing the expertise required for collecting and collating the statistical and other information necessary for projecting trends and setting targets was solved by making the council a two-tier body. The top tier provides the tripartite representation, and the lower tier, staffed with professional economists, operates as a semi-independent office or secretariat to the council, with the Director of that office serving as a link between the two levels.

Some concern was expressed at the outset that the top tier might degenerate into a mere "talking body." This fear was dissipated, however, by the quality of the appointments on both the employer and union sides of the council. The six industrialists were said to include "some of the brightest and most sophisticated businessmen in the country." [24] On the union side the representatives were of equally high caliber. In addition to the six industrialists and six trade unionists, there are two representatives of the nationalized industries, both of whom are well-known public figures, and two leading independent economists. The three representatives of the government are the Chancellor, the Minister of Labor, and the President of the Board of Trade. The council is headed by a fulltime Director General.

The lower tier staff Secretariat is headed by an Economics Direc-

---

[24] *The Observer* (London), February 11, 1962, p. 10, cols. 3, 4.

tor, and has an Administrative Secretary who is also Secretary to the Council. There are two sections in the lower tier, an economics staff and an industrial staff. The latter is composed of business economists from industry and labor, and both sections employ a few young university graduates. It is not anticipated that the entire Secretariat staff will number more than fifty.

The initial reaction of the trade union leaders to the NEDC proposal was one of hesitancy and suspicion. They acknowledged the overwhelming case for planning — indeed, they had been proposing it all along — but they had reservations. In the end the TUC decided to accept membership because of its emphasis on economic growth, the unparalleled opportunity to influence government policy, and the public embarassment of a refusal to cooperate. Moreover, the TUC felt that in the sessions which preceded formation of NEDC it had obtained a number of concessions, including tripartite representation; a relatively small discussion group rather than a larger one; a planning office which was not an arm of the Treasury, with only two independent members rather than the six originally planned; and commitments by the government that no subject would be barred, that union members would have a right to initiate proposals, to declare their views, and to obtain information independently, and that NEDC would be consulted by the government and would not be exploited for arbitrary and unilateral action.

At the same time the TUC made it unmistakably clear that acceptance did not imply endorsement of wage restraint; that it would indeed be willing to discuss wages if other relevant subjects like investments, imports, exports, financial policy, industrial development, profits, and dividends were also discussed; if fairer distribution were accepted as an objective along with economic growth; and if it were understood that wage restraint could at most take the form of inducing a mood, a sense of responsibility, rather than a precise figure and/or time period, since in any case they did not consider wage restraint feasible in view of trade union sovereignty and responsibility to members, and in view of wage drift. Nevertheless it was felt that if the unions could be convinced of the need for restraint and that it would actually be in the interest of the workers, much could be accomplished by a TUC declaration made publicly, and by the machinery of the TUC Congress. Finally, the hope was expressed by the trade unionists that NEDC would be used as a forum for genuine discussion about the "public interest," with argument leading to understanding and thence to agreement, which could then be translated into action since NEDC would be chaired by the Chancellor who would, in turn, be equipped with all the tools of government. The TUC recognized that it was the intention of the government to use NEDC as a means of influencing the unions, but this was not necessarily objectionable since the quid pro quo was an opportunity on behalf of the trade unions to influence the government.

The FBI, the British Employers Confederation, the National Union of British Manufacturers, and the Association of British Chambers of Commerce all expressed approval of the NEDC plan. There was, however, a representation problem on the employer side which did not have a counterpart on the union side. Two of the employer members happened to be officers of the FBI, and one an officer of BEC, but they were not appointed as representatives of those organizations and would presumably remain on the council after their terms of office on the employer organizations expired. There was, therefore, some concern as to the inadequate ties between the council and industry. There have been proposals to form an Industrial General Council to play a similar role in relation to NEDC as that of the General Council of the TUC — perhaps with a small high level secretariat composed of people in a position to command the support of their organizations. Other proposals put forward have included satellite industry committees as links between NEDC and sections of industry; vertical links with industry to provide two-way channels of communication; horizontal committees to maintain liaison with the council on problems like manpower, redundancy, and research which affect all industry; and development councils for each industry which would be representative of producers, consumers, and trade unionists.

Insofar as NEDC has any terms of reference they were worked out at the first meeting, which was held on March 7, 1962. At that time the following objectives were outlined:

1. To examine the economic performance of the nation with particular concern for plans for the future in both the private and public sectors of industry.

2. To consider together what the obstacles are to quicker growth, what can be done to improve efficiency, and whether the best use is being made of the national resources.

3. To seek agreement upon ways of improving economic per-

formance, competitive power and efficiency; in other words, to increase the rate of sound growth.

The first step in the NEDC program was to select a target rate of growth of 4 per cent for the period 1961 to 1966, or nearly 22 per cent over the whole period. In its first report, issued in February, 1963, the second part considered the feasibility of the 4 per cent growth rate, analyzing the various components of the national economy in the light of the results of the general studies by the council, and setting out a balance sheet of the economy as it might be in 1966 if such a rate were achieved.

A second report, published in April, 1963, presented and commented on certain changes needed to stimulate economic growth in the field of education, mobility and redundancy, regional development, balance of payments, taxation, the level of demand, prices and incomes, and the role of government, management, and the trade unions.

From the outset it was an open secret that the extremely touchy issue of a wages or an incomes policy would be temporarily avoided by NEDC, until it had a chance to register some initial successes and acquire a good reputation and some practice in the art of tripartite consultation. Thus the subject was completely bypassed in the first report, and in the second, only the following comments appeared:

From 1948 to 1961 total money incomes per person employed, and wages and salaries per employee, rose by an average of 6 per cent a year; unemployment averaged 1.6 per cent. During the last five years of the period the increase was nearer 5 per cent; unemployment averaged 1.8 per cent. If the price level is to be prevented from rising significantly, incomes cannot rise as fast as this. It is therefore important that ways should be found of limiting the rise in incomes associated with a given level of unemployment to a rate lower than that which would occur on the basis of past experience. The reduction of disparities in regional unemployment would help as would measures to increase mobility of labour and to equate demand for and supply of particular skills.

A satisfactory development of prices and incomes is important for a number of reasons. There is a general dislike of a rising cost of living. Unless costs and prices go up considerably more slowly than in the past it is unlikely that the United Kingdom can maintain her competitive position in world markets. . . .

The 4 per cent programme is based on an increase of about 3¼ per cent in output per head. For the general price level to remain broadly constant, money incomes per head would have to rise at approximately this rate. Even if rising prices abroad permitted a slow increase in our general price level, the rise in money incomes would have to be substantially less rapid than the past average of 5–6 per cent a year.

There will thus be a need for policies to ensure that money incomes (wages, salaries, profits) as a whole rise substantially less rapidly than in the past. If, however, the growth programme can be achieved, *real* incomes per head will increase much faster than in the past. They will increase as fast as output per head, or about 3¼ per cent a year. This is about double the rate achieved between the wars and in the fifty years or so before the first world war, and very substantially more than the rate achieved in the post-war years. If maintained in the future, it will enable real incomes to be doubled in a little over twenty years. The maintenance of this rate of increase even over the next ten years would enable real incomes to increase by nearly 40 per cent.

A policy for prices and money incomes can succeed only if those concerned are convinced that it is a necessary part of a wide programme for growth of real incomes, and that restraint by one section of the community will not merely result in a gain by other sections. The Council regards the solution of the difficult problems involved as a necessary part of its task.[25]

In the autumn of 1963 election fever and the emergence of incomes policy as a major political issue had the effect of postponing any forthright approach to the problem by NEDC. Indeed, as noted below, conflicting views within the labor movement, and particularly between the TUC and the Labor Party leaders, as to the appropriate structure and machinery for economic planning made it unlikely that NEDC would survive in its present form in the event of a Labor victory.

AN EMERGING INCOMES POLICY

However fashionable current interest in an incomes policy may be, implementation of such a policy is hampered by disagreement over content and mechanics. This shows up clearly when one examines the problem more carefully and from different perspectives.

The Trade Union View

There is a reason to believe that British trade unionists are not fully convinced of the need for a wage policy per se. Such lip service as they have paid to the concept may well have been motivated by a political urge to be on record in support of a modern, or at least an increasingly fashionable, economic idea. And, not unnaturally, this urge seems to have been more acute on the part of the

---

[25] National Economic Development Council, *Conditions Favourable to Faster Growth*, April, 1963, pp. 50–51.

TUC, which bears greater responsibility for the public image of the trade union movement than of the leaders of individual unions.

Thus official TUC statements on the need for an incomes policy are interlaced with reservations. A typical example is the supplementary report on *Economic Development and Planning* which became the center of controversy at the 1963 TUC Congress in Brighton in September, 1963.

The General Council recognized from the outset that this subject (incomes policy) would not be excluded from the NEDC's discussions. However, as they made clear when they accepted the invitation to join the NEDC, this did not imply that they accepted the Government's views about incomes policy in general or wage restraint in particular. The fact that their representatives have participated both in the general work of the NEDC and in its discussion of prices and incomes policy does not remove the very great difficulties that would be involved in introducing such a policy. . . .

In their supplementary report on the National Incomes Commission to the 1962 Congress the General Council recognized that it is possible for incomes to get so much out of line with output as to raise costs and prices and accepted that at any one time some groups of people have a greater claim than others to improvements in their incomes. Nor, as they pointed out, is any group of trade unionists entitled to pursue its own interests with complete disregard of the interests of the rest of the community — or of other trade unionists. Congress has also agreed that in conditions of a take-off to faster growth it might be necessary to limit increases in personal incomes in order to make resources available for other purposes such as investment and exports. It has, however, condemned attempts by the Government to lay on working people the blame for Britain's economic difficulties and to impose on industry without consultation an unworkable system of restrictions on wages, emphasizing that this is no way to secure the cooperation of trade unionists in devising methods of jointly promoting the nation's interest.[26]

The TUC position appears to be that there can be a case for restraints on incomes under certain *temporary* circumstances, but not as the keystone of economic policy. In this same report it is stated:

The natural starting point for finding a solution to Britain's economic problems is not from considerations of incomes policy but from policies of making better use of the nation's economic resources including manpower. . . .

The main way of improving the cost structure of British industry — in which incomes are only one of a number of factors, all of which have to

[26] Trades Union Congress, 1963 Supplementary Report A, *Economic Development and Planning*, 1963, p. 12.

be taken into account — is by maintaining a high level of demand and the maximum possible ultilization of Britain's industrial capacity.[27]

In short, TUC leaders look upon wage restraint as a very dubious answer to what is in any event the wrong problem. They object to a formulation of the central economic problems as one of inflation and associated balance of payments difficulties, and the consequent need to moderate "autonomous wage-cost price pressures resulting from the strong bargaining position of trade unions." This they regard as a distorted concentration upon wages as the villain in the piece.

The real problem, as they see it, is one of better utilization of resources, that is, of achieving full employment, faster economic growth, and a fairer distribution of the resulting output. Price stability has only secondary priority in the sense that it is not an end in itself, but at best one of a set of possible methods of facilitating these employment, growth, and distribution objectives. Nor are wages the sole or primary cause of inflation, which stems from restrictive monopoly elements in the economy, the ability and willingness of entrepreneurs arbitrarily to raise prices in order to cover costs, and the failure of government to control excessive demand which provides the climate of expectations in which such cost-plus mentality can flourish. In such a setting, there is no guarantee that lower wages would not be offset by higher profits. Indeed, there are many who, taking note of the rigidities in the economy, have reconciled themselves to "creeping inflation" as a permanent by-product of more rapid economic growth, and as far preferable to the alternative of restrictive "stop-go" regulatory policies and consequent interruption to economic expansion. Their economic prescriptions, accordingly, take the form not of wage restraint, but rather of measures to ensure steady economic growth plus devices to counter the injustices imposed by inflation on a small group of fixed income recipients, for example by tying insurance and savings contracts and social insurance benefits to changes in the price level.

Similarly, trade union economists argue that wage costs are far from being the most important cause of the United Kingdom's chronic balance of payments difficulties; hence the cure for this malady lies elsewhere than in wage restraint. They challenge the figures purporting to show that the increases of United Kingdom export prices have been far out of line with those in other major

---

[27] *Ibid.*

exporting countries, and they argue that other causes of poor export performance have been much more important, for example, deficiencies in design, salesmanship, and delivery time. They suggest that there are other much more significant steps that need to be taken to solve the balance of payments problem, including export promotion councils, better government services to exporters including tax concessions, temporary import controls, assistance to import-substituting industries, selective controls over capital exports, scaling down of overseas defense expenditures and perhaps of sterling balances, improved international liquidity, devaluation, and, above all, faster economic growth which would substantially reduce unit costs of exports.

It is, in fact, the growth theme that dominates the thinking of those who are reluctant to acknowledge the need for a wages policy as such. Reversing the argument about inflation being an obstacle to growth, they argue that it is the inflation-psychosis which has acted as a brake on growth through frequent premature impositions of restraint and consequent business uncertainty and reluctance to invest. Trade union economists never tire of emphasizing that it is only in the framework of a continuously expanding economy that the problems of inflation, of full employment, and of distributive justice can be solved.

Individual trade union leaders are finding it even more difficult than the TUC bureaucracy to accept the need for a wages policy. For one thing, they have less reason to be dissatisfied with the status quo — particularly leaders of the stronger unions who have found it possible year after year to bargain for substantial wage increases. And they are less conscious than the TUC economists of the larger economic context, or even of the interests of the working class as a whole. Such men are not easily convinced that a wages policy could yield tangible results for their workers in the form of higher real wages than they have been obtaining under free collective bargaining.

At the Brighton TUC Congress in September, 1963, the leaders of three of the most powerful unions (Amalgamated Engineering Union, Transport and General Workers Union, and the Miners Union), as well as the colorful leader of the Boilermakers Union, were so touchy about the concept of "restraint" that they insisted on deleting a reference, in the report on *Economic Development and Planning*, to the NEDC view (in its report on *Conditions Favorable*

to Faster Growth) that "it is necessary to ensure that money incomes
as a whole — wages, salaries and profits — rise less rapidly than in
the past," and replacing it with the following:

This was why the N.E.D.C. pointed to the desirability of creating a situation in which money incomes (profits as well as wages and salaries) did
not rise more rapidly than output. As the N.E.D.C. emphasized, the
purpose of this would be to achieve a programme of faster growth, and
to secure a much faster rise in *real* income per head than in the past: even
its present target of 4 per cent per annum (and the aim must be to raise
this target) would enable *real* incomes to be doubled in a little over
twenty years. . . . One of the necessary factors in economic growth
must, indeed, be an expansion of real purchasing power. To restrain real
increases in wages and salaries could defeat such a programme. Equally,
to allow prices and profits to rise unchecked would undermine the foundations of a policy of planned growth. . . .[28]

In addition, these leaders voted both for acceptance of the report,
which was interpreted as endorsement of TUC participation in planning of incomes within the framework of NEDC, and against "any
form of wage restraint"; the latter vote was accompanied by oral
explanations that this opposition was only to imposition of wage
restraint under the prevailing Tory government. A few weeks later
at the Labor Party Conference in Scarborough, some of these same
leaders went much further in the direction of open support for an
incomes policy under a Labor government. This is thought to have
been partly the result of talks during the intervening period between
party and trade union leaders. In addition it was certainly given an
impetus by the skillful handling of semantics from the platform; the
major speakers stressed their interest not in "wage restraint," but
rather in "increasing the real value of the pay packet" and "planned
growth in wages." In the words of Frank Cousins, the militant left-
wing leader of the transport workers, who had led the "rebellion"
at Brighton: "Under a genuine incomes policy we would expect
real wages to rise and that is why we in our union refuse to equate
wages restraint with the economic progress we support."

Clearly, however, there is more than semantics at issue. Trade
union leaders, particularly leaders of the most powerful unions, have
good reason to think twice before committing themselves to an incomes policy. In the first place, such a policy effectively implemented
would constitute a serious threat to their own function in industrial
relations. At best it would imply a secondary role for individual

---

[28] Trades Union Congress, Amendment to Supplementary Report A, *Economic Development and Planning*, replacing paragraph 40.

trade unions in the collective bargaining process in that it would exclude them from direct participation, as negotiators, in the decision as to the overall amount available for wage increases. This implies, further, a significant shift of power from individual trade unions to the TUC, which would necessarily gain a degree of centralized authority in the process, and also to the Labor Party as overall wage bargaining was transferred from the industrial to the political arena.

In the second place, trade union leaders are not in a position to move too far ahead of rank-and-file opinion. Before subscribing fully to a far-reaching program like an incomes policy, they must be persuaded that they can sell the idea to their members whose support they would need in implementing such a policy. This is presumably why the major leaders, some of whom are actually sitting in NEDC and are relatively sophisticated in economics, make a fuss about the the sound of words like "restraint," and "incomes policy" rather than "wages policy." And this is why they stress the psychological importance of ensuring that the program appears to be directed at profits and speculative gains as well as at wages and salaries, and that profits should not be allowed to rise as a direct consequence of wage restraint. Above all this is why, as indicated below, trade unionists from Mr. Woodcock on down insist that trade unions must fully participate — and be seen to participate in — as equal partners in the planning process from which an incomes policy is to emerge.

The View of the Employers

As with politicians and trade unionists, British businessmen have bowed to fashion and are paying lip service to the need for an incomes policy. In conviction, however, they appear to have serious reservations.

Predictably they are opposed to controls on profits. But with respect to wages it is fallacious to assume that employers are eager for restraints on labor costs. True, they are quite prone to ascribe inflation and balance of payments crises to the excessive monopolistic bargaining strength of trade unions. "It is indeed because Trade Unions have succeeded in limiting competition in the labour market that it is possible for wages to run ahead of labour productivity; against this the cases are rare in which profits can for long exceed the measure of the risk-taking and the value to the economy of the enterprise of which they are the reward."[29] For several reasons,

---

[29] Federation of British Industries, *Profits and the National Incomes Commission,* July 24, 1963.

however, they shy away from specific proposals for government intervention to limit wage costs. They do not want to be prevented from bidding up wages when and where necessary to attract scarce workers in a tight labor market. Nor are they unduly worried about rising wage costs in a boom economy in which higher costs can easily be covered by higher prices; the tendency of businessmen to set prices by adding a fixed margin or mark-up to costs has been widely commented on in the United Kingdom. Above all, British employers are as resistant as the trade unions to the threat of any encroachment on their collective bargaining "prerogatives" — in part, perhaps, because a closer official check on wages necessarily implies a closer scrutiny of profits and of monopoly influences and restrictive trade practices. Thus it is being discreetly suggested in industrial circles that employers would prefer offering higher real wages to accepting limitations on profits, and hence would be amenable to a kind of "deal" by which the unions would support favorable treatment of investment incomes in return for improved social security and redundancy arrangements, greater regional investment efforts, and (relatively innocuous) taxes on wealth and higher wages. "Too much attention can be devoted to knocking off the last half-penny rise in wage earnings to the sacrifice of other objectives." [30] "The aim of policy should be to favour high wage-earnings based on competitive wage rates, and high profits based on competitive profit markup. High profits, earned by effort, are in fact the foundation of high wages and job security." [31]

On profits, the official, and apparently the heartfelt, industrial view has been stated in a paper on *Profits and the National Incomes Commission* published by the FBI on the occasion of the most recent NIC report. The memorandum explicitly acknowledges that "any effective national incomes policy must concern itself with all categories of income. Hence we agree that profits and dividends, no less than other incomes, must come within its orbit." "Keeping profits in step with other incomes in broad terms and over the long run may be justifiable." But it then proceeds to "demonstrate" the undesirability and administrative impracticability of every method so far conceived of dealing with aggregate profits.

Profits, it is argued, must be treated differently from wages and other contractual incomes because they are fundamentally different

---

[30] *Manchester Guardian*, September 13, 1963.

[31] Federation of British Industries, *op. cit.*

in nature. "Direct restraining action may often be justified in the case of wages but not normally in the case of profits." Wages and salaries are costs of production; profits are a residual. Contractual incomes are always positive, and they are fixed; profits are uncertain and may be negative. "In an efficient economy the points of economic growth or shrinkage are first shown by changes in profits, only subsequently by changes in contractual incomes." Profits are "in the great majority of instances" earned in competitive conditions; wages are earned through monopolistic bargaining. Dividend restraint is not to be recommended, because dividends are such a small proportion of personal income, because controls would obstruct the market function of dividends in allocating capital, would be inequitable between companies, and would "weaken the penalties for lax control of current expenditure." Any kind of profits restraint would endanger the supply of risk capital needed for growth. Profits statistics are inadequate to permit profits control. Control of prices or of profit margins would be "obnoxious," and would lead to cost-plus pricing or would inhibit the accumulation of capital for economic expansion. The profits tax is discriminatory. The manipulation of tariffs so as to restrain profits is not feasible and would undermine long-term planning by industry.

Thus the conclusion is reached that "the purposes of a national incomes policy are best served by a correct general economic and fiscal policy. If general policy is aptly designed to promote the growth of the economy at the highest rate sustainable over the long-term without inflation, incomes in total will not usually be able to outrun productivity. . . . From the general tone of this memorandum, it is clear that British industry intends to fight very hard against dealing with incomes in isolation; and that it thinks general economy policy . . . is much more important than any quasi-legalistic control of incomes on the NIC model. Mr. Woodcock may have found an ally.[32]

DEFINING THE PUBLIC INTEREST: CRITERIA FOR INCOME DISTRIBUTON

Even if all parties were agreed on the need for an incomes policy, they would still have to reach a decision on what kind of limits to set to acceptable increases in income. There are several facets to this problem, but they all relate to income distribution. With respect to primary distribution of income, a twofold decision is required: how

---

[32] *Manchester Guardian*, July 25, 1963.

to determine the global amount by which private incomes of all kinds can safely be increased, and what criteria to apply in allocating this global amount, that is, how to take account of differentials between skills, between industries and between firms within an industry, and between regions. Simultaneously there arises the issue of secondary income distribution, that is, how much should be taken away from private incomes to be used for collective investment and consumption. Although the term "incomes policy" is usually intended to apply to primary distribution of incomes, the discussions which it provokes invariably lead to analysis of fiscal and monetary policy, that is, of secondary distribution of income.

This is fundamentally a political problem of weighing up the conflicting claims of various interest groups, of defining the "public interest." In the final analysis this process represents nothing more than a compromise between the conflicting claims.

Because the problem is political, it is indeterminate. Just as the practical politician must admit that there is no automatic rule which can serve as standard for noninflationary income determination, so do most economists grant that there is no rigid economic determinancy shaping the pattern of income distribution. Although a relative constancy in capital output ratios and distributive shares has been noted over long periods in the United Kingdom,[33] this is attributed by some to convention and entrepreneurial expectations which can be altered ("full cost-pricing" on the basis of "normal" markup or rate of total profit to total pay) rather than to automatic market forces in the classical sense, while others attribute the phenomenon to historical accident or conjuncture of offsetting influences. Moreover, the ratio *does* change; many observers have pointed to a profits squeeze in recent years in many industrial countries including the United Kingdom. Governments have ample monetary and fiscal tools for altering the secondary distribution of incomes, and these same tools also have an influence, via their effect on expectations and propensities to consume and to invest, on primary distribution of income. Thus there is neither practical nor theoretical justification for suggestions that the bargaining partners or the government are powerless to alter distributive shares.

Accordingly, if the government decides to intervene in this strug-

---

[33] E. H. Phelps Brown, "Some Aspects of the Distribution of Incomes," paper read at Business Economists' Conference at New College, Oxford, April 18–21, 1963.

gle over income shares, in an effort to achieve greater economic stability, it will be faced with the further problem of defining the criteria by which its intervention is to be guided. This must be done in two contexts: (1) a decision as to total amount available for increases in income, and (2) the allocation of this total amount as between income recipients. Both are extremely difficult and complex tasks. Presumably the first decision will be arrived at by economists in line with some kind of measure of increases in overall productivity for the economy as a whole, and will take the form either of a percentage figure or an absolute amount to be subsequently allocated. This process will entail conflict and compromise, and much will depend on the machinery set up for permitting sectional interests to participate in this process.

Conceptually and practically, however, it will be far simpler to arrive at an estimate of global availabilities than it will be to allocate this amount.

The dilemma can be posed more concretely by describing the choices which would confront the unhappy officials charged with attempting to implement a national wages policy. At first blush it might seem that the easiest course, after deciding on the total sum available for wage increases compatible with economic stability, would be to grant equal increases throughout the economy, thereby avoiding the complaint of discrimination or disproportionate concessions to particular groups. Actually, however, this would immediately give rise to serious social tensions. If the "equal" increases were granted on a straight flat-rate basis, they would narrow differentials and would be resisted by higher-paid skilled workers. But "equal" percentage increases, because they would increase differentials, would be considered an unfair "distortion" by lower-paid groups, and would constitute an obstacle to trade union "solidarity" demands. And there is the opposite but equally relevant objection that such a policy of equal increases would unduly cement existing differentials which have evolved largely for historical and accidental reasons, and are not adopted to modern conditions or to actual job content. Finally, there is the argument that equal increases would not make allowances for differences between firms in productivity, in profitability, or in recruitment needs.

Thus it is clearly unworkable to proceed automatically on the basis of equal increases. The alternative is to give more to some groups and less to others, to set forth clear-cut, acceptable criteria for granting exceptions to the principle of equal increases. But what criteria? *Productivity* increases in the firm or in the industry do not provide a satisfactory guide because of statistical and conceptual measuring difficulties, because they contravene the principle of "the rate for the job" wherever performed, because this does not take account of manpower needs, and because it would discriminate against essential services like health, education, research, and government, where productivity is extraordinarily difficult to quantify. Almost the same objections apply, with perhaps more force, to *profitability*. Similarly *manpower requirements* is a difficult standard to apply because of the problem of measuring actual "needs" and "adequate recruitment" in a tight labor market where all employers "need" or "want" more workers except in the context of national planning priorities, and because it may conflict with considerations of equity, of productivity, or of profitability.

Although there has been a great deal of discussion in the United Kingdom as to criteria for wage control, little progress has been made in clarifying the problem, or demonstrating how to reconcile the various requirements that must be taken into account. It may be that they are in fact irreconcilable, and that a completely consistent solution of the problem is not possible. Nevertheless, there have been enough promising suggestions from various quarters to indicate that the difficulty is not altogether intractable. There are ways of at least reducing anomalies in the wage structure and of more clearly defining permissible exceptions to the overall limit for wage or profits increases.

Theoretically, the biggest contribution of this kind could be made by overhauling the wage structure on the basis of a carefully worked out system of work study or job evaluation. The objective would be to classify kinds of work done into a manageable number of "jobs" on the basis of efforts and qualifications required for each, to establish a corresponding scale of wage differentials thereby eliminating anomalies, and then to ensure that increases were granted in such a way as not to disturb these established "relativities." But the difficulties of achieving such a structural reorganization are formidable. Even conceptually, scientific job evaluation is difficult in view of the problem of how to assign weights to such diverse and mutually inconvertible factors of job content as effort, skill, responsibility, prestige or status, and job environment, as well as the need to introduce at some point a nonscientific monetary measure as the keystone of the resulting wage structure. Moreover, it can be argued that the wage structure based solely on the concept of "the rate for the job" would not be economically viable since it would fail to reflect differences in supply and demand for labor between firms, or industries and regions. And practically there are problems of how to get the assorted lot of employers and trade unions in various industries to accept and enforce the resulting scale of job definitions and wage differentials — both in national negotiations and at the plant level. Even though the idea of scientific work study has a vague appeal to workers as corresponding to their notion of "justice" and objectivity, it is certain that an attempt at complete reconstruction of the wage structure would be defeated by British conservatism plus genuine conflicts of interest and in social and economic philosophy.

Nevertheless, if it were made clear to both employers and unions that anomalies in wage structure are a threat to economic stability, it might be possible to devise ways of "tidying up" that structure on a smaller scale at the plant level by establishing more equitable earnings relations between time workers and between time and piece workers, bringing wage rates into line with actual wages, making incentives more genuine, and reducing anomalies (as distinct from planned differentials) through work study within a firm or an industry. Conceivably also there might be some progress in the direction of wage solidarity by restricting increases for higher-paid workers in favor of those in lower brackets, thereby reducing the "inequity" justification for leap frogging. *Within* an industry this might be accomplished by use of what the British have labeled "pro tanto agreements," designed to grant larger increases in the lower-wage brackets, a device that was once tried unsuccessfully in the engineering industry, but which is again being proposed in several quarters. As *between* industries it is sometimes suggested that "solidarity" might take the form of tapering off increases for those industries in which earnings or productivity are above average, and granting relatively larger increases in less dynamic industries, for example, railways and the public services, in order to compensate for higher drift in the former. This, however, presumes an unlikely degree of coordination by the TUC and central employer organizations.

Another proposal is that anomalies in the wage structure — as well as leap frogging and wage drift — could be reduced by a shift away from payments by results which are regarded as unfair in that technological progress has made it increasingly difficult to relate increased output to the physical efforts of individual workers. A withering away of payments by result would certainly be favored by all those who dislike it on other grounds. For example, it is argued that incentive schemes are an irritant in worker-management relations in the plant, that they involve waste, additional clerical work, more resistance to changes in production methods, less freedom in allocating work, less internal mobility in the plant, and that they engender worker suspicion that new machines will mean new time allowances and reduced pay, with a consequent tendency to "go slow," "fiddle," and to penalize "rate busters." On the other hand many still feel that incentive payments can make a major contribution to productivity, and hence to combatting inflation, by enhancing worker care and attention to machinery, rewarding the exercise of responsibility, and stimulating greater effort and efficiency.

In the public sector there is a current controversy in the United Kingdom concerning the appropriate role of arbitrators in formulation of national policy on wages. As matters stand, arbitrators do not have any mandate to take account of interests other than those of the parties. Moreover, since arbitrators report only their decisions, but not the grounds on which they were reached, the decisions do not provide a corpus of case law which could serve as a guide to negotiators or precedent for subsequent arbitration awards. In the view of many, this is quite satisfactory, since, they feel, it is not the function of the arbitrator to guard the national interest or to dispense justice, but merely to settle disputes. "The arbitrator's job is to find a settlement that the disputants can with advantage accept, not to impose a solution that seems to him fair and just."[34] Indeed, the argument continues, arbitrators could not hope to stay in business unless they aim at compromises that please both sides, or at least provoke a minimum of resistance; otherwise they would be open to the charge from both sides of "not judging cases on their merits." In a sense, therefore, awards reflect the actual balance of bargaining power, and are not very different from what would have been obtained under free collective bargaining.

There are others, however, who reject this interpretation of arbitration as an objective, neutral reflection of the balance of bargaining power, and point out that it is precisely because arbitration bolsters the bargaining strength of weaker, less well-organized groups

[34] J. R. Hicks, *The Theory of Wages* (New York: Macmillan, 1932), pp. 149–150.

and thereby alters the wage structure that would be obtained by free collective bargaining that it is so widely used. They note that the argumentation in the arbitration chambers is conducted in terms of ethical standards, and the whole atmosphere is judicial. Their objection is not to the exercise of value judgments by the arbitrator, but to the absence of any consistent and explicit set of criteria as a guide to these value judgments. Indeed, it is argued, if there were an agreed national wages policy arbitration, tribunals could make an invaluable contribution to such a policy by publishing the reasons for their decisions and even, perhaps, by making their hearings public and thereby clearly enunciating the underlying criteria and guides for exception. This would have widespread repercussions on wage negotiations, since each side would find it necessary to demonstrate that its objectives were consistent with declared national policy.

For perspective in this conflict of views it should be borne in mind that so far there *is* no agreed national wages policy in the United Kingdom — no definition of the public interest, no explicit set of generally accepted principles for wage determination, and no criteria for exceptions which arbitrators could reasonably be asked to take into account. In this context it is patently unthinkable to ask them to try to moderate wage claims in order to combat inflation; this would clearly constitute an indefensible and arbitrary kind of intervention and would undermine the functioning of the arbitration system. On the other hand, it is conceivable that the context might change to one in which a national wages policy and objective had been hammered out, perhaps in NEDC, with the participation of all parties concerned, so that there was an explicit definition of the public interest with respect to wage increases acceptable to both sides. In such a setting it would be feasible and legitimate, and probably very helpful to implementation of the wage policy, to ask arbitrators to operate within this agreed framework.

MACHINERY FOR CONTROL OF INCOMES

Even assuming a genuine urge on the part of employers and trade unions to have wages controlled, and at least moderate success in defining workable criteria for distributing the overall amount available for increases in incomes, there would still remain a basic issue as to whether the trade unions, the employer organizations, and the government could develop the requisite controls for implementing such a policy. The specific types of control that might prove effective in the British context are largely unexplored territory beyond the scope of this chapter. It is possible, nevertheless briefly, to indicate the kinds of problem that are likely to arise in this connection.

Could the British trade union movement exercise the kind of control required to implement an incomes policy? Structurally it is clearly not equipped to do so, and prospects of a drastic change in this respect are far from bright. The TUC has little centralized authority over constituent unions, which are free to do as they wish. Disorderly trade union structure embitters interunion relations by engendering intensive wage competition and leads to jurisdictional disputes as rival unions attempt to protect skills, membership, and prestige. Nor is there much chance of achieving the kind of reform in trade union structure that would make for greater cohesion. Theoretically, for purposes of implemeting a national wage policy, the TUC's lack of constitutional authority could be remedied by working through trade union federations. There are difficulties, however, in attempting to achieve via federations the degree of coordination required for an effective national wage policy. For one thing, it is an extremely loose form of organization in which the individual unions retain their autonomy; the alliance is intended merely for more effective bargaining vis-à-vis employers' organizations, but final decisions rest with the executives of individual unions. Moreover, neither the constituent unions nor the federation officials tend to favor tighter links with the TUC. So far TUC suggestions for closer ties have made little headway.

However there is still the possibility that a great deal can be accomplished through mobilizing the considerable potential for moral authority at the disposal of the TUC General Council. The General Council is composed of leading trade union officials, and within the council a handful of general secretaries, representing the most powerful unions, are dominant. It is said that the leaders of the six largest unions, whose aggregate membership is in excess of that of the remaining TUC affiliates, and who thus yield more than half the votes at the congress, are able to shape trade union policy provided they are backed by their executives and their members. Whether they will do so depends, as is so often the case, on the personalities and capabilities of the leaders. Ernest Bevin, that dominant figure in the postwar Labor government, did a great deal to strengthen the authority of the TUC. And from the end of World War II until the death of Mr. Arthur Deakin in 1955, TUC policy was effectively controlled by the Deakin-Lawther-Williamson "triumvirate." In more recent years the TUC leadership has been less vigorous, inhibited apparently by the urge to keep their influence discrete, "to persuade rather than to compel; always to avoid taking a step that might seriously embarrass an affiliated member."[35] Nevertheless, Mr. Woodcock and various other TUC officials and staff members have indicated that given an agreed wages policy objective to which the TUC could fully subscribe, ways could be found of coordinating union activity in order to implement that objective. Exactly what they have in mind has not been disclosed, but past experience suggests ways in which "moral suasion" can be exercised by the leaders of major unions once they have agreed upon a goal. One of these is the system of block voting at the annual Trades Union Congress and at the annual conference of the Labor Party. Each union casts a vote for the whole of its membership regardless of any internal differences of view. If the rank and file have not expressed their wishes, the General Secretary of a union can decide how the union's block vote shall be cast. Candidates for the General Council and for the Labor Party offices are nominated by individual union groups, but voting is by a ballot of the whole congress or conference. This means that each union votes not only for its own group, but for every group, with the result that the big unions exercise a dominating influence on the result in every group. The arrangement is defended on the grounds that each electee will represent the movement as a whole, thus making it possible for small unions to obtain representation. Because of this system candidates for election to major office are conscious of the fact that they cannot hope for success without the support of the big unions. Also it is generally assumed that there is an understanding among the larger unions that they will normally support each others' nominees.

Another maneuver which has been utilized in cases of urgency — for instance, in the case of the wage restraint program of 1948 — is the convening of a special ad hoc conference of union executives. If the emergency nature of a situation can be clearly established, it may be possible to agree on coordinated action without formal approval from the membership of the constituent unions.

Finally, various proposals have been made from time to time for

---

[35] B. C. Roberts, *Industrial Relations, Contemporary Problems and Prospects* (London: Methuen, 1962), p. 21.

enhancing the moral or persuasive authority of the TUC. These include building up a well-staffed research and planning department to study the long-range trends and implications of a rising rate of economic growth, and making this research available to the federations; regular consideration by the TUC Economic Committee — or a specially constituted committee — of tactical policy for the trade unions as a whole on wages and other bargaining terms; and provision for consultation by union executives with the General Council at the beginning of the bargaining year *before* major policy decisions are taken by their union conferences — an arrangement that might eventually lead to simultaneous settlement of wage claims in the major sectors of the economy.

Also the very process of discussing an incomes policy has already had the effect of strengthening the ties between the TUC and the Labor Party, and easing internal tensions within the labor movement. Fundamentally the cleavage between the more extreme Socialists and the more conservative or pragmatic trade union wing of the movement has been the result of ideological conflicts over planning. Already it is clear that the kind of economic planning now being attempted in NEDC, and the consideration of wage levels in relation to other incomes and to economic growth and inflationary pressures, provides common ground for the Socialists and the more conservative trade unionists.

To place the matter in perspective, however, it should be kept in mind that the potentialities for moral suasion and domination by a minority of leaders of the largest unions depend on achievement of a consensus of views. Unless these executives see eye to eye, centralized control will not emerge, and unless they can sell the policy objective to their membership, they will not be in a position to commit themselves to such an objective. Ultimately, therefore, the viability of a wage policy, so far as the unions are concerned, will depend upon convincing individual workers that they are likely to gain from such a policy, in short, by offering a quid pro quo for restraint on their part.

Similar considerations apply to prospects for greater centralization and cohesion *within the ranks of employers*. Structurally there is at present even less centralization here than in the trade union movement, and internal tensions, resulting from differences between firms with respect to size, dynamism, capital structure, technological development and degree of monopoly, are at least equally great.

However, prospects for early structural reform are perhaps brighter in view of the consideration being given to a merger of the three major organizations, BEC, FBI, and NABM. Such a development would facilitate the implementation of an incomes policy by enabling businessmen to speak with one voice, forcing industrialists to think through and integrate their views on wages in relation to profits and pricing, and increasing cohesion by enlarging opportunities for exercise of moral suasion and (fairly loose) sanctions against nonconforming firms. Also, as with trade unions, actual participation by leading employers in the planning process via NEDC and any other institutional bodies that might be established will inevitably clarify and unify the collective industrial view on the incomes issue and the importance of cohesion and cooperation.

The effectiveness of an incomes policy will depend in the last analysis on the nature and quality of economic planning, and particularly on the *planning machinery*. An incomes policy is by definition an exercise in planning, but it is only a sector of planning. It cannot by itself achieve steady growth without inflation; this objective calls for careful meshing of an incomes policy with all of the other vital elements in overall economic policy.

Current British discussion on machinery for economic planning is taking place primarily within the Labor Party and the trade unions on the assumption of a Labor victory in 1964. The Conservatives, having launched NEDC, are letting the matter rest there, and have said little about mechanisms for transforming NEDC's indicative targets into a program for action. To be sure, the new Prime Minister has created a new Ministry which subsumes the Board of Trade and the programming for less developed regions of the United Kingdom. So far, however, no overall planning functions have been entrusted to the new ministry.

Within the labor movement, however, there has been a lively discussion on planning machinery, with a sharp division of opinion between two distinct views, roughly attributable to party leader Harold Wilson on the one hand and to the TUC on the other. The controversy centers on the issue as to whether economic planning should be done in the first place by a professional body of experts operating as an integral part of the machinery of government, for example, in a Ministry of Planning and Production, or whether it should evolve out of deliberations, outside the departmental orbit, by the private interests groups concerned plus representatives of the public interest.

The issue goes far deeper than that of mere machinery or apparatus for planning. It is basically a question of the extent to which the government is prepared to accept ultimate responsibility for formulating and implementing national objectives. Wilson's view seems to be that this responsibility requires that the economic plans should be drawn up within and by the government, after which they might be submitted to an advisory group representing labor and management for advice as to adequacy and feasibility, perhaps modified accordingly, and then submitted to Parliament for final approval as a government plan. It would obviously be of immediate and crucial importance to a new Labor government to ensure that economic planning conformed to the changes in policy and direction to which it is politically committed.

Among the supporters of government planning as opposed to interest group planning, there is a lesser although still major dispute as to the appropriate location within the government of the planning function. Harold Wilson, and at least some of the economists who work closely with the party, are reported to feel that this function should be assigned to a new Ministry of Production and Planning, and perhaps also an Investment Council, rather than to the Treasury.

Until the advent of NEDC such overall economic planning as there was took place in the Treasury — presumably as an offshoot of its responsibility for government revenues in relation to expenditures and its special role vis-à-vis the Bank of England and the money market. The Treasury's planning staff consisted of seven senior officials including the Economic Advisor, and seven businessmen and trade unionists, meeting under the chairmanship of a Joint Permanent Secretary to the Treasury responsible for economic affairs. Its activities had the effect of linking in a close network of discussions about 100 key officials of the economic departments, including the heads of divisions concerned with governmental revenues and expenditures, the capital market, international trade, employment and manpower, officials of the Bank of England and of the nationalized industries. A recent reorganization of Treasury structure has given the economists a more definite place in the hierarchy. A new Economic Unit is expected to provide a link with NEDC by supplying the independent opinion once given by the Treasury's Economics Section.

The argument for removing the planning job from Treasury, thus leaving it with its original responsibilities for monetary policy, tax reform, the national debt, and some control over expenditures, rests fundamentally on the conviction that its traditionally restrictive attitude would seriously hamper economic expansion. And this conservatism, according to one observer, stems from the

. . . monolithic organization of Government Departments which is forced upon the Civil Service structure by Cabinet responsibility. The Minister responsible for a department is advised by the Permanent Secretary who ultimately concentrates in his hand the sum total of the official views which are rising up from below. It is he, as an administrator, who sums up the argument. . . . The monolithicism of the command structure of British Government means that the Minister will get an administrator's advice. The Treasury's main administrative task is to safe-guard the balance of payments and monetary stability. In a conflict between expansion and reticence, reticences will always win within that Department.

Unless the expansionist, physical planning point of view, and the view of the economic expert can be matched against the Treasury at the highest level, planning will remain a limp affair, biased towards contraction rather than expansion. Yet to get balance it is equally necessary that there should be a powerful Department, paying primary attention to the requirements, especially of the balance of payments.[36]

At the Labor Party conference in September, 1963, Wilson succeeded in wedding the concept of a Ministry of Planning and Production to the motif of economic growth based on scientific progress in a way that captured the imagination of the public and the press — and even, apparently, of the Conservative Party which subsequently set up a new ministry directed to the same end, but without the stress on planning.

The trade unions, however, are not impressed by this line of thought. Although initially reluctant to cooperate in NEDC, they now feel that this kind of planning offers them an unparalleled opportunity for exercising direct influence on government policy — an opportunity that would clearly be lost were the planning function to be transferred to a government ministry. The TUC wants "the plan" to be drafted by an independent staff (like the NEDC office) in consultation with employers and unions, submitted for amendment and not mere advice to a tripartite body, and then sent to Parliament for approval; *not* drawn up by the government with the

---

[36] Thomas Balogh, *Planning for Progress, a Strategy for Labour*, Fabian Tract 346 (July, 1963), p. 35.

advice only of unions and employers and then approved by Parliament.

The advantage of this method . . . is that it recognizes that planning, to be effective, must be largely based on consent. The more . . . representatives of industry at all levels are involved in creating a plan, the more committed they will be to implementing it.

When the General Council were discussing whether they should join the N.E.D.C. they made it clear that they were not interested in membership of a body whose job would be to exchange economic banalities or to transmit to trade unionists the Government's views of the needs of the economic situation. The potential value of the N.E.D.C. lies in the fact that it provides a forum in which agreements can be reached between the Government and the two sides of industry. Such agreements can only be based on thorough and objective studies carried out by a staff which is responsible directly to the Council and is not open to the suspicion — as a Government Department would be — that its work is influenced by predetermined Government policies. . . . [This] is entirely in keeping with British democratic practice of encouraging voluntary groups to participate actively in the formulation of decisions which affect their interests.[37]

To effectuate this policy of participation in the planning process (and transform trade unionists "from critics into architects"), the TUC has been pressing for immediate action to establish machinery for bipartite (trade union and employer) representation and consultation at the industry level. These "industrial councils," or "industrial commissions," or "little Neddies" would serve as the focus for translating NEDC's descriptive forecasts into specific performance targets for major industries or industrial sectors. Indeed, they are viewed by some trade union members of NEDC as the principal "instruments of purposive planning" necessary to give effect to NEDC decisions.

Such bodies are seen as having a threefold function. They would provide a two-way flow of ideas and statistical information between NEDC and industries on such matters as investment and rationalization plans, manpower requirements, redundancy arrangements, costs, profit margins, and prices. They might provide a mechanism for cooperation with respect to research, standardization, marketing and export promotion, credit facilities, and perhaps even be entrusted with funds for promoting industrial rationalization. Finally they could serve as a channel for the exercise of industrial self-discipline and persuasion in relation to "recalcitrant" employers, for example,

---

[37] Trades Union Congress, *Economic Development and Planning*, p. 10.

those who consistently failed to meet targets, to give required information, or to adhere to prescribed profit margins. This is seen as a
more practicable and immediate kind of pressure than the ultimate
sanctions of state control over profit margins, tax measures, or threat
of take-over of inefficient firms or competition from new publicly
owned enterprises.

Predictably there is a conflict of views as to the merits of the suggested industrial commissions. The Director General of NEDC is
on record as favoring such working groups in each industry, and for
several industries discussions were well advanced in November, 1963,
and prospective members of the commissions have already been selected. Some of the employer members of NEDC, however, were
inclined to block this development for fear of encroachment on the
sanctity of trade secrets and on the prerogatives of employer associations and of management itself.

Labor Party leaders are reported not to be fully convinced of the
soundness of the proposal. This stand accords with their general
preference for governmental as opposed to bipartite or tripartite
planning. Although official party pronouncements stress the desirability of a *blend* of the two approaches, and the indispensability of a
representative body like NEDC, this should not be allowed to obscure
the fundamental principle at stake. This is whether control over the
formulation and execution of overall economic policy, including incomes policy, shall reside with the government or with the interest
groups themselves. In this sense the extent to which a representative
bipartite or tripartite body renders *advice* is irrelevant; the vital issue
is one of ultimate power.

CONCLUSION

Italy and Germany have relied almost exclusively on indirect controls over wages and prices in the postwar years. Perhaps because
her economic situation was less favorable than theirs during this
period, Britain has gone further and experimented with ways of persuading private groups to exercise restraint in their economic demands. These experiments have not, however, involved formal
controls. On the contrary, every effort has been made to achieve compliance on an entirely voluntary basis. Devices which have been
used include appeals by high public officials, special reports by
study commissions, "wage pauses" at the instance of the government,
the focusing of public attention on private bargaining by postsettle-

ment examination at the hands of a National Incomes Commission, and the current experiment with the formulation of broad economic policy through a National Economic Development Council.

If success is measured in terms of evidence that the government's campaign elicited acquiescence and/or support, failure is quite clear. Never, except for one brief period from 1948 to 1950, did the trade unions find it possible to agree, and even then a "wage pause" was put into effect without announcement. Our analysis further suggests that local managements have continued to put into effect wage increases despite national bargains which presumably settled the wage question, that national labor and management organizations are incapable of exerting other than moral influence over their members, and that in any event there is very great difficulty in defining and formulating an equitable wage policy.

The logical next step, following British efforts at acquiescence without controls, is a system of controls. For this reason, the experience in the Netherlands provides an interesting contrast. It is with formal controls that the Dutch have been experimenting since World War II, as will be seen in the next chapter.

5   The Netherlands

Each of the countries which we have reviewed is, not unnaturally, unique in some respects. Certainly this is true of the Netherlands. It is tiny (hardly larger than the state of Maryland), heavily populated, short of natural resources (except for the recently discovered sources of natural gas), terribly vulnerable to international economic pressures, characterized by a social system in which Catholic and Protestant religious organizations and concepts play an unusually important role, and inhabited by a people who show extraordinary tolerance and harmony in dealing with points of tension. For our purposes Holland is unique in another respect. It has, since 1945, had a formal wage-price policy far beyond anything found in any of the other countries. True, the Dutch system of cooperative labor-management-government action is constantly evolving, and has only recently taken a startling turn. Nevertheless, in contrast to the Italians, Germans, and British, who are only at the threshold of an incomes policy, the Dutch have now had about two decades of experience. It is this experience which is the subject of this analysis.

One must know something about the country, its people, and its institutions before the postwar economic program can be understood.

In area Holland approaches 16,000 square miles (a steady program of land reclamation causes the figure to vary). Its greatest length is but 175 miles and its greatest width is only 115 miles. Most of its people live in cities, some of which number more than 100,000 people. The population has been growing extraordinarily fast.[1] Prior to

---

[1] Population was 5,000,000 in 1900, 9,300,000 in 1945, and 11,000,000 in 1957; the estimate for 1970 is 13,000,000 and the forecast for 1980, 14,300,000.

1961 the labor force increased at the rate of about 1.5 per cent per year, and in 1961 and 1962 the rate was 2 per cent. In a small country with meager natural resources such a rapid rate of growth poses the threat of unemployment. This is a major reason why the Dutch have put so much effort into land reclamation and into industrialization programs.

(Because of its size and limited resources, plus its heavy population, Holland has always been heavily dependent upon foreign trade.) In 1958 imports represented 45.3 per cent of the gross national product. No other OECD country except Norway even approached such a ratio.[2]

Religious alignments permeate Dutch economic and political life, yet since World War II almost no tensions have resulted therefrom. This is so despite the fact that historically the Netherlands has been subject to as many external and internal religious pressures as most of the other European countries. The battle for supremacy between Catholicism and Protestantism was fought for eighty years in the form of the war of liberation from Spain from 1568 to 1648. The Protestants emerged victorious and Dutch Catholics were isolated in the two provinces of Limburg and Brabant, which had not revolted against the Spanish rule. Thereafter Catholics were tolerated as second-class citizens until the franchise was widened in the second half of the nineteenth century.

The interests represented by Calvinism and Catholicism were embodied in political parties during the gradual extension of suffrage between 1848 and 1919. (Universal suffrage for men came in 1917, and for women in 1919.) Both groups believed that religion should be the essence of public as well as private life. Accordingly, they were thrown together against the anticlerical liberals at one extreme and socialists at the other. The issue of state support for denominational schools dominated the politics of the last half of the nineteenth and the first decade of the twentieth centuries. By the time the religious groups won that battle, the organizational and emotional ties between religion and politics, which still prevail, had been forged. A collateral effect, along with the late arrival of the industrial revolution in Holland and the fact that the bulk of the working classes did not have the franchise until early in the twentieth century, was to deter the establishment of a Socialist Party until 1894. Even after

---

[2] Organization for European Economic Co-operation, *The Problem of Rising Prices,* C(61)12, May, 1961, p. 119.

1894, when the Socialist Party gradually grew to be one of the leading political parties in the Netherlands, it did not have the solid support of the working-class people, for trade unions also came to be formed along religious lines. Before World War II the Socialist Party had changed its name to the Labor Party, and had attempted to steer away from an active Marxist course and become a people's party. In this it has not been altogether successful because of the strength of religious convictions and voting traditions, but it is the second most powerful political party in the Netherlands, and in several coalition governments between 1945 and 1959 it furnished the Prime Minister.

The Dutch electoral system promotes the establishment and survival of many parties. Voting is compulsory in the sense that the voter must at least make an appearance at the polls. The total number of votes cast in elections for the Second Chamber is simply divided by 150, which is the total number of seats in the Chamber. The quotient roughly represents the number of votes a party needs in order to obtain a seat in the Parliament. Any party obtaining this number of votes (usually around 40,000 to 50,000) gets a seat. This means that in addition to the main parties there are always splinter parties having one or more seats in the Second Chamber.

A multiplicity of parties often makes parliamentary government difficult. The problem perhaps is a little less acute for the Dutch because three of the five main political parties (KVP, which is the Catholic Party, AR, which represents the orthodox wing of the Calvinist church, and CHU, which represents the liberal wing of the Calvinist church) are church-oriented and thus tend to be a bit closer in their political view.

The percentage of votes obtained by each of the five main parties in the postwar elections are shown below.

	PvdA[a]	KVP[b]	AR[c]	CHU[d]	VVD[e]
1946	28.3	30.8	12.9	7.9	6.4
1948	25.6	31.0	13.2	9.2	8.0
1952	29.0	28.7	11.3	8.9	8.8
1956	32.7	31.7	9.9	8.4	8.8
1959	30.3	31.6	9.4	8.1	12.2
1963	28.0	31.9	8.7	8.6	10.3

[a] Partij van de Arbeid (Labor Party)
[b] Katholieke Volkspartij (Catholic Peoples' Party)
[c] Antirevolutionaire Partij (Anti-Revolutionary Party, Orthodox Calvinist in view)
[d] Christelijk-Historiche Unie (Christian Historical Union, less Orthodox Calvinist)
[e] Volkspartij voor Vrijheid en Democratie (People's Party for Freedom and Democracy, the former Liberal Party)

Since the 1963 elections provided no party with a majority, the usual coalition was once again required. Complications in forming a new government occurred because the Catholic Party (KVP) is split into right- and left-wing groups. The former did not wish to collaborate with the Labor Party (PvdA), which had the next largest vote, while the left-wing group was oriented toward the Catholic trade union movement, which was in turn allied with the trade union group having Labor Party affiliations. A seventy-day crisis followed the election. A coalition government which did not include the Labor Party finally emerged.

Despite the failure of the Labor Party to gain recognition in the new government, the trade unions remain a uniquely powerful pressure group in the Netherlands. This is because, as will be shown later, trade unions are partly organized along confessional lines. Thus they are not dependent upon the political fortunes of any one party in order to retain influence in government. In every coalition government there are people in influential policy posts who are oriented toward the trade union position.

THE ORIGINS AND INSTITUTIONS OF POSTWAR POLICY

Three points are fundamental to a grasp of postwar economic and social policy in the Netherlands. The first is that World War II and the subsequent five years of occupation left Holland devastated, and in response to this critical situation the Dutch closed ranks to agree that any internal differences they might have could not stand in the way of recovery for the nation. It is extremely doubtful that the degree of unity and cooperation in economic and social affairs which has characterized Dutch life since World War II could have been achieved in the absence of this common bond.

Second, a wage-price policy as such has never been the focal point of the Dutch economic policy. On the contrary, the Dutch (like most of the other Western European governments) have seen wage-price stability as only one of many objectives including full employment, rapid economic growth, balance of payments equilibrium, equitable distribution of income, industrial peace, and economic planning to ensure an orderly, coordinated development of all the factors contributing to national economic policy.

Third, Dutch institutions have been strongly influenced by the principle of "private responsibility," which in turn stems from Protestant and Catholic religious concepts. When Parliament first was asked to consider social legislation, the confessional parties took the position that where social control was needed, it should be exercised by private groups rather than through the government. Over a period of time an accommodation was reached between public and private regulation under which smaller geographical and economic communities within the national community participate in the enactment and administration of such controls as are needed. "That private groups should eventually take part in the administration of regulations that are of particular interest to them has never been a subject of serious political controversy. It was generally acknowledged, even by the Labor and Liberal Parties, that the anticipated growth of government regulation in social and economic fields would create a danger of a power bureaucracy. It was also argued that the regulations would better accomplish their purpose if those to whom they would apply would in some way cooperate voluntarily in their preparation and administration. . . ."[3]

In 1944–45, the Dutch government was in exile, materials and equipment had been ransacked, large parts of the industrial installations and nine-tenths of the traffic facilities were destroyed, the labor market was disorganized, employer and trade union groups were disbanded, there were acute shortages of food, commodities, and housing, and the currency was inflated.

Mutual hostility to the Germans during the wartime occupation first led labor and management leaders into a form of clandestine cooperation. The approaching end of the war brought the leadership in both groups to the realization that the country could not recover unless they put aside their differences and worked closely together. Thus they were prepared, in May, 1945, when the war ended, with the announcement that they were forming a Labor Foundation as an instrument for joint consultation between labor and management in the sphere of social affairs, "both individually on behalf of each industry and within the framework of national and central organizations."[4]

The foundation, embracing all organizations of importance on both sides with the exception of the small United Trade Union

---

[3] G. J. Balkenstein, "The Netherlands Industrial Organization Act of 1950," *University of Pennsylvania Law Review*, 106, No. 4 (February, 1958), p. 502.

[4] P. S. Pels, "Development of Collective Employment Agreements in the Netherlands" in A. Sturmthal (ed.), *Contemporary Collective Bargaining in Seven Countries* (Ithaca, N. Y.: Cornell University, New York State School of Industrial and Labor Relations, 1957), p. 105.

Centre, almost immediately became the advisory body for the government on all important measures of social policy. Increasingly, however, it has become especially concerned with wage policy.

The board of the foundation, consisting of the presidents of federations on both sides, numbers twenty. But the day-to-day work is done by members of the two wage committees: a "big" committee to handle industry-wide agreements and a "little" committee to handle plant agreements. Much work is also done by the secretaries of the various federations. One of the secretaries of the Social and Economic Council is also secretary of the "big" wage committee. Many committees of the council and of the foundation have members in common.

The legal basis for postwar wage policy emerged with the enactment of the Extraordinary Employment Relations Decree of 1945[5] and the directive of the Board of Government Conciliators[6] which designated this board as the official body responsible for determination of wages and working conditions. Employers were thereafter prohibited from altering wage rates or other conditions of work without the approval of the Board of Government Conciliators, every collective agreement between employers and workers required such approval, some provisions of collective agreements could be declared binding throughout the industry concerned if both parties so requested and the Board of Conciliators approved, the board could impose provisions regarding wage rates and other conditions of work, either at the request of associations of employers and employees, or on its own initiative, it could issue norms regarding wage rates and other conditions of work, within the framework of general directives given by the Minister of Social Affairs, it could grant permission to employers to pay wage rates different from those laid down in collective agreements, or the board's provisions or directives, and finally, the board had to ask the advice of the Labor Foundation before taking a decision of "more general" importance.

Members of the Board of Conciliators are appointed by and receive their general guidelines from the Minister of Social Affairs. Except for the chairman, they are not regular civil servants and they do not serve fulltime; traditionally they are men of great personal

---

[5] Extraordinary Decree on Labor Relations (Buitengewoon Besluit Arbeidsverhoudingen), October 5, 1945, Staatsblad 178.

[6] Directive of the Board of Government Conciliators (Beschikkling van het College van Rijksbemiddelaars, October 15, 1945), Staatscourant 96.

prestige. Appointments to the board are carefully allocated to ensure representation for major political and religious groups, and close relations with the Cabinet are maintained. The board no longer performs an official conciliation function. Its name is a legacy from the Labor Disputes Act of 1923,[7] which provided for the appointment of four conciliation officers. These men were not civil servants, but independent persons of great personal authority who were to perform conciliation functions in addition to their normal pursuits. In the immediate postwar years labor and management leaders were in agreement that the country could not afford strikes, and that far-reaching wage and price controls were required. Out of this conviction evolved a governmental wage policy administered by the Board of Conciliators, and kept realistic by advice from the Labor Foundation.

In 1950 a new body was added, the Social and Economic Council (SER), as a result of the Industrial Organization Act of 1950.[8] It was meant to be the apex of a comprehensive new system of industrial organization in which labor and management would join with the government in regulating the nation's economic and social affairs.

The SER consists of forty-five members, fifteen of whom are nominated and appointed by the government, fifteen by the central and other representative organizations of employers, and fifteen by the central organizations of workers. The fifteen government appointees are independent Crown members and are *not* representatives of the government. They include professors of economics and of law, the Director of the Central Planning Bureau and the President of the National Bank. It is understood that their choice will be made in such a way that no political party can have reason to object. The chairman is appointed by the Crown, on advice of the council. The council has the power to collect its own revenue and is therefore financially independent.

The SER has both administrative and advisory functions. In connection with the former it can issue binding decrees, though these require specific authorization and the government has the right to annul or suspend them insofar as they are thought to be in conflict with the law or with the interests of the community. These administrative functions relate largely to the supervision of vertical and

---

[7] Labor Disputes Act (Arbeitsgeschillen wet), 1923, Staatsblad 182.

[8] Industrial Organization Act (Wet op de Bedrifsorganisatie), January 27, 1950, Staatsblad 22.

horizontal organizations within industry. The advisory functions, on the other hand, were intended largely as a transfer to the council of various functions performed previously by various advisory bodies and by the Labor Foundation (which was originally thought of as temporary and which had no staff or headquarters). The advice of the SER has by no means been confined to industrial relations questions. Ministers are obliged to take the advice of the council on all important social and economic measures unless in their opinion it is not in the national interest.

The operation of the Social and Economic Council has been described in illuminating detail by a man who was, at the time of writing (1958), its secretary. He says:

Unlike the Foundation of Labor, the organizations [Labor and management] as such are not represented; their role is confined to appointing members who, in accord with the Industrial Organization Act, are to vote independently of previous instructions or consultations. Formally, therefore, the organizations are not bound by the Council's decisions. This distinction from the Foundation is accentuated by the presence of the government appointed experts, which stresses the personal responsibility of those who participate in the deliberations. Of course, members appointed by the organizations, generally their leaders, vote as a rule according to their organizations' views. . . . Nevertheless, there is a clear distinction between the Council and the organizations. An organization has no direct responsibility for an advice of the Council even if its appointees vote for it, though morally those members are bound to defend the advice within their organizations. . . .

Another distinguishing characteristic of the Council as compared with the Foundation is the membership of experts whose participation has several important consequences. It compels the members appointed by the entrepreneurs and employees to justify their views before independent men, which helps prevent the discussion from lapsing into negotiations between parties. . . .

It should be understood, however, that the Social-Economic Council does not operate as a tripartite body in which labor and the employers vie for the experts' support. This would be impossible, if only because the experts are not a homogeneous group. The same lack of homogeneity characterizes the entrepreneur and labor factions. . . . There are, therefore, many more distinctions among the members than the tripartite scheme would suggest; deliberations do not have the character of a battle of interests as much as might at first be expected. These interests are nevertheless present, and there are instances, as for example in the preparation of advice on the wage-policy, in which they dominate. There are, however, many issues on which other considerations than immediate interest are preponderant.

·   ·   ·   ·

The predisposition of the government and parliament to comply with the Council's advice which has been adopted by a substantial majority rests on obvious grounds. Any government action in accord can expect support from large sections of the population, which is very often needed to give the measures their intended effect. There is the further, more fundamental argument that the very institution of the Council as such implies that its advices should be followed excepting only where they appear contrary to the public interest. This view assumes that material governmental functions have been delegated to the Council, so that the qualification of its activities as "advisory" is an understatement. This broad proposition is, however, far from being generally accepted. It is felt, nevertheless, that too frequent departures from the advice would imperil the Council's valuable contribution in shaping policy.[9]

It should be noted that the SER was intended as the apex of a new system of industrial organizations based on bipartite bodies, industrial boards (schappen) which were to be set up in all industries to discuss various technical, administrative, and commercial problems and to issue binding regulations. In practice, only relatively few boards have been established, mainly in agriculture and allied processing industries, and the retail trades, and they do not deal with wages (except in mining) or prices. "The inspiration behind this organization is strongly ideological; generally speaking the Catholics are in favor of it, so are most socialists. The liberals are not so enthusiastic, although some lip-service is paid to the system. The institutional pattern and ideology is reminiscent of the corporate state, although it is not the done thing to remind people of it. The establishment of new 'schappen' has ground to a halt; at the moment the organization is not as comprehensive as its advocates have wanted."[10]

Dutch wage policy has largely pivoted on the interplay among the foundation, the board, and the SER. And changes in the pattern of interplay have shaped the postwar evolution of that policy, an evolution that has been consistently in the direction of an ever more important role for the foundation.

Until 1959 the pattern of relationships represented careful balancing of responsibilities among the three bodies based on a process of endless discussion, negotiation, and compromise, with each acting as a buffer for the other two. The board operated with a considerable margin of independence of the government. The Minister of Social

---

[9] Balkenstein, op. cit., pp. 511–514.

[10] J. Pen, "The Strange Adventures of Dutch Wage Policy," British Journal of Industrial Relations, 1, No. 3 (October, 1963), p. 321.

Affairs had general responsibility for its activities, but actually issued directives only in exceptional circumstances. Thus the board protected the Minister when he reported to Parliament, relieving him of responsibility for details. Similarly, the board enjoyed a kind of internal protection in the legal requirement that it obtain the advice of the foundation on matters of more general importance. In practice the board was so conscious of the need for support by organized groups that it took this obligation very seriously, and in most cases followed the foundation's advice. In all important questions concerning a specific industry, decisions were the result of discussions and negotiations between the foundation and the board. Up to a point the foundation could filter and mediate the specific demands of individual branches of industry in the interest of the common welfare. Beyond that point, however, it found it necessary, as the representative of private parties, to defend these interests vis-à-vis the government. At this stage the responsibility for applying the brake passed to the board, which did not have to answer in detail either to the government or to private interests. Thus final decisions were "the results of deliberations taken step by step and by degrees, which, psychologically, increases the likelihood of their being readily accepted. The same applies the other way around. If the board wants to start a given policy, it is first laid before the foundation, which, by reason of its being in closer touch with the feelings of the organizations, may by its advice change or mitigate this policy. Besides, being an organization of the organizations themselves, it is more apt to win for this policy the approval of the rank and file on both sides." [11]

Similarly, the foundation had an advisory function vis-à-vis the SER, a responsibility which it took very seriously. The foundation tended to become

. . . the place where a joint labour-management point of view is evolved for presentation to the Council, which bears the responsibility for reconciling the sectional attitudes with the national interest in the formulation of wage (and other) policy suggestions to the Government. The typical, but not invariable, sequence of events in the implementation of a wage increase was for prior discussions in the Labour Foundation to be followed by a report by the Social and Economic Council at the request of the Government, which then (decided) whether to put into effect a mandatory wage increase, a permissive wage increase, or no wage increase. When a permissive wage increase was authorized, the emphasis shifted

[11] M. G. Levenbach, "Lönebildningen i Holland," *Svensk Sparbankstidskrift*, February, 1957, p. 66 ff.

to the normal collective bargaining process and then to the Wages Committee of the Labour Foundation, where agreements are examined before the final stage, which was approved by the Board of Government Mediators. Before the new wage policy was introduced in 1959, approval was generally a formality, since members of the Board participated in the discussions of the Wages Committee.[12]

From 1959 on, however, there have been developments, described below, which altered this delicate balancing of authority as between the three bodies, and, it appears from the perspective of events in the autumn of 1963, in so doing undermined the very foundation of Dutch wage policy.

Still another institution plays an important role in Dutch wage-price policy. The Central Planning Bureau, established in September, 1945, was designed to serve as an advisory body for the coordination of the government's economic, social, and financial policies. Its primary function is to make recommendations to the government in the form of economic plans, published at the beginning of each year. In addition, the bureau also makes confidential studies on its own initiative or on request, and does more or less continuous long-range studies. Its statutory base was not established until 1947,[13] and it is now formally under the Minister of Economic Affairs, although its activities are of an interdepartmental nature.

At the head of the Central Planning Bureau is a managing board, consisting of a director and two deputy directors. The Minister of Economic Affairs is empowered to appoint and dismiss members of the managing board of the CPB, and they are answerable to him. The bureau has three sections dealing with (1) structural problems, involving long-term research and developments abroad; (2) short-term macroeconomic planning; and (3) branches of industry, with technical experts for the various sectors of industry. There is also an advisory committee to the Minister and the Central Planning Bureau, known as the Central Planning Committee. It is composed of representatives of various ministries and government agencies, central employers' and workers' organizations, other businesses, and some general economic experts.

The Central Planning Bureau is charged with preparing an annual report which is an important factor in the formulation of govern-

---

[12] OEEC, *op. cit.*, p. 365.

[13] Act of April 21, 1947, on preparation for adoption of a Central Economic Plan (Wet van 21 April 1947), houdende de voor bereidnung van de vaststellning van een Central Economisch Plan), Staatsblad 127.

mental policy. These annual economic prognoses are forecasts on the basis of policy directives adopted by the government. They summarize, on the one hand, national production and imports, and on the other hand, private consumption, government expenditures, investments, and exports. The totals on both sides must be equal. For this forecasting purpose an econometric model has been evolved over the years, comprising several different types of equations.

Preparation of the plan is an involved process comprising consultation at various stages with the Central Bureau of Statistics, various ministries, the Central Planning Committee, and the Council of Economic Affairs.

The Dutch concept of "planning," embodied in the annual report of the Central Planning Bureau, is limited. It is short range, as compared either with the National Economic Development Council approach in Great Britain, or the well-known French medium-term planning. It does not involve a clearly defined growth policy with specific production targets or elaborate development programs, and its reports are neutral or at most advisory, based on expert diagnosis and prognosis of the economic situation according to alternative assumptions. Interest groups do not participate in the preparation of the report, although they are represented on the Central Planning Committee. Final decision on economic priorities and the choice of appropriate measures for implementing the plan are not vested in the CPB. Its function is limited to showing the consequences of various possible alternatives. The CPB does, nevertheless, play a key role in defining the "national interest." Its annual reports constitute a first and major step to the process, a step which is then followed by consultation with interest groups via the SER, the Labor Foundation, various ministries, the Board of Conciliators, and the central employers' and workers' organizations in the course of the complicated procedures described below.

Though the Central Planning Bureau does not make the ultimate policy decisions it has great influence on businessmen, trade unions, and the general public by way of rationalizing the discussion on wages and prices and diffusing what has come to be known as "macroeconomic consciousness," or a grasp of the interrelationships among economic processes. Through expert opinions based on systematic documentation and analysis by a staff which has acquired a reputation for outstanding competence and impartiality, people have been taught to think globally in terms of national resources, the limits to these resources, and the necessity of setting priorities for allocating them to expenditures, in short, to understand that gains for one group may mean losses for another.

The influence of the CPB on government departments and on official planning decisions has been equally significant. There is no central economic executive agency in the government charged with the coordination of policy formulation and implementation. This responsibility is, rather, diffused among a number of relatively independent ministries, with the Cabinet, Council of Economic Affairs, and other interdepartmental committees as consultative rather than executive bodies. This splitting up of economic policy enormously enhances the importance of the coordinating, even though only advisory, function of the CPB, but it at the same time limits that bureau's direct influence on economic policy.

DUTCH MANAGEMENT AND LABOR ORGANIZATIONS

Management and labor are both organized, in the Netherlands, along ideological and denominational grounds. On the employer side associations cover separately the fields of industry, commerce, and agriculture. In the industry sector the two denominational groups are small, and about 80 per cent of the employers belong to the non-denominational Centraal Sociaal Werkgevers-Verbond (CSWV). Thirty to 40 per cent of the trading middle classes belong to the commerce association, and probably 70 per cent of the farmers belong to the agriculture associations. Of the employer organizations the CSWV is by far the most powerful, though it is politically weak because it has ties to the former Liberal Party (now the VVD), which in the 1963 elections attracted only 10.3 per cent of the vote. In the Labor Foundation the CSWV has only three of the nine employer organizations' votes.

Employer federations put great emphasis on cooperation among their respective member organizations with respect to collective bargaining. There are contact committees in all instances, and all employer organizations in a given industry bargain jointly. Though the moral commitment to associational solidarity is apparently very strong, there are almost no formal controls or sanctions; until 1963 not even the threat of expulsion was operative. On the other hand, it appears that members have made a firm commitment with respect to the process of "internal coordination" described below. This coordination is facilitated by the fact that the CSWV represents such a large proportion of the total employment in industry that it can speak with a good deal of authority.

Labor is split along denominational lines more than is management. There are three significant union federations: (1) the Socialist and nondenominational NVV (Nederlands Verbond van Vakverrenigingen); (2) the Catholic Trade Union Federation, known as the NKV (Nederlandse Katholieke Arbeidersbeweging); and (3) the Protestant Labor Federation, CNV (Christelijk Nationaal Vakverbond). Of these, the NVV is the largest with 507,666 members, followed by the NKV with 417,780, and the CNV with 224,865 as of 1962. Another 269,202 are said to be organized in other unions, and the total number of organized workers in 1962 was listed at 1,420,-000.[14] This represented about 40 per cent of all employees — a significant increase over the 30 per cent who were organized in 1947.

The three labor federations cut indiscriminately across industry lines. No effort has been made to merge them, but they cooperate closely, especially in the Labor Foundation.

Relations between the denominational unions and the NVV are again close, after a rupture in 1954. In the 1930's the NVV and the Socialist Party began to shed their Marxist tenets in the hope of broadening their base, and appealing to individual Catholics and Protestants. But there was no serious attempt at a unified movement. In 1946 a pastoral letter promulgated by a Dutch Catholic bishop prohibited Catholics from joining the NVV. When this was reaffirmed in 1954, with a blast against the "socialist and Materialist" NVV, the Council of Trade Union Federations, which had been the forum for an agreed labor attitude, was dissolved. Regular consultation was restored in 1958, however, although the council was not revived, and currently the NKV and the NVV are working very closely together, especially after the NVV dropped its resistance to the recent change in wage policy; recently they issued a joint policy statement.

The labor federations are, of course, made up of individual unions. Because wage policy has been centralized since the war, the constituent unions need the federations. Nevertheless, most of the funds are still held by the national unions so that they are in no sense subservient to the federations. Nor are the services offered by the fed-

---

[14] Central Bureau of Statistics, *Omvang der vakbeweging in Nederland op 1 januari 1962*, 1963, p. 6.

erations significant enough to exercise any important degree of
control through threat of withholding.

Within the national unions the real power is exercised by the
executive boards. There are no shop stewards' committees, and
there are local unions only for the city or region. Even these are not
very vigorous. There is great concern over member apathy, poor attendance at meetings, and insignificant turnover among union officials — though corruption is virtually unknown and all the outward
forms of democracy are meticulously observed. The unions are generally well financed, and officials earn about twice as much as a
manual worker.

Federation officials claim that there is strong control exercised
through the federation. This appears to be less the consequence of
constitutional authority than a by-product of the wage determination system, which will shortly be discussed. Not only do the member unions need the federation for wage purposes, but there is the
problem of engaging in joint action in order to keep any one union
from asking for too large an increase to the detriment of the others.

There are many national unions in the Netherlands which are not
affiliated with the federations. However, 81 per cent of all organized
workers belong to one of the three federations, and because the
"big three" are the only ones having representatives on public bodies
or even on labor-management consultative bodies, they end up representing all organized and unorganized workers in the country.
There are two Communist unions, but their membership is insignificant. Moreover, the Collective Labor Agreements Act of 1927[15] spec-
ifies that organizations of employers and workers wishing to negotiate collective agreements must be recognized by the government
as legal persons, and the Communist unions have never requested
recognition.

COLLECTIVE BARGAINING

At the end of 1962, 2,000,000 workers were covered by collective
agreements in Netherlands, and another 241,000 workers in industry
were covered by binding regulations, so that about 79 per cent of
the wage and salary earners were covered by collective agreements
and related arrangements.[16] Since only about 40 per cent of the

---

[15] Collective Labor Agreements Act (Wet op der Collective Arbeids Overen-
komst), December 24, 1927, Staatsblad.

[16] Central Bureau of Statistics, Regulations of wages and other conditions of
employment in the Netherlands on December 31, 1962.

employees are organized, there is an obvious discrepancy between the number of workers belonging to unions and those covered by collective agreements or related arrangements. The difference is accounted for by Section 14 of the Collective Agreements Act which stipulates that unless the agreement provides otherwise, the employer must observe the provisions in the agreement in his relations with individual employees who are not bound by the collective agreements. The same applies to provisions of a collective agreement which are declared by statute to be generally binding.

Before the war there were a fairly substantial number of agreements between unions and individual firms. Now there are relatively few. Industry-wide agreements have become much more important. Contracts tend to be for only one year. Little use has been made of the cost-of-living principle.

Outwardly collective bargaining looks much the same as it does in other countries but the existence of a statutory wage determination procedure leads to profound differences. Decisions on wage increases are made not on the local level but rather in the course of discussions centralized within the Labor Foundation. Lower level negotiations relate to application of decisions reached at the national level, and collective agreements reached at the firm or industry level must be approved by central authorities before they are valid. Furthermore, the subject matter of negotiations is circumscribed by the fact that the agreement reached through the centralized procedure covers not only wage rates, but paid holidays, pensions, other fringes and compensation for increases in rents and social security charges.

As in the other European countries in which the wage bargain is reached on an industry or national level, the Netherlands have their problem of wage drift. Indeed, a good deal of research is being done on the subject. However, in the context of a comprehensive, formal and centralized procedure for wage determination, wage drift is even harder to define and to measure than it is under free collective bargaining. This is partly because a portion of the drift is officially "consolidated" into the agreed wage increases under the category of "incidentals" (which include increases due to upgrading, reclassification of jobs, merit rating, piecework, bonuses and other incentive payments, and changes in occupation involving higher levels of pay), and thus are not reflected in drift, which is the difference between officially negotiated increases in wage rates and actual earnings. Even more it is due to the difficulty of obtaining accurate data on actual earnings under a system which condemns wages higher than the agreed level as "illegal." (Since January, 1964, it has been possible for the parties to a collective agreement to depart somewhat from the terms of the agreement which applies to that branch of the industry.) So-called "black" wages have been serious in the past, and there is a marked correlation between "black" wages and shortages of manpower.

The Dutch appear to have realized from the outset that compliance with the law would depend upon the willingness of employers and unions to cooperate rather than upon formal legal controls. Thus the enforcement officers view their function as one of "educating" the parties rather than prosecuting them. Theoretically, violations are punishable by heavy fines, or even the closing down of enterprises. In practice fines are usually light, and the judges have been reluctant to convict. It is difficult to know just how widespread violation is, but it appears to be substantial. Businessmen are quite open about violations, justifying them on the basis that "everyone else does it too."

Various estimates on the dimensions of drift are available,[17] but they all differ substantially, and there is no way of ascertaining the extent to which black wages are reflected in the official drift figures.

WAGE-PRICE CONTROLS IN ACTION

It is difficult to talk about public-private cooperation in a knowledgeable way without viewing it in action. The institutions which are involved in the Dutch system of economic controls — the Labor Foundation, the Central Planning Bureau, the Social and Economic Council — have already been described. What remains is an overview of the way in which these institutions have operated over the years.

It would make a neater package if one could describe wage and price controls separately. The fact is that they are interrelated and

---

[17] OEEC, op. cit., p. 370.

Wage drift, adult male workers in industry, October to October

1953	1954	1955	1956	1957	1958	1959
1.6	0.3	2.7	3.1	−0.4	−2.7	1.1

Line 1 below: Central Planning Bureau, Monograph No. 8, Conjunctuurpolitiek in en om de jaren vijftig, 1963, p. 28, calculated from table 6; line 2 provided by Central Planning Bureau in November, 1963.

	1950	1951	1952	1953	1954	1955	1956	1957	1958	1959	1960	1961	1962
Line 1:	0	2.4	3.3	2.8	2.2	4.3	.5	5.2	3.2	2.1	6.4	5.3	7.5
Line 2:	−0.6	1.9	2.2	1.5	−2.5	3.7	−0.5	3.9	1.5	−0.4	0.7	1.1	0.8

to describe one without the other is but an exercise in fantasy. There are, of course, some general comments which can be made about each.

The desperate economic situation arising from five years of occupation, with destruction of railroads, canals, dikes, roads, factories, and mines, the shortage of capital and skilled labor, scarcity of food, large national debt, and an inflated currency clearly called for a comprehensive system of government controls. In this setting all parties were agreed on the need for a marked degree of state intervention to ensure what the Dutch refer to as "equitable distribution of poverty." Accordingly the "social minimum" became the foundation of the wage structure. The starting point was a calculation of the minimum required by a worker with a wife and two children to buy the necessities of life. Five different cost-of-living categories were recognized, ranging from industrial and commercial regions to rural towns in agricultural provinces, with differences of two to three cents per hour in standard rates from zone to zone. Although these differentials were modified from time to time in later years, the maximum difference between the highest and lowest zones rarely exceeded twelve cents per hour (approximately 10 per cent of the 1953 wage rate for unskilled workers). Since the system was based primarily on rent differentials, it eventually became obsolete as costs of housing tended to equalize.

The unskilled rate was considered the social minimum, and a 10 per cent adjustment was allowed for the semiskilled worker and 20 per cent for the skilled employee. Since the social minimum and the resultant semiskilled and skilled rates were the same for all trades, it followed that there must be a way of comparing jobs across industries. This was to be done on the basis of job content, irrespective of profits. A certain amount of work on job analysis and job classification already existed within plants. Now the concepts had to be extended and generalized to whole industries, and then across industries. Naturally this has been a long process and has taken place gradually over the years.

Incentive payment plans were to be regarded as permissible in the interest of increased productivity. However, incentive systems had to be based on work measurements and standards stipulated by the Board of Conciliators, in which case average earnings could rise up to one-third above the basic hourly rate; or, if the parties used a simple piece-rate system without work studies, the ceiling could not go higher than 15 per cent above basic rates. Where incentive systems were not applicable, merit rating could be used with a 10 per cent ceiling on adjustments.

Postwar price policy, as contrasted with wage policy, has placed much greater reliance on indirect than direct controls. This does not reflect any indifference to price movements. Indeed, in the words of the Economic Ministry, "The whole social and economic policy since the second world war has revolved around the need to keep prices relatively low," and "to keep price levels as steady as possible."[18] Price stability has been regarded as crucial in order to maintain both internal and external economic equilibrium. Internally, sharp rises in costs might slow down the rate of economic growth. Externally, the country was, and is, extremely dependent on exports — which in turn made competitive prices imperative. Moreover, a wage policy without a price policy would be impossible.

Immediately after the war the government did, for a time, maintain a system of direct price controls. This took the form of a general prohibition of price increases and was carried out in conjunction with rationing. By 1948 shortages eased and it was possible to free most prices. Controls were retained on certain strategic items like coal, textiles, and crucial foods. In late 1949, following devaluation, a general price freeze without rationing was imposed for a few months to permit a more gradual adjustment of the price level, but the order was withdrawn after about six months. In 1950 price controls were applied without rationing to selected items such as metals, fuel oil, coal for industrial use, several chemicals, and coffee. Subsequently, however, price policy has been largely in the form of price supervision rather than direct control. The essence of the policy has been an attempt to persuade both employers and workers to exercise vigilance in such matters.

For all practical purposes, indirect price measures taken by the Dutch have been more important than direct price controls. The most important of these have included monetary and fiscal policies, subsidies, measures designed to enhance price competition, and the wage policy itself.

Monetary policy has been conducted by the Central Bank and the Treasury. The Central Bank has made its influence felt through relatively moderate changes in discount rates, through individual control of lending by banks prior to 1951, and subsequently a more

---

[18] Memorandum on price controls from the Ministry of Economics, 1962.

general qualitative system of control including minimum limits to legal reserves, maximum limits for loans outstanding, a "gentlemen's agreement" concerning cash reserves held at the Central Bank, and through open market operations.

Food subsidies were an important feature of price stability until March, 1951, when the government decided to cut them drastically. Subsequently the only important subsidies were for bread-grain, which was dropped in 1955, and for milk, which was dropped in the spring of 1959. Housing subsidies were also important, but these were drastically curtailed in 1959.

Some steps have also been taken by the government to promote competition and to prevent or abolish restrictive trade practices which would exercise an upward push on prices. Cartels emerged relatively late in the Netherlands, as a result, partly, of the comparatively late development of industrialization, the individualistic character of Dutch businessmen, and the traditional policy of free trade. In the mid-thirties, however, the depression and marketing crises led to increases in import duties and quantitative import restrictions in some sectors, thus facilitating cartel agreements among Dutch manufacturers.

In 1935 the first cartel law, the Enterprisers' Agreement Act,[19] was passed. This law was actually designed to encourage cartelization as a protection against unrestrained competition. It authorized the Economics Minister to declare specific agreements generally applicable to all entrepreneurs in the industry or branch of business concerned, if this seemed to be in the public interest. It also authorized the government to nullify agreements, but this negative power was not exercised prior to World War II.

During the wartime occupation there was little occasion to apply cartel legislation because the Germans controlled the economy. Nevertheless, in 1941 the Act of 1935 was superseded by a Cartel Decree which enlarged the powers of the government to intervene either to declare agreements binding, or to invalidate them. The decree also introduced the compulsory registration of all cartels.

The immediate postwar years were characterized by shortages and lack of competition; hence there was little incentive to regulate competition. From 1948 on, however, rapid economic recovery was accompanied by a noticeable tendency toward cartelization and

---

[19] Entrepreneurs' Agreements Act (Ondernemersovereenkomstenwet), 1935, Staatsblad 310.

concentration. It has been suggested that this was attributable partly to the growing acceptance of the collective approach brought on by the necessity for cooperating after the war, and partly to the growth of heavy industry with its higher proportion of fixed to variable costs. In any event, the emphasis of government action with respect to cartels has shifted from encouragement to control. Since 1941 no use has been made of the power to declare agreement generally binding. Meanwhile action against cartels has been accelerating, with particular emphasis on cases of exclusive dealing in relation to freedom of entry, and on agreements regulating prices.

In 1956 Parliament passed the Economic Competition Act, which considerably enlarged the authority of the government to act against cartels. Compulsory registration now extends beyond commerce and industry to include all economic sectors such as banking, insurance, and transport. Action is also authorized by way of publicity, and by making it possible to prohibit certain categories of agreements. In general, however, Dutch cartel legislation is still based on the "abuse" principle. Cartels as such are not probihited, but only abuses of monopoly power by individual firms or combinations. The attitude of the government is still one of neutrality; it is felt that there are circumstances in which the public interest can actually be served by cartels and monopoly power.

Insofar as direct price controls are concerned, until 1961 the government derived its legal power from the 1939 Law on Price Raising and Hoarding.[20] However, since 1949 this power has been used only in rare and exceptional cases. Instead the government has appealed to businessmen, held discussions with them, enunciated guiding principles, and in general tried to convince them that price restraint was in their own self-interest. Sometimes this exercise in persuasion has been fortified by requirements for notification of price increases, insistence on promises not to cover wage increases by higher prices, actual price stops, and official limits to trade margins. In the background lurked the seldom used power to freeze prices.

The 1939 price law was replaced in 1961 by a new Law on Prices[21] which gives the government somewhat less power than it had before. The powers of the government under the new law are threefold: (1) it can issue decrees imposing maximum prices, and can at the

---

[20] Law on Price Raising and Hoarding (Prijsopdrijvings en Hamsterwet), June 24, 1939, Staatsblad 634.

[21] Law on Prices (Prijzenwet), June, 1961, Staatsblad 135.

same time stipulate how maximum permissible prices are to be calculated; (2) it can issue regulations requiring particular accounting methods designed to clarify the calculation of prices; and (3) it can issue regulations governing the price labeling of goods and services. The last two powers are deemed important because the crux of effective price control is the ability to determine how particular prices were calculated, and it is thought that price labeling will encourage the public to be price conscious.

The government's price policy is carried out by a price office in the Ministry of Economic Affairs, consisting of three divisions, each covering a certain number of industries. The same office is responsible for the administration of cartel legislation. Notifications of intent to raise prices are sent to this office, and it also has the duty of conducting spot checks throughout the country in an effort to discover unreported price increases. Price policy is based upon informal agreements with employer organizations, after consultation with trade unions and sometimes consumer groups, as to rules of behavior. Thus legal enforcement cannot be based on penal sanctions. Price officials tend to think of their job as educational. If a case of price increase without notification is reported to the office, the violator is sent a letter asking him for his justification. If his response does not prove acceptable, an attempt is made by letter, telephone, or personal confrontation to persuade the entrepreneur of the correctness of the Ministry's position. Usually this is said to be effective, but in the event it is not, the case is passed on to a higher level in the Ministry.

Neither wage nor price policies have been regarded as fixed or inflexible. Both have been groping, pragmatic, trial-and-error processes involving continuous discussion and reassessment in an effort to reconcile legitimate interests of the various groups with the ever changing economic situation. In this light the innumerable changes in policy which have characterized the process do not reflect a feeling of inadequacy so much as responsiveness to changing attitudes and requirements. The trend in direction has always been toward less governmental intervention.

For a more intimate view of how wage and price controls have worked, it is convenient to identify four separate periods. The broad stages in this development have comprised movement from (a) uniform wage increases imposed by the government and limited to rises in cost of living, to (b) increases in real wages with limited differentiation under strict government control, to (c) differentiation by industrial sectors on the basis of productivity subject to government approval, to (d) the present system comprising a number of criteria for differentiation, and a shift of the major responsibility for implementation and sanctions from the government to the bargaining partners themselves. In addition to and cutting across this general pattern of development, there was a continuous process of refining and improving the wage structure through application of scientific job evaluation and work study procedure and incentive systems of remuneration.

EARLIER PATTERNS OF CONTROL

The Period 1945 to 1954

This first period has been characterized as one of wage stops. This it was only in the sense that although special wage increases were allowed to improve the wage structure, the general level was permitted to rise only in response to increases in the cost of living. The first general increase in 1945 was associated with the general revision of the wage structure on the basis of the social minimum referred to earlier, with adjustments for semiskilled and skilled workers; the resulting level was 35 to 42 per cent higher than in 1940.

The next three increases, which came in November, 1948 (one guilder), January 1950, (5 per cent), and September, 1950 (5 per cent), were in response to changes in the cost of living. The first was related to a reduction in subsidies, the second followed devaluation, and the third was associated with the continued rise in the cost of living.

In early 1951, faced with a balance of payments crisis, the government attempted to elicit voluntary cooperation of employers on the price front. The representative national organizations of industrial employers, as well as of the craft and retail trade organizations, promised their cooperation and committed themselves not to pass on wage increases or increases in the cost of nonessential materials in the form of price increases. Increases in the cost of essential materials were allowed to be reflected in price increases. In addition, traders undertook to maintain trade margins in absolute terms at pre-Korean levels, a promise which later had to be enforced through compulsion in a number of instances. At the same time the government asked the unions to accept an increase in wages of only 5 per cent, despite the fact that the cost of living had gone up 10 per cent since September, 1950. This the central trade union federation reluctantly accepted on condition that the cut not exceed 5 per cent. For the record they protested within the ranks of the Labor Foundation. By November, 1951, the cost of living had slightly exceeded the 5 per cent limit and a small adjustment was then permitted.

The next two wage rounds, in July, 1952, and January, 1954, were again compensatory. The first one was 2 per cent and was to cover the cost to workers of a new compulsory unemployment insurance scheme, and the second of 5 to 12 per cent was to cover a rise in house rents, to liquidate the balance of the sacrifice which workers had made in 1951, and to adjust wages to the changing geographic differentials in the cost of living. At the same time a small part of the increase was aimed at increasing skill differentials in order to attract workers to jobs for which substantial training was required Wages in agriculture were increased 12 per cent to bring them into parity with industrial rates.

Gradually throughout this period the crude initial job classification, which divided all jobs into unskilled, semiskilled, and skilled categories, was replaced by a more detailed system of job evaluation under the aegis of the Board of Conciliators, but actually administered by the Netherlands High Commission for Standardization. Decisions to introduce job evaluation were arrived at by negotiation between employers and unions, but the resulting proposals were subject to the approval of the board. All different types of work in an industry were allotted points on the basis of hardship, skill required, technical characteristics, and so forth, and grouped into classes. Thus it was possible to translate points into rates of pay on a basis designed to ensure equal pay for equal work, as between firms and industries.

Further flexibility was introduced into the wage structure by permission to pay production bonuses and to introduce incentive payments as a stimulus to productivity. Since 40 to 45 per cent of all workers were on a piece-rate basis, their rates were closely supervised, with earnings for the average worker linked to statutorily controlled time rates.

The Period 1954-59

From 1953 on, with the recovery of the prostrate economy, accelerated growth, and accumulation of a balance of payments surplus, there was apparent a growing restiveness with wage controls. All three trade union federations felt that workers should begin to share in growing national prosperity through wage increases going beyond mere cost of living adjustments, which occurred only after a time lag and were then absorbed by new price increases. Moreover, all agreed on the need for a greater degree of industry differentiation. The confessional unions, particularly, argued that uniform wage increases had led to unjustified profits in some industries which ought to be shared with workers in those sectors. In addition, they objected on principle to continued extensive governmental interference in wage negotiations.

The favorable economic situation, and the fact that Dutch wages were low relative to those in the rest of the Benelux area, led to serious discussions as to the feasibility of revaluing the guilder. In the end, however, a choice was made in favor of wage increases, and there then followed a series of "prosperity" rounds designed to permit workers to share in economic growth with some degree of differentiation by industry.

The shift to "limited differentiation" involved breaking the wage negotiation process into two stages. This first involved the central discussions between employer and union federations in the Labor Foundation with respect to maximum or average permissible overall increases. The second called for collective bargaining at the industry (or, in some cases, firm) level to determine the specific measures appropriate to the individual case. A consequence was that a succession of "wage rounds" emerged with a succession of separate negotiations in which certain pace-setters — notably the metal industry — determined patterns. Permissive, rather than mandatory, increases also became more numerous since limits had to be stated as maxima to permit negotiation of industry differentials. Until 1959, however, industry differentials were still held in check by the reluctance of the largest of the unions (the socialist NVV) to abandon the principle of "solidarity," that is, moderation of extreme differentials in the interest of social justice, and by the reluctance of the government to relinquish its firm control over wage levels.

In 1954 the cost-of-living index again began to rise, and the Economics Minister became concerned over the threat of a price-wage spiral. Accordingly over the next few years price supervision was tightened up in a number of different ways. For one thing, repeated appeals for price restraint were addressed to employers. In March,

1955, the Minister persuaded the national associations of industrial employers to circularize their members urging them to stabilize, or where possible, to reduce prices. This appeal was repeated in February, 1956, and again in November, 1957. Since the Minister had the legal power to fix maximum prices, the appeal to employers appears to have met with some success.

The new price policies during this period carried certain specific rules relating to price increases. Wage increases were not to be passed on in price rises. Price increases could be justified only by increases in external costs, which were generally interpreted to mean the costs of raw materials. On the other hand, a drop in these costs was supposed to be passed on immediately in the form of price reductions. Even where prices were raised because of external costs, nominal trade margins (in money terms) were supposed to remain unchanged. Exceptions to these rules were to be granted only in hardship cases.

Meanwhile, in October, 1954, the government permitted a 6 per cent maximum increase in wage rates for all workers. Actually, increases had to be approved by the Board of Conciliators, but approval was only a formality if the increase was within the limit. The intended industry differentiation did not emerge since practically every employer gave the maximum allowable increase.

In 1955 there was no official wage round, but in September the government permitted an improvement of fringe benefits — paid holidays, holiday benefits, bonus payments — up to the annual value of 3 per cent of annual wage rates. These were to be gradually incorporated into collective agreements.

In March of 1956, in response to growing demands by employers and the denominational unions for greater differentiation, the government permitted another 6 per cent maximum increase, 3 per cent plus differentials amounting to a maximum of 3 per cent. The passing on, via prices, of wage increases of more than 3 per cent was prohibited, but those of less than 3 per cent could, upon appoval, be covered by price rises. The idea was to encourage higher increases by more prosperous industries, but again practically all employers, under the pressure of a tight labor market, gave the maximum increase.

The background of the 6 per cent permissive increase in 1956 is rather interesting. In response to a union claim that wage increases had been lagging behind national income, the government sought the opinion of the Social and Economic Council. In its February, 1956, "margin report" the council confirmed this claim, although its members could not agree on the magnitude of the lag. This gave rise to difficult negotiations in the Labor Foundation, and at one time the employers threatened to walk out. In the end the government settled the matter by the 6 per cent permissive increase.

At the end of 1956 the Economics Minister issued a general prohibition against raising prices without his consent — or rather, his statement of "no objection" (the word "approval" being avoided because the Minister feared that it would give the price the stamp of official sanction). The prohibition took the form of a communication by the Minister to the national employers' organization indicating that he should be consulted about price increases *before* they were applied. It was not a prohibition in the legal sense since it was no more than an arrangement between the Minister and the employers' organizations. It was felt by individual employers to be a prohibition since it had the strong endorsement of the national federations, and because the Minister had the power to fix maximum prices if he chose to do so, and has indeed exercised it on a number of occasions over the years.

By 1957 the country was once again faced with a serious balance of payments problem which some insisted was attributable to the increased purchasing power resulting from the 1956 wage increases. Another cutback in expenditures appeared to be necessary, and the government, for the second time since the end of the war, called on the unions to accept a cut in real earnings. Since it seemed impossible to reduce the wage level, the government decided to cut consumption by reducing government expenditures, pushing up prices, and syphoning off extra profits through fiscal measures. Representatives of employers and trade unions accepted the program and agreed to a stipulated rise in index without compensatory wage increases. By this agreement the unions lost heavily in membership because the conviction of the leaders that the economic situation required such action did not carry over to the rank-and-file members.

Later in 1957 two compulsory wage increases were authorized. One was to cover additional payments for old age insurance, and the other to cover a rise in rents. Neither of these compensated for the drop in purchasing power accepted by the unions as a result of the program for restriction of consumption. This brought the wage round phase to an end. There were no further wage increases in 1957, 1958, or the first part of 1959.

During these years dissatisfaction with the existing wage policy accelerated. Economic differences between industries were becoming more pronounced and shortages of skilled workers in 1959 began to turn into general labor shortages. As a result employers' organizations were increasingly vocal in demanding a wage policy which would permit more prosperous employers to pay more to attract workers, and they were supported by the confessional unions which were increasingly irked by governmental interference and concerned about the atrophy of the union bargaining function. But the dominant Socialist union (NVV) remained adamant in opposing a differentiated wage policy. It has been suggested by some observers that the NVV actually preferred a freer wage policy, since its members were also asking for it, but the union felt an obligation to support the Labor Party which was participating in the coalition government under Socialist Ministers of Social Affairs and of Finance. These ties were broken in the general election of 1959 when the Labor Party lost seats and left the government coalition, largely as the result of an earlier dispute over a tax issue. Under the new non-Socialist Minister of Social Affairs frictions began to develop over wage policy, and these had an influence on the attitude of the NVV.

The Period 1959-63

In 1959 there was a new government without Labor participation for the first time since World War II. There was also a substantial jump in the gross national product, a growing labor shortage, and a continuing increase in the balance of payments surplus as the result of the disinflationary measures of 1957. The new Prime Minister announced a broad policy of economic expansion involving restraint of government expenditures and corresponding tax reductions, and on the wage front, differentiated wage increase (and/or fringe benefits) geared to output per worker in various industrial sectors rather than exclusively to national overall productivity.

[The new approach] was based on the notion that labour's part of the national income should not be allowed to decrease and wage costs not allowed to increase. The role of productivity fitted in nicely with both objectives. Labour's share equals the quotient of real wages and labour productivity, given a constant share and given stable prices. In this case, wage costs also remain constant, which is a condition for stable prices. This philosophy suited the Minister of Economic Affairs, who is responsible for price policy, and his colleague the Minister of Social Affairs, who has to see to it that everybody gets his share of the cake.

It also suited the trade unions, and the employers could not reasonably object. It looked as if this criterion — wage rises in accordance with increasing productivity — could produce the basis for wage differentiation and institutional decentralization. The rule of the new game became: wage increases, wherever possible, without rising prices. This rule was supplemented by another one. Wages were allowed to diverge, but not too far. This is typically Dutch restriction. The harmonious wage structure was not to be upset. In those branches of industry that were expanding rapidly, the increase in wages should be moderate, and there would be some room for a price cut. This would come in handy, for in the sectors that were lagging behind pay rises were necessary for the sake of harmony, but since they were not covered by productivity they would consequently lead to rising prices.[22]

Thus the new emphasis on productivity in individual sectors of industry carried with it an even closer link than before between wage and price policy. Under the new productivity policy it was expected that in those sectors in which productivity rose sharply wages could be raised more than in sectors in which there was only a slight rise, or even none in productivity. Employers were permitted to increase wages in their industry or branch of industry only on the condition, made explicit in a written pledge by the employees' association, that the increases would not lead to higher prices. Furthermore, the Economic Minister tried to ensure that in sectors in which the rise in productivity was well above average, a proportion of the gain in productivity was passed on to consumers in the form of price reductions. With this in mind the Minister held talks with employers on ways of bringing about price reductions. These discussions were only partially successful; the impact on prices appears to have been slight. It was hoped that, while maintaining a stabilized price level, room would be created for a possible wage increase for those workers employed in branches of industry for which only a very slow rise in productivity or none at all was noticeable, even if the increase had to be coupled with a rise in prices. This was the so-called coordinating principle inherent in the new system of wage determination.

The Economics Minister also obtained the agreement of the employers' organizations that notice of price increases should be sent to the Ministry, accompanied by justification. This was notification *after the event*. Exceptions were made for several necessities (bread, milk, liquid and solid fuels, and margarine), for which the advance

---

[22] Pen, *op. cit.*, p. 324.

consultation procedure remained in force. In cases where a price increase appeared to have been made without sound justification, the company or sector concerned was asked to cancel the increase on threat of legal action by the Economics Minister.

In trying to administer the new wage program, the government after consultation with the Labor Foundation, issued complex and somewhat vague instructions which promptly gave rise to misunderstandings. Subsequent "clarifications" only seemed to further confuse the issue. Frictions were thereby created between the Board of Conciliators, which was under pressure from the government to restrain wage rates, and the bargaining partners who resented official intervention in the form of repeated rejection or downward revision of wage proposals that had been negotiated and signed by them. A former Director of General Economic Policy of the Ministry of Economic Affairs has described this period as follows:

[Another] reason for the failure was that the Government, startled at its own generosity, and at the marked wage increases, tried to keep the lid on, by issuing directives to the Board. This was something new. Under the old system, directives had been restricted to general wage rounds — for specific wage proposals to the Board, together with the Foundation, were given a free hand. But now directives started to pour from the Government. Personal elements also played a part; the Secretary of State for Social Affairs, who (under an unusually weak Minister) really determined the wage policy, was an able as well as energetic man. He had come from the Protestant trade union movement, and set to work in his new job energetically and pugnaciously. He clearly thought it unnatural to stay aloof from such important business as wage negotiations. This made for some opposition, not only from the industry, but also from the Board. The opposition took the shape of a rebellion. This was met by new instructions, further instructions and supplements to further instructions. Ministers never went to bed so late, there were so many nightly meetings on the question of wages.[23]

In addition to problems of interpretation there was the inherent difficulty of measuring productivity in individual industries and firms. The intention had been to make use of statistics provided by the General Statistical Bureau, but these did not provide complete coverage of more than 40 per cent of the economic sectors concerned. A perhaps inevitable consequence was that arbitrary productivity figures were "negotiated," resulting in wage increases that added up to much more than the overall national productivity increase.[24]

---

[23] *Ibid.*, p. 325.
[24] *Ibid.*, p. 324.

The situation was further complicated by the fact that working hours were reduced from forty-eight to forty-five during these years. This was in line with the trend in Europe, but the government had hoped that the reduction would come slowly in accordance with a philosophy of differentiation and liberty. On the contrary, the movement was immediate and without regard for a priority as between wages and shorter working hours. Costs were naturally increased and greater strain placed on the wage policy.[25]

The situation was sufficiently tense in October of 1960 to cause the government to ask the Social and Economic Council to recommend criteria in addition to productivity that might be taken into account in determining the permissible rate of wage increase in each industry. Meanwhile, pending completion of the report, the government consulted the Labor Foundation on interim principles. The result was the Oud-Wassenaar agreement of November 17, 1961, on a formula designed to keep average increases in line with national productivity, taking into account both the average productivity increases in an industry over the past decade plus the Central Bureau of Statistics estimate of the average national productivity increases for the coming year. Unfortunately such a formula could not compensate for inadequate statistics, nor could it meet the problem of critical sectors like construction, which showed almost no productivity increases. As to such industries the board had allowed an arbitrary 4 per cent increase in 1960.

The long-awaited report from the Social and Economic Council finally came out in July, 1962. As it turned out, the report was not responsive to the government's request, for the government had not asked for a new system of wage determination but for new criteria to supplement productivity as a guideline for future increases. Nevertheless, it carried so much weight, and came on top of so much dissatisfaction, that the government could not resist a major shift in policy. Thus an agreement on a new system of wage determinants was reached in December, 1962.

THE NEW WAGE-PRICE POLICY — 1963 AND ON

The essence of the new system for administering wage controls in Holland is that it drastically curtails the functions of the Board of Conciliators and transfers the key role to the unions and employers represented in the Labor Foundation. Emergency powers are re-

---

[25] *Ibid.*, p. 325.

served to the government in the event the new system will not work. It is assumed that the new wage policy carries with it the possibility of still greater industry differentiation based, in addition to productivity, on general economic criteria like profitability, demand and supply for labor, and shifts in the shares of various productive factors in national income.

The *motivation* leading to the recent abrupt change in wage policy was complicated in the sense that it represented a compromise between the wishes of the various interest groups involved. The majority view, which more or less prevailed in the end, largely reflected the thinking of the denominational unions, NKV and CNV, but also happened to accord with the interests of a majority of individual employers, although not of the largest employers' federation, the CSWV. The predominant strand in this rationale was the "subsidiary" principle, inherent in the basic philosophy of the denominational unions, that is, the doctrine that every organized group should have the right and opportunity to perform the function for which it was established, with minimum interference from higher echelons; hence the emphasis on private rather than public controls. Applied to wage policy the implication is that wages should be determined by those who are directly concerned; further, that if primary responsibility is to be given to the bargaining parties, government intervention must be minimized. Guidelines can be established by public authorities in advance of negotiations, but the government should not exercise a retroactive control. Organized employer and union groups cannot be asked to exercise the responsibility, that is, wage restraint, unless they are given the requisite authority and controls.

This theoretical approach is closely related to a practical problem which has been of concern to the Dutch trade unions in recent years, namely, how to retain membership and justify their existence under a control system which tends to deprive unions of their primary *raison d'être*, wage bargaining. This explains their urge for greater differentiation in the granting of wage increases — a policy which they also justify on economic grounds as a stimulus to productivity and a way of permitting workers to share in the profits of more prosperous and dynamic sectors of the economy. The denominational unions were no longer so committed to the solidarity principle once economic recovery had obviated the necessity for "sharing poverty."

Perhaps much of the above argument is mere rationalization. In blunt terms, unions could in periods of boom, when the labor market is tight, negotiate higher increases if they were allowed to do so. In this sense the drive to eliminate the Board of Conciliators stems from a conviction that the board has supported the employers in restraining wages.

The position of the dominant Socialist union (NVV), on the other hand, has been ambivalent. From 1953 to 1959, when the denominational unions were clamoring for relaxation of wage controls, the NVV, because of its commitment to the principle of solidarity and a planned economy, and also because it was supporting the Labor Party which was then in the government, strongly supported the prevailing system of centralized wage guidance coupled with strict price controls. NVV argued against any retreat from the principle that wage increases should be based on social rather than economic criteria. However, in 1959 the Labor Party went into opposition, and the NVV began to reverse its position. The official NVV explanation for this change is that a centralized wage policy is not compatible with an economy in which most other controls have been eliminated. The explanation of outsiders, and particularly the confessional unions, is that the NVV leaders were always in favor of freer collective bargaining as a reflection of the wishes of their members, but were inhibited from expressing these views as long as the Labor Party exercised governmental responsibility. The truth may lie somewhere in between the two explanations. Certainly it appears that the NVV, as well as the other unions and the employers, was increasingly irritated by the inadequacies of the differential productivity system and the "arbitrary government intereference" which it entailed.

On the employer side, the major organization, the CSWV, stubbornly opposed the new scheme. It agreed that there should be greater freedom in wage negotiation, that differentials should be increased, and that the bargaining parties should be given more responsibility. It did not agree, however, that the Board of Conciliators should be eliminated, at least for the time being, and it argued that the Labor Foundation was not equipped, in terms of staff or of objectivity, to review collective agreements. CSWV thought that the organizations concerned would feel freer to express their differences of opinion if they did not have responsibility for the final decision, and that retention of the Board of Conciliators as the final arbiter, even if it operated on the basis of the same criteria proposed for the foundation, would guarantee more uniform objectives and equitable decisions, plus more reliable wage guidance.

Many observers believer that the CSWV's position was motivated primarily by the "acute internal tensions" which would be created within the employers' federation if it had to assume responsibility for policing negotiations. The federation lacks control over its members, and there are few sanctions available to it in the event of recalcitrance. Failure to observe wage guidelines does not constitute a violation of the federation's constitution nor until late 1963 was it thought to give grounds for explusion. Internal cohesion within the CSWV is far less than in the trade unions, or even in the other denominational employer associations. Thus CSWV is said to have feared that if it were placed in the position of having to overrule the claims of employers it would simply lose members and the organization would disintegrate. Despite its initial reluctance, once the decision was taken in the Labor Foundation to utilize the new system the CSWV accepted the new system and indicated its willingness to cooperate in implementing it.

Government officials, particularly the Ministers of Social Affairs and Economics, also resisted the erosion of government control over wage policy. When it became clear that they could not block the shift of authority to the Labor Foundation, they managed to incorporate in the system the right of consultation at all stages in the new procedure as well as certain reserve powers for the government, and to have the Confrontation Committee as a sort of watchdog over the whole operation.

The mechanics of the new system as it was expected to operate can be described as follows:

1. The starting point is a report published by the Social and Economic Council, based on the macroeconomic estimates of the Central Planning Bureau, and on data from the Central Bureau of Statistics. It covers items other than wages, and it indicates how wage proposals would contribute to achievement of other economic objectives such as full employment, stable prices, and a satisfactory balance of payments. With respect to wages, the report indicates, in the form either of a specific percentage, maximum and minimum percentages, or vague guidelines, the permissible increase in wage rates in the near future. It also suggests other facts, like changes in controlled rents or social insurance contributions, which should be taken into account.

There have been differences of opinion as to whether the guidelines should take the form of a specific percentage or rather a more flexible range. The unions prefer vague guidelines because this will help in negotiating larger increases, and in the present tight labor market individual employers tend to agree with them. The large employer federation feels, however, that a more specific figure would minimize conflict in employer ranks. And the government also prefers a more concrete guideline on the ground that it is both more workable and more realistic. On the latter count it is felt that a vague indication would soon shake down to a specific figure at which the Labor Foundation was approving proposed contracts.

2. The second stage of the new policy is that a consultation takes place between the government — represented by the Ministers of Social Affairs and Economics and other Ministers as well — with leaders of labor and management operating through the Labor Foundation. The hope is that an agreement will be reached at this point, either on the figure proposed by the Social and Economic Council, or on a lower figure if the views of the government are more restrictive than those of the council. Even if no agreement is reached, it was expected that awareness of the government's views would induce a certain degree of caution in subsequent negotiations.

Aside from wages, the above consultations also include such subjects as fringe benefits, hours, holidays, profit sharing schemes, and price policy.

3. Following the meeting with the government, the next step is for consultation within the Labor Foundation between the employer and union federations. This is for the purpose of translating the agreed percentage figure or range into a pattern of increases, that is, to discuss in a general way such issues as the principles of differentiation between industries and the allocation between cash increases and fringe benefits. Of this stage of the process it may be said that the employers try to secure from the unions as firm a commitment as possible, and the unions try to avoid being pinned down any further than possible.

4. The novel feature of the new arrangement, and a crucial step in the entire procedure, is the process of so-called "internal coordination." This is the stage, prior to actual negotiations for renewal of agreements, during which the central federations of the employers on the one hand, and of the workers on the other, attempt through special and ad hoc committees to persuade their respective affiliates

to stay within the agreed guidelines. Since the three major trade union federations and the various employer federations always bargain jointly, these committees are representative of all employer and union federations.

The method of achieving this internal coordination was not prescribed in legislation or in the original recommendations of the Social and Economic Council. The discussions offer a forum for familiarizing the actual bargaining partners with the macroeconomic possibilities, and for arriving at agreements as to differentials between industries and firms, and as to fringe benefits. They also provide a two-way channel for informing the central federations of the views of the individual firms and branches of industry, and of ensuring that the latter are aware of the consequences of failure to stay within the prescribed limits.

5. With the stage set for bargaining, the employers and unions, through their federations, begin to negotiate. The ensuing agreements must then be submitted to the Labor Foundation for review. The power to approve, reject, or revise now resides with the foundation rather than the Board of Conciliators. An independent wage bureau will be set up, which will be in charge of the technical preparations for decisions in matters of wage policy. It will be at the disposal of the Minister of Social Affairs and Public Health, the Labor Foundation, and the Board of Government Conciliators.

At the time that negotiated agreements are submitted to the foundation, a copy is also sent to the board. Within a three weeks' period after receiving this copy, the board is authorized to warn the foundation that it might have to advise the Minister to declare it invalid and nonbinding. If no warning is issued, the foundation may approve the agreement three weeks after receiving it. If there is such a warning, the agreement, even when approved by the foundation, cannot come into force until two weeks after such approval, in order to permit action by the Minister.

The board is also authorized to ask the foundation for a special investigation of proposed agreements which it feels require deeper analysis. This is not a warning like that described above, which the Dutch call the "red light," but only a "yellow light." The board actually made use of the "yellow light" a number of times in the autumn of 1963, much to the irritation of the foundation which felt that it was competent to recognize dangers without such interference.

It may happen that the foundation will fail to reach a conclusion concerning a proposed collective agreement. This can occur when an adequate majority of 13 out of 18 cannot be found either for approval or for disapproval. In such a case the proposed agreement is submitted to the Board of Conciliators together with a record of the opinions held by the various members of the foundation, and the board is then responsible for deciding whether the agreement can be accepted. If the decision is favorable, the agreement comes into force immediately. If it is unfavorable, the foundation informs the parties concerned and they can reopen negotiations. Should the parties still be unwilling to modify their proposed agreement in such a way as to meet the approval of the foundation, the latter can ask the Board of Concililators to impose a wage settlement binding on both parties. A similar application can be made if the parties to a collective agreement refuse to revise it following rejection by the foundation.

6. There are various points in the procedure at which the government may intervene either directly or via the Board of Conciliators. Some of these have already been described. In addition the Minister of Social Affairs has the power in exceptional cases, when so advised by the Board of Conciliators, to declare agreements approved by the foundation to be nonbinding (which implies not only that employers need not apply the provisions of the agreement, but also that they must not). In such cases the board must inform the foundation within three weeks after having received the text of the collective agreement.

Governmental influence over the system is also enhanced by the establishment of what is called the Confrontation Committee. This committee is composed of representatives of both the public and the private sector, with an independent chairman (currently the Director of the Central Planning Bureau) whose task it is to follow the current development of wage claims and to report to the government four times a year in the form of a "confrontation" of the participating parties in the foundation with a comparison of the intended effects of the agreements and their actual impact to date.

Finally, there are two types of situations in which the government is authorized to promulgate a cooling-off period during negotiations and/or a definite wage freeze, and to restore to the Board of Conciliators its former powers of approval or rejection of collective agreements. The first is during consultations with the foundation on the Social and Economic Council's report if a fundamental disagreement developed which the foundation refused to take into account. The second is in case wages get out of hand, or if the economic situation develops in such a way that the government considers it necessary to impose wage measures.

Price Implication of the New System

The shift to an entirely new system of wage determination naturally had price implications. Since wage increases are not to be based upon productivity in individual firms or branches of industry, it is no longer assumed that prices will remain stable when wage increases are given. Accordingly, employers are not required to commit themselves in advance in this respect. They are expected, however, when presenting their proposals for wage increases to the foundation, to mention possible price repercussions. Moreover, the foundation has agreed to inform the Economics Minister as soon as possible so as to enable him to make allowances for such increases in working out his policies. Similarly the foundation will make allowances for possible price repercussions when judging wage proposals, but this does not mean that possible price consequences will necessarily imply that a proposed wage increase will not be approved.

Postwar price policy in Holland has always, in the eyes of the Dutch, rested primarily on acceptance by the groups concerned. And there are a number of reasons, despite irritation and resistance, why there was often an inclination to cooperate in price controls. (All parties were more or less convinced that they were essential to economic expansion.) Also, there is a disposition toward conformity among the Dutch, and a sense of discipline which inclines them toward the advice of their employer federations. Irresponsible price increases might damage the business community as well as the general public. The Common Market increasingly exposed Dutch businessmen to the presssures of competition. In this connection, many employers recognized that wage and price controls were logical corollaries, and that one could not expect wage controls without a significant gesture in the direction of price controls. Finally, it has been suggested in an OEEC report that "price control, on the whole cannot have been very oppressive. This may be deduced from two facts: profits were, by and large, quite good during the period when price control was strongest (1955, 1956, beginning 1957); and there was no overall shift of sales from the home market where prices were controlled to foreign markets where they were free." [26]

Nor have the trade unions been resistant to price supervision. Their sophistication on price issues has been enhanced by the work of top level economists employed by them and by their active participation in official decisions on price policy. In addition, the absorbing union concern over full employment, and hence over industrialization and economic growth, have given them a vested interest in profits high enough to permit adequate investments. They are convinced that an effective price policy can make a contribution to balance of payments equilibruim, economic growth, and equitable income distribution. Finally, it appears that some leaders of the national trade union confederations look upon stable prices as a way of checking pressure for higher wages, thus easing their task with the Labor Foundation.

Within the ranks of government there are differences of opinion as to the efficacy of price controls. In the Economics Ministry in recent years, and again under the new Minister appointed in 1963, there has been a conviction that direct price controls made a major contribution to economic stability. In other parts of the government on the other hand, there are those who feel that direct price controls are unworkable and harmful. The latter group would put more stress on indirect methods of changing the price climate. This view seems to predominate in a recent report of the Social and Economic Council, which reads: [27]

Recognizing that changes in prices relative to one another constitute a main element in the normal functioning of the economy, and also recognizing the importance of developments in price-cost relationships abroad, the Council believes that the government should pursue a policy designed to prevent the general price level from rising in an unjustified way. In carrying out this policy the government should rely primarily on monetary and budgetary policy. In addition, an effective policy to encourage economic competition should be pursued. In cases where price developments appear to be in danger of getting out of hand, the government under the Prices Act retains a final power of intervention.

How the New System Has Worked Out: The First Test

Much has happened to the Dutch wage-price scene since July, 1963. The Central Planning Bureau's (CPB) macroeconomic esti-

[26] Cornelius Westrate, *Economic Policy in Practice; The Netherlands 1950/57* (Leiden: H. E. Stenfert Kroese, 1959), p. 96.

[27] Social and Economic Council, translated from Sociaal-Economische Raad, *Advies Inzake het Systeem van Loonvorming*, July 6, 1963, p. 33.

mates, which were supposed to provide the framework for discussion in the Social and Economic Council (SER) preliminary to publication of its semiannual report (which appeared on November 5), were drawn up at the beginning of August (although they were not published until September 17). These projections assumed a 4 per cent increase in wages as a result of renegotiation of expiring contracts, plus another 2 per cent for incidentals and overlap from 1963. Since productivity was expected to rise 3 per cent, this would imply an increase in wage costs per unit of 3 per cent. On the assumption of an unchanged price policy, it was thought that consumer prices would rise 2 per cent and prices of investment goods 3 per cent. The increase in total demand was expected to center on domestic products, so that a balance of payments surplus of 500 million florin was projected, the same as 1963.

This was how it looked to CPB in early August. Since then a marked increase in the already considerable pressures on the labor market has resulted in a veritable explosion of industrial unrest. The subsequent rapid sequence of events has completely bypassed the new system of wage determination set up in early 1963. The first test, in short, has been an utter failure. And the resulting large increases to be expected in wages and in prices have made the CPB estimates quite obsolete.

In August and September, 1963, there were three cases in which the Board of Government Conciliators intervened in the process of approval of contracts submitted to the Foundation of Labor. In two of these the government's decision was to declare the contracts nonbinding; in the third it did not do so. But these cases, like the CPB estimates, have been overtaken and obscured by the swift pace of events during recent weeks. By the time the government had reached its decisions, there was so much pressure for really drastic wage increases that these pronouncements were greeted with something like contempt. At a time when everyone was already thinking in terms of 10 per cent or more increases, it seemed the height of irrelevance for the government to be quibbling about whether a 3 per cent increase was too high; this, indeed, further weakened the "grip" of the government over the wage determination procedure.

The labor market has for some years been under severe pressure with demand for workers greatly exceeding the available supply. According to the Ministry of Social Affairs, the labor market could already be characterized as tight in 1956 when there were shortages of 97,000 workers as compared with a registered labor reserve of 40,000. Only in 1958 was there any slight relaxation; by 1962 the situation had worsened with a registered labor reserve of only 34,000 and a labor shortage of 110,000, and provisional figures for 1963 indicate an even greater disparity.

Although there are many factors, foreign and domestic, that contribute to the demand for Dutch goods and services and the current labor shortage, four appear to have been particularly important in recent months: (a) growing inflation in Western Europe which has widened the gap between the level of costs and prices in Holland and in other countries and thus swelled the demand for Dutch exports; (b) the drain of Dutch workers to Germany in response to high wage levels there — on March 31, 1963, some 24,229 Dutch workers were employed abroad (24,000 of them in Germany) as compared with a total of 19,484 a year earlier, 12,124 two years earlier, and only 4,628 in March 1960; (c) the boom in the construction industry; and (d) the fact that, according to many observers including SER and the Ministry of Social Affairs, wage increases have been so moderate in recent years that capital investments have tended to be channeled to investments that are "capital broadening" rather than "capital deepening" (labor displacing), thus increasing the demand for workers relative to the potential supply.

Recent visible manifestations of the extremely tight labor market situation have been a marked increase in black wages and open industrial unrest. A report on black wages presented to the Parliament by the Ministry of Social Affairs in October noted a sharp increase for the period from January to the end of September, 1963, especially in border areas. The payment of wages higher than legally permissible has been stimulated by the activities of "labor brokers" (Koppelbazen), who contract with employers, particularly in the metal industry and also in chemicals, construction, and mining, to supply them with extra workers. The practice arose from the legitimate need for a pool of workers to be made available to meet fluctuating peak demands in various industries. As developed in recent years, however, it has become a device for evading the wage ceilings prescribed by the foundation in conjunction with the board, since the broker who actually pays the men in his pool at levels much higher, sometimes almost twice the stipulated norm, is not strictly a producer subject to the wage determination procedure; and similarly, the producer who contracts for the services of the labor broker is not, strictly, the employer of the workers involved. The result has been to increase black wages as workers are attracted to the payroll of the labor broker, where they can earn considerably more than their fellow workers in the same shop. Thus the producers are increasingly under pressure to pay more than the legal wage in order to retain their workers.

Such a situation has made for restiveness in all quarters. *Employers* find it almost impossible to operate within the prescribed wage norms and still retain their manpower and sustain worker morale in the shop. *Workers* are tempted to accept higher offers elsewhere, and those who stay object to working side by side with Koppelbazen staff who earn considerably more for the same work. Also in recent months there has been evident an acceleration of the smoldering resentment against the many incomes which escape the strictures of the wage determination system, such as salaries of executives and staff employees, and, in fact, "any wages which at the moment exceed £800 per annum," [28] to say nothing of profits and particularly speculative incomes. By the same token *trade unions* find their influence and prestige ebbing away as the official wage level to which they have committed their members diverges evermore from the much higher earnings available to those who do *not* respond to trade union appeals for restraint. Similarly, *employer associations* feel their "grip" (the current top hit among jargon words in Holland) over affiliates weakening as individual employers find it increasingly difficult to conform to official wage levels. One manifestation of the resulting unrest was a jump in the number of strikes from seventeen, involving 1,500 men, for the period January 1 to mid-August, 1963, to fifty-two involving 16,700 men for the period from mid-August to mid-October.

In September these tensions were blasted into the open by the decision of a major metal employer in Amsterdam openly to acknowledge the de facto situation by publicly announcing a wage scale considerably above that established by the relevant collective agreement, partly as a way of combatting the Koppelbazen. This forced the government to take legal action, and the firm was subjected to a fairly heavy fine. At about the same time it was expelled from its employer association. The resulting glare of publicity on the evils of Koppelbazen led the metal industry to take action by adding to

---

[28] Pen, *op. cit.*, p. 319.

collective agreements a clause providing that approval of the Vakrad (Industry Advisory Council) would be required for subcontracting for workers. At the same time the government tightened its supervision over subcontracting firms and declared universally binding the new clause of the agreement for the metal industry. Meanwhile the foundation recommended that other industries should follow the example of the metal industry, and the Ministry of Social Affairs started preparation of a bill designed to counter the evils of Koppelbazen.

These developments in August and September had the effect of focusing public attention on the accelerating problem of labor market tensions and black wages. At the end of August the Ministry of Social Affairs discussed the situation informally with representatives of the foundation and proposed a joint consultation on measures to reduce tensions, even prior to the talks scheduled in the course of the agreed procedure for wage determination. Accordingly on September 25 there was a formal discussion between the government and nine members of the executive board of the foundation, and on September 30 another with the full board. These talks centered on the possibility of a wage increase considerably higher than that projected by the CPB in its macroeconomic estimates, but the government constantly took the stand that the determination of actual magnitudes would have to await publication of the SER semiannual report. In actual fact, however, the simultaneous deliberations of the SER were rendered farcical in the sense that the employer and trade union members of the SER, largerly the same individuals as in the foundation, refused to make any commitments in the SER pending the outcome of the discussion in the foundation.

According to press reports, negotiations in the foundation proceeded somewhat as follows. The trade unions posed a demand for an 8 to 10 per cent wage increase plus a lengthening of vacations by two days in 1964, the right to immediately reopen collective agreements due to expire at the end of December, 1963, pressure for "plantwise differentiation," that is, increases above the established norm in branches of industry and in individual firms whose productivity and/or profitability are above average, payment in 1963 of an extra week's wages, a minimum wage, corresponding benefits for civil servants, and a 10 per cent increase in social expenditures.

The employers rejected the increase in vacation benefits, the breaking open of collective agreements, and an extra week's pay in 1963; suggested somewhat smaller wage increases with some "absorption" of black wages; and asked for a rent increase on January 1, 1964, consideration of limited plantwise differentiation, greater price discretion, more overtime supported by legal provisions and better facilities for overtime workers, and postponement of the provisions for a minimum wage and increases in social benefits.

Gradually over the months mutual concessions on both sides as a result of internal discussions within the respective organizations led to an agreement which was accepted in the foundation in a meeting on October 29 and submitted to the government for its "information." To a large extent this agreement represented a victory for the trade unions, although their demand for a week's wages bonus in 1963 was eliminated.

The major provisions of the agreement are as follows:

On *wage increases*, the possibility was opened for an increase of 10 per cent (which most observers feel will stretch to 14 per cent once incidentals and such are added), in two phases, a general across-the-board adjustment of 5 per cent on January 1, 1964, and a further negotiated increase of up to 5 per cent upon expiration of existing contracts. Partners to agreements expiring after April 1, 1964, can, if both parties wish, advance the date to April 1. The second 5 per cent is intended to include any increases resulting from extensions of holidays by two days at the most; for this purpose each day of extension is to be valued at 0.4 per cent, unless the parties agree on a higher figure.

On *plantwise differentiation*, the parties in individual branches of industry are to be permitted to decide methods and magnitudes of limited plantwise differentiation resulting in increases over the agreed level. However, an effort should be made to prevent consequent significant rises in the general wage level, that is, increases above the norm should average out.

On *minimum wage*, it was agreed that discussions would be continued in the foundation and the SER on ways of guaranteeing a certain minimum wage. As a beginning, it was agreed that further measures would be based on a minimum norm of 100 florin a week for male workers and also that implementation of the minimum wage should not result in a rise in wage level above the 10 per cent.

On *social benefits*, an accord was reached on a 10 per cent increase as of January 1, 1964, regardless of the extent of actual wage increases, for general old age pensions, health benefits, children's allowances, widows and orphans, fixed pensions, and workmen's compensation. The purpose is to enable recipients of social benefits, usually in the lowest brackets, to absorb the anticipated price repercussions. The SER noted that the outside *limit* should be 12 per cent, since the last increase was in May, 1963, and between then and December 31 the increase in cost of living was expected to be between 1 and 2 per cent. Appropriate legislation is to be introduced.

On *rents*, no agreement was reached in the foundation, but it was noted that if rent increases for 1964 should be decided upon by the government, they should be compensated for by an increase of not more than 1 per cent in wages. The Ministry of Social Affairs has indicated that a bill will be introduced for increasing rents on July 1, 1964, but the nature and extent of the increase will be discussed with employers and trade unions.

On *pricing policy*, it was noted that the large increase in wages in excess of the rate of growth in productivity would make inevitable adjustments in prices, on the other hand, foreign competition plus the character of the demand for certain domestic goods and services sets limits to feasible price rises. Thus in many cases the rise in wage costs will have to result in lower profit margins. Since some branches of industry have been lagging in price adjustments, however, they may have to be given special consideration.

This agreement was promptly given official government approval. The SER, in its semiannual report published November 5, deplored the bypassing of prescribed procedure for wage determination, but nevertheless based its recommendations on the agreement.

The Council, taking cognizance of the course of events, regrets that it involved the bypassing of an essential stage in the procedure provided by the current system of wage determination. . . . the Council notes on the positive side that cooperation between trade unions and employers on the central level has not collapsed, and that as a result the prevailing wage determination system, which the Council considers to be the most acceptable system available, can still function in the future. The Council feels that a repetition of the current situation should if possible be avoided in the future.

Although as a result of these developments the semi-annual report has lost its influence in the shaping of views as to the most desirable future wage developments, this does not discharge the Council from its obligation to take a stand on this issue. . . .[29]

---

[29] Social and Economic Council, translated from Sociaal-Economische Raad, *Derde Halfjaarlijks Economisch Rapport*, November 5, 1963, printed as appen-

Similarly, at the scheduled meetings of the government with the foundation to discuss the semiannual report of SER, the October 29 agreement was fully endorsed.

Finally, on November 13 the Minister of Economics, at the conclusion of discussions with employer organizations, trade unions, and consumer groups, endorsed the section of the agreement on price policy by announcing his plans for a flexible price policy comprising a price pause until January 1; an adjustment of prices at that time to the first 5 per cent wage rise in line with the labor intensity of individual industries though not by enough to negate real wage increases (firms which might delay their price adjustment, e.g. those subject to seasonal fluctuations, would be permitted to do so provided they notified the Ministry); and then a further price pause but with special consideration for firms, particularly smaller ones in retail trade whose profits have been lagging in recent years. "My idea is that firms should be able to earn a reasonable return on their investments. On the other hand, I also want these large wage increases actually to prove an advantage for workers." [30] At the same time the Minister announced his intention of consulting representatives of employers, trade unions, and consumers preparatory to drafting of legislation to prohibit collective vertical price fixing (collective resale price maintenance).

Actually the government had no choice but to accept the *fait accompli* of the agreement reached in the foundation; the SER has no vote on the final decision. Although some members of the SER expressed their view that the increase ought to be lower, they did not propose rejection of the agreement.

Part of the Council places great stress on the fact that workers and employer organizations on the central level could agree. They think that it is extremely difficult to stipulate the exact wage rises that the economy can tolerate. From a strictly economic viewpoint they agree that a rise of the magnitude indicated by the CPB would be best. But they recognize the acute situation on the labor market, and feel that policy must aim at easing those special tensions and that such a policy, assuming a fixed rate of exchange, implies increases higher than indicated by the CPB. . . . Thus this group prefers an agreement on a lower figure, but nevertheless are unwilling to reject the agreement reached in the Foun-

dix to Letter from Minister of Social Affairs, G. M. J. Veldkamp, submitted to the President of the House on November 8, 1963 (Brief van de Minister van Soziale Zaken en Volksgezondheid aan de Heer Voorzitter van de Tweede Kamer der Staten-General, Zitting 1963–1964, 7400), p. 11.

[30] Cited in several newspapers, November 14, 1963.

dation, feeling that this . . . would lead to chaos . . . and bring great harm to the economy.[31]

Similarly, the Ministry of Social Affairs: "The expected rise in wage costs in 1964 involves serious economic risks. However, given the increasing black wages, it seems that a wage increase that is economically desirable cannot be realized. . . . Given the particularly tight situation on the labor market and the importance which the Government attaches to an agreement reached in the Foundation, the Government will acknowledge the agreement." [32]

The point is that given the tense psychological situation created by publicity on black wages, Koppelbazen, and open employer defiance of wage limits, once the government took the initial step of asking for a discussion in the foundation *prior* to SER deliberation, the prescribed procedure for wage determination was irrevocably undermined. From that moment the pace of developments was so swift that there was no opportunity for the government to retrieve its former hold over the process of wage determination. Even in the normal— or rather, newly prescribed — procedure the government's influence could only be exercised indirectly through the persuasiveness of the CPB estimates and the influence of the Crown members of the SER — who, indeed, are independent and represent the public interest rather than a strictly governmental point of view. But once the deliberative process was initiated at the other end between the private interests represented in the foundation, it was clear that the *decision* would also be taken there free from the influence of more "objective" pressures for moderation. This is because the employer and trade union representatives in the SER are largely the same individuals who constitute the foundation. Accordingly, while negotiations were still in process in the foundation, the members refused to seriously participate in SER discussions, much less to commit themselves to any position. Thus the procedure there was in effect stalemated pending an agreement of the foundation level. As the SER itself stated in the report:

Clearly, members of the Council feel themselves committed, because of their role in the Foundation of Labor, to the contents of the agreement. Hence the Council finds it the most acceptable procedure to take that agreement as a basis for its consideration. . . .

The Council feels that . . . (current) developments endanger the role

---

[31] Social and Economic Council, *Derde Halfjaarlijks Economische Rapport*, p. 12.

[32] Letter from Minister of Social Affairs, *op. cit.*, pp. 4–5.

of the Foundation as the top organ of organized industry charged with execution of wage policy. True, it would be conceivable for the leadership of top organizations to take on responsibility for wage policy, but the Council excludes this possibility because it feels that under the circumstances the "grip" on wage determination must be restored through a body further removed from the parties directly involved than are the central organizations.[33]

It added somewhat pathetically: "The Council sees the most important shortrun goal as retaining 'grip' on effective wage determination in order to ensure the role of wage policy as an instrument of economic policy."

Interestingly, there appears to have been no consideration given, at any point, to use of the government's "big stick" which had been so widely referred to in the discussions preceding the setting up of the new system as the ultimate guarantee of the government's influence over wage policy, namely, its right to intervene and order a temporary wage stop, and then, if necessary, to follow that with restitution to the Board of Conciliators of its former authority. Clearly when it came to the test, it was obvious that having taken the first step to institute discussions within the foundation on ways of coping with an urgent situation, it was not possible for the government subsequently to resist the drastic wage increases agreed upon in those discussions, and it would have been even more unrealistic to attempt to reinstitute as final arbiter a board whose prestige had been irretrievably undermined by the original withdrawal of its authority.

There was, of course, some attempt at face-saving in the comments of both the SER and the Ministry of Social Affairs. For one thing, great stress was put on the serious risks involved. "They recognize that (higher incomes than those projected by the CPB) involve a certain risk . . . in the short run . . . the danger of overspending and balance of payments deficit, and in the longer run, of unemployment." [34] These dangers, it was pointed out, arise initially from the possibility that in the very short run, before price adjustments have been widely diffused, wage increases could, if not countered by appropriate monetary restrictions, result in increased overall spending for consumption and investment. This might lead to an increase in imports at the very time that exports were beginning to be ad-

---

[33] Social and Economic Council, *Derde Halfjaarlijks Economische Rapport*, p. 11.
[34] *Ibid.*

versely affected by increasing prices, and thus create a balance of payments deficit. The hope was that gradually higher costs and prices, and a squeezing of profit margins in some cases would brake exports and investments sufficiently to relieve the pressure on the labor market — but not so much as to create unemployment. In Holland, with its rapid population growth, limited natural resources, and consequent dependence on foreign trade, both exports and investments are crucial to full employment, and by the same token, both are major sources of "excessive" demand and pressure on the labor market. Thus there is always at issue a delicate balancing of long- and short-run objectives. "Clearly the risk from excessive wage increases lies in too great a check to investment activity to the detriment of employment and economic growth over the longer run." [35]

Accordingly, the SER stressed the importance of (a) a restrictive, but not too restrictive, monetary policy that would permit the assumed balance of payments deficit to absorb liquidity, (b) of limiting the demand for construction workers, (c) of moderating public expenditures, increasing rents and indirect taxes, and reducing subsidies, and (d) above all, of exercising caution with respect to wage increases in order to avoid an inflationary spiral. Both the Ministry of Social Affairs and the SER mentioned a number of times that employer and worker organizations had stated their readiness to take certain measures if the risk proved too great. "The Government, realizing that responsible industrial circles are conscious of the risk which large wage increases carry with them, finds it easier under these circumstances to accept the agreement." [36] "It is of great importance that all parties, employers, workers and the Government, should proceed with caution, especially since no very great relaxation of the labor market can be expected in the immediate future. Self-control is required particularly for those parts of the agreement which have still to be worked out in detail. The agreed limits must be observed." [37]

Still, the reports of both the Ministry and the SER were a curious admixture of caution and optimism. They were clearly trying to convince themselves that despite the risks, the following developments were likely to result from the large increases in wages.

[35] *Ibid.*
[36] Letter from Minister of Social Affairs, *op. cit.*, p. 4.
[37] Social and Economic Council, *Derde Halfjaarlijks Economische Rapport*, p. 9.

Higher labor costs, and in some cases lower profit margins, would check investment and exports and considerably alleviate the pressure on the labor market.

The balance of payments deficit resulting from higher imports and lower exports would be only temporary until overall spending was absorbed by higher labor costs, and there would be no lasting effect on the structure of exports.

At the same time productivity would increase because of the stimulus to "capital-deepening" investments, the reduction of labor turnover and industrial unrest, and greater labor mobility as a result of wider wage differentials.

"Black wages" would be at least partially absorbed by the wage increases and the possibility for plantwise differentiation.

With elimination of black wages and relaxation of labor market tensions, the central federations of employers and trade unions, and the Foundation, would regain their "grip" on wage policy, and thus the new system could again function as it was intended to.

EVALUATION

Dutch wage policy has, since its inception in the immediate postwar period, evolved into an elaborate system of consultation, checks and balances, and cumbersome machinery for policy-making. Many observers, looking at the enormous time and effort involved, the frequent shifts in direction, and increases in wage-price levels not markedly different from those in neighboring countries without such controls, are inclined to question the value of the experiment. Can the Dutch wage policy be considered a success?

In terms of wage-price stability the Dutch performance has been fairly good. Over the last decade the only major upward thrusts in prices were in 1954 and 1957, as shown in Table 5-1.

In 1954 the price rise was the result of a conscious decision, in view of a favorable balance of payments, employment, and price situation and of low wages relative to other countries, to achieve external equilibrium by letting prices and wages rise, rather than by revaluing the currency. In 1957 prices and wages rose faster than intended as a result of earlier tax reductions, mounting investments and public expenditures, and large wage increases, and had to be reversed by fairly drastic restrictive measures. Otherwise price increases have been fairly steady and moderate.

The rise in cost of living between 1953 and 1961 was less than in

France, the United Kingdom, Sweden, or Norway, although more than in Germany, Italy, and Belgium, all of which had much greater sources of labor in terms of foreign workers or reserves of unemployed

Table 5-1.[a] Consumer Prices (Per cent change over previous year)

1953		−0.6
1954		4.3
1955		2.0
1956		2.0
1957		5.5
	Average	2.6
1959		1.1
1960		2.2
1961		1.6
1962		2.5
1963		2.5
	Average	2.0

[a] Table from OECD, *Netherlands*, 1963, p. 26.

Table 5-2.[a] Consumer Price Index (1953 = 100)

	1950	1956	1957	1958	1959	1960	1961
Neth.	88	108	115	117	118	121	123
France	77	103	106	122	129	134	137
W. Germ.	93	104	107	109	110	112	114
Italy	86	109	110	113	113	115	118
Belgium	91	104	107	108	110	110	111
UK	81	112	116	119	120	121	125
Sweden	79	109	113	119	120	124	127
Norway	77	109	112	118	120	121	124
Denmark	87	111	115	117	—	—	—

[a] Provided by Central Planning Bureau, based on General Statistics OECD, 1962.

In terms of wholesale prices, which of course are strongly influenced by external prices, the Dutch record is much better than most of the rest of Western Europe, or even the United States, with lower increases only in Italy; Belgium experienced about the same rate of increase.

Wages, on the other hand, have risen considerably faster than in Italy, Belgium, and Norway, and somewhat faster than in the United Kingdom, Sweden, and Germany, but only slightly more than in France.

In interpreting the wage data, however, several points should be noted. First, it is very likely that wage increases would have been considerably greater in the absence of a wage policy. This follows from the fact that through the process of conscious wage coordination in the framework of economic planning, the familiar phenomenon of wage-price spiraling has been largely avoided.

Second, whenever the government found it necessary, because of balance of payments difficulties or excessive increases in internal demand, to restrain wage increases, the employers and the trade unions cooperated. On two occasions, in 1951 after Korea and in 1956, workers consciously accepted cuts in real earnings in order to prevent further cost pressures on the price level.

Third, in assessing Dutch export competitiveness vis-à-vis other countries, the relevant comparison is not so much changes in costs

Table 5-3.[a] Wholesale Price Indexes (1953 = 100)

	1950	1954	1955	1956	1957	1958	1959	1960	1961
Neth.	87	101	102	104.5	107.4	105.2	105.9	103.2	102.8
France	78.3	98.3	98.1	102.4	108.2	120.7	126.5	129.7	132.4
FR Germ.	85	98	100	102	103	103	102	103	105
Italy	—	99	100	102	103	101	98	99	99
Belgium	93	99	101	104	106	102	101	103	102
UK	85.3	100.3	103.4	107.3	110.7	111.4	111.8	113.3	116.3
Sweden	78	99	103	108	110	107	107	111	113
Norway	77	102	104	109	113	111	111	112	113
Denmark	—	—	100	103	103	102	102	102	104
US	93.6	100.2	100.5	103.8	106.8	108.3	108.4	108.6	108.2

[a] Provided by Central Planning Bureau, based on General Statistics OECD, 1962.

Table 5-4.[a] Hourly Wages in Manufacturing (1953 = 100)

	1950	1956	1957	1958	1959	1960	1961
Neth.	88	128	145	151	153	167	182
France	—	130	143	158	168	182	—
W. Germ.	77	119	129	138	145	158	174
Italy	85	117	123	128	131	137	—
Belgium	—	115	125	131	133	138	—
UK	81	124	133	137	142	155	164
Sweden	68	120	128	135	140	149	162
Norway	75	120	127	—	—	—	—
Denmark	80	117	124	129	139	148	—

[a] Provided by Central Planning Bureau, based on General Statistics OECD, 1962.

and prices over a period of time, but in the absolute level of comparative costs. A major reason why the Dutch authorities have found it possible to raise wages as fast as they have was the wide gap between Dutch wages and those in Western Europe, a gap which has considerably widened with respect to Germany. This is indicated in the following data on indexes of hourly labor costs, including basic wages and all additional labor charges, for Germany, Great Britain, Italy, and the Netherlands relative to those in Belgium.

Table 5-5.[a] Indexes of Hourly Labor Costs, Including Additional Charges (Belguim = 100)

Yearly Average	Germany	Great Britain	Italy	Holland
1938	210.5	168.4	77.4	142.3
1948	77.5	110.0	72.2	76.6
1949	84.1	103.7	78.6	72.8
1950	81.9	89.3	78.5	63.2
1951	84.0	86.7	79.0	63.8
1952	83.6	86.7	78.5	60.7
1953	85.8	90.9	82.0	63.9
1954	86.0	94.3	83.7	69.0
1955	88.2	98.4	84.2	71.9
1956	87.0	97.6	82.4	72.5
1957	90.6	93.7	78.7	70.4
1958	94.0	95.0	80.4	70.2
1959	97.4	95.0	80.7	70.4
1960	102.8	98.4	81.5	74.8
1961	114.8	100.6	82.0	([b])
Aug.–Oct., 1960	106.7	99.5	81.4	75.5
Feb.–April, 1961	112.8	100.0	82.8	78.0[c]
Aug.–Oct., 1961	116.7	101.3	81.7	79.2[c]
Feb.–April, 1962	120.0[c]	100.3	83.6	80.0[c]

[a] Table from Federation des Industries Belges, *Industrie*, December, 1962.
[b] Not available.
[c] Provisional.

Finally, a comparative evaluation of wage restraint is meaningful only in terms of unit labor costs, since the obvious purpose of wage restraint is not to keep wages low as an end in itself, but to keep relative wage costs competitive with those in other exporting countries. Unfortunately comparative data on unit labor costs are hard to come by. According to estimates made by the OEEC,[38] in the decade from 1950 to 1960 the Netherlands remained roughly on a par with Germany and the United States with respect to average

[38] OECD, *Netherlands*, p. 27.

annual percentage increases in unit labor costs, and did strikingly better than the United Kingdom. Moreover, rough guesses based on rates of economic growth and wage trends in France and Sweden would also indicate a considerable advantage for the Netherlands.

It cannot be overemphasized, however, that wage and price stability as such have not been a major objective of Dutch economic policy. As a matter of fact, leading economists in the Netherlands argue that their system has little to do with wage inflation or cost-push theory. The wage policy evolved not from theorizing, but from the desperate postwar economic situation and the sheer necessity for cooperation on the part of the interest groups. In the face of economic prostration it was obvious that all efforts must be directed toward expanding investment and economic growth to achieve full employment, that export prices must be kept competitive, that strikes were a luxury that could not be afforded, and that a degree of distributive justice was imperative to share the poverty in such a way as to ensure minimum standards of subsistence for all.

Thus wage policy was conceived and developed within the framework of multiple objectives, including not only wage-price stability, but also, and much more important, rapid economic growth, full employment, balance of payments equilibruim, equitable distribution of income, industrial peace in a framework of industrial democracy, and economic planning to ensure an orderly, coordinated development of all the factors contributing to national economic policy.

But it is extremely difficult to measure the degree to which these various objectives have been achieved. For one thing, none of them lends itself to precise, quantitative formulation. Another difficulty in measuring performance stems from the interdependence of the objectives. The links between them are so close and so intricate that almost any action taken in pursuit of one has repercussions on all the others. Full employment is clearly related to the rate of economic growth. Exports and imports and the balance of payments situation can have profound effects on prices and on the rate of growth. Rapid price rises can create balance of payments crises and threaten industrial peace, but as the same time restrictive price measures may be at the expense of distributive justice, full employment, and economic growth.

The exigencies of practical policy require continuous shifts in priorities; yet if priority at one point is given to a particular objective,

it may be said that other objectives have failed. Moreover, the interdependence of objectives gives rise to the familiar problems of
ceteris paribus; since "other factors" never are held constant, it is
never possible to be sure how well a particular part of the program
has worked. Always one ends up with the question, "What would
have happened if there had not been a wage-price program?"

Still, some quantitative indications are in order. One is the fine
record of *economic growth* in the Netherlands. From 1950 to 1960
real gross national product increased at a rate of 5 per cent a year,
as compared to 4.3 for France, 5.8 for Italy, 7.4 for Germany, 2.9 for
the United States, 2.6 for the United Kingdom, and 3.5 for Sweden.[39]
This is an impressive record for a small country with few resources,
no large reserve of manpower, and extreme vulnerability to external
influences. In 1962 there was a 3 per cent increase over the previous
year, and for 1963 the increase is estimated at 4.5 per cent.

Also in terms of *unemployment* the Dutch record is far better than
that of the United States and Italy, and compares favorably with
Great Britain, West Germany, and Sweden; only France has done
slightly better. Under any definition of the term "full employment,"
the Dutch can surely claim that they have had it.

Table 5-6.[a] Average Level of Unemployment as Per Cent of Labor Force

	1950–60	1960	1961	1962
Netherlands	1.9	1.4	1.0	1.0
France	1.2	1.0	0.9	0.9
Italy	7.1	8.2	7.6	6.3
FR Germany	4.1	1.2	0.8	0.7
United States	4.6	5.6	6.7	5.6
United Kingdom	1.4	1.6	1.4	1.9
Sweden	1.8	1.4	1.2	1.3

[a] Table from OECD, *Netherlands*, p. 27. Also Robert Myers, Remarks at Conference on
Unemployment and the American Economy, University of California (Berkeley), April 20,
1963.

Balance of payments equilibrium has also been maintained. In
order to finance their heavy imports and to maintain a high level
of investment abroad, the Dutch export about half their gross national product. Planning authorities aim at a slight surplus on current
account, in recent years about 2 per cent of the national income,

---

[39] *Ibid.*

designed to offset capital exports and to maintain reserves. As indicated earlier, wage restraint has more than once proved useful in achieving this goal. In recent years the balance on current account (trades and services) has been as follows in billions of guilders: [40]

1958	1959	1960	1961	1962 estimate	1963 forecast
1.6	1.8	1.2	0.52	0.50	0.70

Distributive justice has been a major feature of Dutch economic policy. In the first postwar years wages were deliberately increased in line with rising real national income. In more recent years increases in excess of productivity have resulted in a gradual rise in the workers' share of national income.

Table 5-7.[a] Employees' Percentage Share in National Income

Year	Per Cent	Year	Per Cent
1953	68.2	1959	68.1
1954	67.7	1960	68.3
1955	66.0	1961	70.4
1956	67.5	1962	72.9
1957	68.8	1963	73.6
1958	70.0		

[a] Table from Central Planning Bureau, Centraal Economische Plan 1963, February, 1963, p. 45.

In addition, a key feature of wage policy has been the attempt through scientific job evaluation and equal pay for equal work to eliminate unjustified differentials and keep wages from lagging in less dynamic or less highly organized sectors of the economy.

Industrial peace. Contrary to the usual assumption that economic controls and state intervention leave the bargaining parties restive, in Holland the impact of strikes, which was minimal even before the war, has (with exceptions in 1956 and 1960) remained slight. Until a new formula for wage increases was reached in 1963, however, it appeared that there would be a rash of strikes.

Far more significant for industrial peace, however, has been the forging of a flexible and realistic framework for active participation and cooperation at many levels by the bargaining parties themselves, not only in the crucial decisions concerning wages and working conditions, but in all aspects of national economic policy-making.

[40] Data supplied by Central Planning Bureau in November, 1963.

Table 5-8.ᵃ Work Stoppage Loss; in 1,000 Man-Years (One man-year = 300 working days)

Year	Because of Unemployment	Because of Strikes
1936	480	0.258
1939	300	0.416
1947	47	0.678
1950	80	0.542
1953	102	0.100
1956	40	0.709
1957	52	0.240
1958	96	0.124
1959	77	0.047
1960	49	1.549
1961	35	0.082

[a] Provided by Ministry of Social Affairs.

Economic planning was imperative in the chaotic situation of the immediate postwar period, and has over the years since continued to be necessary for coping with recurrent price and balance of payments pressures which endangered economic expansion and full employment. It has, moreover, proved to be consonant with the Dutch inclination for organization and orderliness, and, more important, with growing interest in industrial democracy and participation by functional groups in economic policy determination.

All this adds up to an impressive performance in terms of expressed goals — reasonable price stability, minimum cyclical and structural unemployment, a splendid growth record for a small country with limited natural resources, considerable narrowing of income differentials and an increasing share of national income for workers, industrial peace, and a rational, objective, democratic approach to overall economic planning which is greatly facilitated by the ability, as a result of wage and price policy, to apply the brakes temporarily whenever internal and/or external pressures so require.

This at least was the record up to the autumn of 1963. But recent events have raised a question as to whether the Dutch still have a viable system of wage-price control. The first test of the new system resulted in its near collapse. Is this the end, or does it reflect nothing more than "growing pains" associated with the process of adjustment to a shift of authority from the Board to Government Conciliators to the Labor Foundation? Obviously no answer at this stage can be more than conjecture; nevertheless, a few generalizations are warranted.

First, there has been operative a very strong impetus toward more "freedom" for the bargaining parties, an urge which will persist so long as there continue to be serious strains on the labor market. In essence this pull boils down to the drive on both sides to make the most advantageous adaptation to an excessive demand for labor. Workers inevitably want to cash in on their strong bargaining position in a tight labor market, and unions inevitably lose their grip over members if they are not in a position to respond to this pressure. Similarly, employers feel impelled to offer higher wages, illegally if it cannot be done through the established bargaining procedure, in order to retain their workers, and failure on the part of employer associations to respond to this basic need inevitably leads to loss of prestige and influence over members.

Another kind of irresistible pull in the direction of "freedom" to negotiate higher wage increases has been the trend toward economic integration within the framework of the European Economic Community, and growing restiveness over the low level of Dutch wages relative to those in the rest of Western Europe. To some Dutchmen this has seemed an incontrovertible justification for substantial wage increases, and to the Common Market partners it has looked like an unfair competitive advantage in world markets.

Second, certain basic features of the postwar system of wage-price determination appear to be irretrievably lost. One is the psychological impulse arising from the sheer urgency of wage moderation. The economy has moved far from the state of prostration which made it possible in the first place for the bargaining partners to cooperate in laying the foundations for wage-price controls. Indeed, it may have been inevitable that the system would gradually erode, or at least drastically alter in nature, as the problem shifted from the "sharing of poverty" to the "sharing of prosperity."

Nevertheless a return to completely free collective bargaining in the Netherlands is unlikely. Those elements of the postwar wage policy which remain are so basic that, even without government authority to intervene, they add up to far more of a wage policy than presently exists in any other Free World country (with the possible exception of Austria). These features include overall economic planning; the pervasive influence of professional economists on economic policy; macroeconomic consciousness on the part of workers, employers, and the public in general, that is, a tendency to think in terms of real incomes and of "reasonable" solutions within the potentialities of the economy; both the habit of, and the machinery for, consultation and cooperation between interest groups with respect to wage determination; and the inclination of the Dutch people to be unemotional, objective, orderly, rational, and socially conscious, and to allocate responsibility to functional groups. Moreover it is likely that decision-making authority over wage levels will remain with the central federations of employer associations and trade unions within the framework of the foundation, rather than revert to the individual organizations. This follows from the strong pull of vested interests and reluctance to surrender authority, and also from the acknowledged probability that individual organizations "out of harness" would not succeed in pulling together to keep control of the wage-price situation.

Much will depend on the next test, that is, the repercussions of the current relaxation of wage restraint. If through a combination of luck, restraint by private groups, and good fiscal management by the government the economic results do not prove disastrous, the next "wage round" might well be left again to the discretion of the central organizations in the foundation. If, on the other hand, an inflationary wage-price spiral develops, or a serious balance of payments crisis, or a significant increase in unemployment, the ultimate outcome will surely be a reappraisal of wage policy, with at least a partial restoration of the authority of the government, via the SER and/or the board, or possibly in some new form.

The low wage level certainly was one of the causes of the rapid growth of Dutch exports, which account for half of the national income; and so of the satisfactory expansion of the Dutch economy. We need this extra growth in view of the rapid increase in population. In the last resort the reason for our special wage policy lies in the high rate of population growth (1.5 percent) and in the Dutch inclination to set up perfect rules. A slight abatement of economic expansion with its repercussions on investments would lead to structural unemployment. Therefore we have to avoid wage inflation or be prepared to devalue. Both evils compel us to be prudent, which explains the unusual character of our wage arrangements.[41]

---

[41] Pen, *op. cit.*, p. 330.

Generalizations drawn from cross-country analysis should be preceded by an acknowledgment that the data is not additive. This is true not just with respect to statistics, which may be figured from a different base, but in terms of institutions and social conventions. Thus we have tried, in some course of the individual country chapters, to point out differences as well as similarities. Some of the basic differences may be worth highlighting once more.

Italy is the only one of the four countries which has a strong Communist movement with all the ideological conflicts which that implies. Unlike Great Britain or the Netherlands, it has not had balance-of-payments difficulties until very recently. Relatively high unemployment prior to 1960 combined with weak unions to largely eliminate wage-push as a factor in the economy. Like Germany, but unlike either Great Britain or the Netherlands, it has had to readjust to democratic institutions following the collapse of the Fascist dictatorship. State holding companies, which have been used in an original way to purchase a controlling interest in numerous areas of industry, give rise to some special bargaining problems which one does not find elsewhere.

Only in Germany has the same political party had a firm grasp of the governmental reins (sometimes in coalition with a small party to its right) for the entire postwar period, though the Italian Christian Democratic Party has managed to retain the prime ministership through a series of shaky coalitions with several other parties. The

German people have seen the disasters of inflation, in the days of the Weimar Republic and again before the currency reform in 1948, perhaps more sharply than any of the others. Her workers seem more inclined to accept the word of those "who know what is best for them" than do their counterparts elsewhere. Job security and status are more attractive than wages to the employee, though the experience elsewhere appears to be to the contrary. German and Dutch workers seem less inclined to strike than their colleagues in Great Britain and Italy.

Great Britain and the Netherlands look more alike, in some respects, than does either when compared with Germany or Italy. Both have been continuously troubled with the balance of payments problem, both had Labor governments for a period after the war, and both have had to adjust their economies to the loss of colonies. But there are significant differences, even as between Britain and Holland. Britain is still a major world power, with all that that implies, while Holland is not. Britain relies heavily on conciliation and arbitration techniques, while these same devices are largely unused in the Netherlands. And on the other hand, no other country except the Netherlands has an institution like the Labor Foundation which has so closely involved labor and management in helping to plan the social and economic life of the country.

There are then important differences among all these countries. Moreover, as one looks back over their respective postwar histories two other strong impressions emerge. The first is that troubled times often call forth leaders who then dominate the period, and the second is that the best laid plans may suddenly look very good, or very bad, depending on external events over which the planners have no control. Konrad Adenauer towers over all the events in West Germany during these years. Arthur Deakin, Sir William Lawther, and Thomas Williamson brought off the "wage pause" in the United Kingdom between 1948 and 1950. Luigi Einaudi, while still Governor of the Bank of Italy, insisted upon a tight money policy which ended the Italian inflation and brought him the Presidency of the Republic. Meanwhile, Germany benefited enormously from world events which were completely beyond her control. Probably the most hated nation in the world in 1945, the East-West conflict forced the West to not only revive Germany, but welcome her into the ranks of a consolidated Western Europe. The currency reform which put Germany on its feet in 1948 was undertaken by the Allied military governments, thus sparing a native government the anguish and hostility which such drastic, but effective, surgery could bring. And when the Germany economy might have faltered in 1950, the Korean crisis produced orders which she was in the perfect position to fill.

Despite the differences in the social and economic institutions in these countries, there is much that is common to all of them. Most important, perhaps, is the universal policy commitment to full employment and relative wage-price stability. Such a commitment necessarily involves the use of governmental power to attain the desired objectives. Since such power must in each of the countries be exercised within a democratic framework, it inevitably provides an overlapping experience. Each of the countries has, for instance, relied on certain monetary and fiscal controls. All but Italy have gone through currency devaluations or revaluations at least once. Budgetary deficits no longer hold any terror for any of the countries. Taxes have often been used, as in the Netherlands in 1957, to complement other economic policies. Direct wage and price controls have been used everywhere at one time or another as a response to widespread fears of runaway inflation or severe hardship (although the uniform experience is that abandonment of such controls is desirable as soon as this is feasible). Exhortation to private pressure groups to restrain their demands appears (though in varying degrees) in all of the countries, and in the Netherlands and Great Britain strenuous efforts have been made to involve private interests in developing and administering a system of controls.

MANAGEMENT AND UNION DECISIONS

Policies affecting wage-price levels are in large measure management and union decisions. An analysis of decision-making in this field must consider both the influences that flow from the management and union organizations and those that operate through governmental mechanisms.

In our studies governmental intervention has been least significant when the international balance of payments problem was not bothersome. Germany and Italy found themselves in this fortunate position throughout most of the fifties, and it was in these two countries that management and union decisions were least affected by government controls. In England and the Netherlands there were recurrent balance of payments deficits, signaling economic tensions that produced a stop-go pattern in England and an elaborate control structure in Holland.

The balance of payments condition in Germany and Italy correlated with particular sets of pressures within the management and union organizations, some of which tended to keep wage-price levels low and others to raise them selectively. In both countries high unemployment levels through part of the period weakened union bargaining power and minimized wage push. The collective bargaining structure prevalent in Western European countries contributed to the same result, for industry-wide or national bargaining meant that negotiated rates were set at relatively low levels which the weaker firms could afford to pay. At the same time the concern of the more efficient and more profitable firms in Italy with winning new foreign markets for their goods had important effects on the wage and price decisions of these companies. Able to modernize their productive equipment and introduce labor-saving machinery, they could easily afford to "pull" wages to levels well above the national negotiated rates, and repeatedly did so. This not only brought them the cream of the labor market and minimized strikes, but reinforced the economic docility of the union organizations (though it did not always make for rhetorical docility) and in some cases gave important companies like Fiat a determining role in the organization of its own workers. The European system of "drift" above negotiated rates served as well to modify the kind of pattern setting by industrial giants which one frequently finds in the United States. In its extreme form, in Italy, this helped preserve a dualistic economy.

On the price side the concern of the large companies for foreign markets helped keep price increases relatively small and in some lines led to price cutting. Competition for foreign product markets thus proved a more effective price control weapon than the anti-monopoly gestures of the German and Italian governments. Economic growth and large foreign sales also made it possible for industries to engage in massive autofinancing, which in turn gave managements greater maneuverability in wage and price decisions and freed them to a degree from the credit controls which were virtually the only forms of German and Italian governmental intervention in the decade of the fifties.

By the early 1960's this special set of conditions in Germany and Italy that had maximized management maneuverability at the expense of union and governmental influence was disappearing. Unemployment had vanished in Germany and was low and dropping in Italy. Foreign demand for goods was softening somewhat, and the Common Market itself was showing serious strains centering around disagreements on agricultural tariffs and the admission of Great Britain. Balance of payments problems appeared. Wages and prices began to rise at more rapid rates. Not surprisingly the politics of wage-price decision-making in both countries began to move toward governmental intervention. Germany revalued its currency in 1961, Italy established a Commission on Economic Programming, and in both countries governmental appeals for restraint grew louder and more frequent.

GOVERNMENT ACTION

Government action in the wage-price area in all four countries is roughly divisible in terms of indirect and direct controls. Included in the former are monetary, and tax policies, while the latter encompasses all direct attempts to persuade employers and unions to exercise restraint. Because our focus is on the interaction between public and private decision-makers, we have been more interested in direct controls. Nevertheless, a few words need to be said about indirect measures.

INDIRECT CONTROLS

Indirect controls are the working tools of the economist. Their design and intended effect need no discussion here since they are already well known and it is not the purpose of this study to calculate their precise success. In general terms, our recitation of the postwar histories of these four countries certainly documents the effectiveness of such controls. However harsh the devaluation of the German currency in 1948, it was clearly the turning point which led to a sound and prosperous economy. Italy's tight money policies in 1947 and 1948 were, by common consent, one of the important factors in ending runaway inflation. Great Britain has not hesitated to run budgetary deficits where to do so would relieve unemployment. When the Dutch government faced a recurring balance of payments crisis in 1957 it made a conscious decision to cut consumption by pushing up prices and syphoning off profits by manipulation of the tax level.

Indirect controls have one great advantage over direct controls. That is that they are so much more easily enforced. The value of the currency can, for instance, normally be changed by executive order. Once changed it is an accomplished fact. If the action proves unwise there may be political repercussions, but the calculation which the executive is asked to make does not include the factor of enforceability. Currency revaluations are, as a matter of fact, not even likely to be discussed in the legislature since the inequities which they inevitably inflict would be even greater if it were known that a change was about to be made.

Fiscal policies normally relate to the budget and are therefore often fiercely discussed in legislatures, and may, as in Italy, be the final product of party compromise. Even so, the policy once enacted does not require widespread public cooperation in order to be effective. The same may be said for monetary controls, except that they are less likely to be a subject of legislative debate. To use the Italian example once again, the powers of the Central Bank in Italy are not subject to very effective pressure from either labor or management interests.

Indirect controls are not removed from politics, for, as the Kennedy Administration's efforts to get a tax bill through the American Congress in 1963 show, tax and budget policies may be highly controversial. There is, however, little opportunity for the mass public directly to influence these measures. For that very reason we have been more interested in direct controls.

DIRECT CONTROLS

The most obvious, but least interesting, form of direct controls is found when a government simply imposes wage and/or price ceilings, and then attempts through some kind of administrative agency to maintain them. There are times, most often associated with a period of war, when such controls seem essential. Each of the four countries covered by our study has used them. Invariably such controls are unpopular and extremely difficult to administer. Evasion becomes a way of life. For the most part democratic governments have not sought to maintain such controls over extended periods of time if any other alternative seemed possible.

One of the alternatives to flat compulsion on the wage-price front is "voluntary" restraint. The word "voluntary" must be put in quotes because it encompasses not only the situation in which willing compliance is forthcoming, but also the situation that one finds in the Netherlands where legal penalties are provided but where the program is consciously and actively based on uncoerced cooperation.

Voluntary restraint is a revealing phenomenon because it parades in close view the problems of a free people in adjusting conflicting self-interests. It involves not only philosophical overtones which go to the heart of the theory of democracy, but also the grubby problems which arise when one is asked to give up something within his grasp in order to benefit an alleged larger or longer term interest. Direct controls are nonetheless direct because they are largely voluntary, in fact if not in law, and such controls are unenforceable unless there is a high degree of willing compliance. The number of potential violators is staggering. Civil or criminal penalties may be adequate for the occasional miscreant, but they will founder if the law is widely disregarded. Thus direct controls seem to have a role to play only when a sufficient consensus can be brought about to cause people to police themselves.

For one who would bring about a consensus the evidence clearly suggests that events are more important than planning. The country chapters show this in detail, but a few highlights will make the point.

The Dutch freely concede that their postwar record of cooperative action has been possible only because military occupation of the homeland during the war and the shared poverty of the postwar years brought them together. Moreover, the two occasions in which the Dutch trade unions were asked to make real wage concessions, in 1951 and 1957, were both occasions on which the economic situation of the country was demonstrably difficult.

The highly successful postwar German economic policy, which now has the support of practically all segments of the population, is largely attributable to the fact that Germany has been the beneficiary of East-West tensions over which she has had little control. Full employment has given employers an incentive to pull wages up and a weak trade union movement has not been inclined to push further.

In Italy the end of the war found industry with a backlog of technological improvements which, when put into use, gave productivity a sudden spurt. This was augmented by the importation of machinery which was not available earlier. Greatly increased productivity made industry much more willing to grant wage increases. This fact, combined with the desire of management to fight strong Communist inroads in the union movement, brought collaboration between industry and non-Communist unions on economic matters.

Governmental efforts to get the cooperation of the trade union movement in the United Kingdom have been influenced by which of the two major political parties happened to be in power. In the period 1948 to 1950 a Labor government persuaded the trade unions to observe a wage pause, while in 1963 a Conservative government could not get the cooperation of the trade unions on a wage policy. Since the trade unions form the backbone of the Labor Party's support it is not surprising that greater cooperation is forthcoming when that party is in power than when the Conservatives find themselves in office. Which of the two parties is in power at any given moment, however, may be little influenced by the economic policies of that party, especially in an age when foreign policy is of such overriding importance.

Short of, or coincident with, events which contribute to a consensus there are a number of deliberate measures open to a government. The first might be labeled "exhortation," and is found in varying degrees in all of the countries. Prior to 1960 Italian leaders offered fewer appeals for restraint than did any of the others, but one must remember that until the sixties Italy did not have balance of payments problems and that she relied very heavily on monetary and fiscal controls. Even so, Governor Guido Carli of the Bank of Italy has written and spoken on the subject often, though not for popular audiences, and Prime Minister Fanfani and Budget Minister La Malfa occasionally urged restraint in public speeches in 1962 and 1963.

In Germany Ludwig Erhard has, particularly since 1962, bombarded both labor and management with "Masshalten" appeals for moderation in wage concessions on the theory that price increases would inevitably follow. Though the statistics do not show that the appeal has been successful, it has been popular, even among workers.

British prime ministers, whether Labor or Conservative, have issued frequent appeals to the trade unions and to management not to let wages get out of hand. Like the German example, there is little evidence that these public appeals have had any significant effect, but this has in no way changed the probability of their issuance.

The Dutch have institutionalized their appeals for cooperation, though high government officials have not ceased commenting publicly on the country's economic condition or the need for continued cooperation through the Labor Foundation.

One can hardly review "exhortation" techniques as used in the

Italian, German, and British contexts without concluding that they are ineffective in bringing wage-price movements to a halt. The Dutch experience is irrelevant to the question since it must be judged on other bases. The well-known American example of President Kennedy's successful appeal to the steel industry in 1962 not to raise prices does nothing to belie the British and European experience, since the massive pressure which the United States government brought to bear in that case could rarely be duplicated and the American steel manufacturers were divided and ambivalent in any case.

With respect to appeals for restraint, it can never be proven that the increase would not have been more had the head of government not spoken out. Silence from the executive office could be interpreted as approval for the ulitlization of unrestrained power. Furthermore, if the need is genuine the government will almost certainly be resorting to a number of fiscal and monetary controls which are likely to be effective. Some of these controls can be accomplished by executive action and some must be enacted with the help of the legislature. In either case, the government will wish to promote understanding of the necessity for such controls. Finally, an elected head of state simply has to be "on the right side." His statements are often doomed to be ineffective, whether he is discussing juvenile delinquency or the Indian-Chinese border dispute. Effectiveness in bringing about a desired end result has not been in the past, nor is it likely to be in the future, the test of whether high government officials should or will orate on a given subject.

Short of a direct effort to involve labor and managment groups in the planning and implementation of an economic policy, there is at least one other step which governments can take by way of directly influencing the wage-price level. It looks directly at wages, but proceeds on the theory that wage increases lead to price increases and a continuing spiral. The method is to try to exert some special control over wages and salaries in the public sector. The central government in any major country is likely to be the country's single largest employer even if one looks only at those persons who are directly employed by the government. In addition, it has an important influence on various related enterprises. Italy has the novel IRI and ENI state holding companies, Germany until recently had Volkswagen, much of Britain's steel and road haulage industries are still nationalized, and in the Netherlands the government accounted for approximately one-fifth of all wages and salaries which were paid.

However sound the idea of influencing wage levels through direct control of the public sector might appear to be, in practice it has failed. The reasons lead one to doubt that such a plan can ever succeed.

The British made the most determined effort to exert a moderating influence on wages through their control of the public sector, but the Germans also undertook some modest experiments. Neither succeeded. In the full employment market of Germany able government employees readily found other jobs in the private sector. The implications of this development, plus inability to recruit, shortly became so clear to the government that the scheme was not pressed. The British experience was somewhat different. It already had in existence a well-established system of conciliation and arbitration for the settlement of disputes in public enterprises. Nothing was done to curb this outlet, with the result that arbitration commissions shortly found themselves caught between following the established principle of relating public to private wages, and accepting the government's policy of wage restraint. The choice fell to the past practice, and the government then had to choose between repudiating its system of conciliation and arbitration or abandoning its wage policy. As between the two, the practical choice was to abandon the wage policy, and this was done.

The Italian public service already suffered from wage depression and inability to recruit so that it was an unlikely source of control. IRI and ENI, as state controlled enterprises, might have offered possibilities but their distinguishing characteristic was that they were to be allowed to chart their own courses without interference from the government. It is doubtful that Enrico Mattei, the genius who headed ENI until his death in 1962, would have brooked any interference with his operations.

The Italian experience with IRI and ENI enterprises offers a clue to possible pressures through government owned corporations which will operate against, rather than for, wage controls. It will be remembered that the Italian unions long sought, and were finally successful, in breaking these enterprises away from the industry association for purposes of bargaining. In a country governed by a tenuous coalition of political parties, such demands offer good political bait.

DIRECT INVOLVEMENT OF LABOR AND MANAGEMENT

Sooner or later, if the economic situation is sufficiently serious, or the balance of political forces sufficiently even, an effort may be made to directly involve private groups in the formulation and implementation of economic controls. Great Britain and the Netherlands have the most experience in this respect. Italy is experimenting with an Economic Programming Commission on which labor and management are both represented, but sufficient time has not yet passed to make any judgment of its success. The German government has shown the least interest, though it reluctantly agreed in mid-1962 to the introduction in the Bundestag of a bill proposing the establishment of a "Gremium" or committee to make annual income projections, analyze economic tensions, and pinpoint threats to healthy economic development.

If and when a government undertakes to work with private groups such as labor and management, some immediate structural problems present themselves. Specifically: (1) how does one find the appropriate representatives of labor and management?; (2) can such representatives, once chosen, forego the interest of their members?; and (3) if so, can the organizations from which such representatives come produce on their agreement?

Individual employers and employees are obviously too numerous to deal with. The only feasible solution is to deal through their representatives. Since there are well-established employer and union organizations in every industrial country, they become likely representatives. The trouble is that there are almost always multiple employer organizations, and in many instances the same thing is true of the unions. Where this is so the organizations on each side may be friendly and cooperative, or they may be quite the contrary. In either event a problem of choice is posed for the government. One alternative is to choose distinguished individuals, who will almost inevitably have a tie to an important organization, and rely on their personal prestige to carry their colleagues with them. If this is done it has a tendency to alienate the organization because it was not itself asked to make a choice of representatives. A second alternative is to call upon the organizations to cooperate and let them name their own representatives. This has the advantage of getting the organization's support, but it holds less promise for the caliber of the individual who will be appointed. Many considerations other than the man's qualifications for the job at hand may enter into the choice.

A third alternative is to combine the two above approaches so that there are labor and management individuals who are present by choice of the organizations, and others who are present by direct governmental appointment.

Actual practice has not been uniform. In the Netherlands the organizations are represented in the Labor Foundation and they choose their own representatives. In Britain the government appointed individuals to the National Economic Development Council, but this was certainly done on consultation with the representative organizations.

Upon appointment the more serious second question arises, namely, can such representatives be expected to forego the interests of their group? The Dutch have answered that question for themselves by frankly admitting that they cannot. The "subsidiary" principle, to which the Dutch so often refer, does not require that private representatives act in the public interest; it suggests only that the public interest may be served if their demands are moderated. But this is on the level of theory, and it is useful to know what happens in practice.

Twice, in 1951 and again in 1957, the Dutch trade unions did knowingly accept a cut in real wages. They did this after studying the economic picture, and at least on the second occasion their cooperation resulted in a loss of members. During the balance of the period they cooperated in the formulation of wage policy and accepted the jurisdiction of the Board of Conciliation over settlements without strikes.

Dutch employer organizations have likewise cooperated with the system, and there is no charge that they have not done so in good faith. How effective the cooperation of either the labor or management organizations has been is another question which remains to be discussed.

The British results have been much more spotty, partly because they have never attempted anything so formal or continuous as have the Dutch. The only period of real wage restraint was from 1948 to 1950 and this was not attributable to any formal policy. The Labor Party was in power and a triumvirate of powerful union leaders managed to effectuate a two-year pause in wage increases without ever raising the matter to a major policy level. Thereafter restraint fell by the wayside, and has never again been made really effective on the trade union side.

Employers in Britain have on several occasions indicated a willingness to cooperate in a government wage policy. One such occasion occurred in 1951 when Chancellor of the Exechequer Butler proposed a method of relating wages to national production. The trade unions rejected the government plan and ultimately substantial awards were made through arbitration tribunals. Again in 1957 the employers got the impression that they would have the support of the government in resisting wage demands, after then-Chancellor Macmillan said that another round of wage increases would be disastrous. But once again major strikes in shipbuilding and engineering were settled by awards from Courts of Inquiry which were interpreted as undermining the government's wage position.

Only the Netherlands offers a sustained experience in labor-management cooperation toward a wage program. Therefore one ends up turning back to it to see what more he can learn about the ability of private groups to forego their own interests in connection with a government sponsored program. And after some reflection the observer is tempted to state the Dutch teachings in three general propositions: (1) the movement has been steadily in the direction of uncontrolled bargaining; (2) four major changes of policy have been required since 1945 to make the system viable; and (3) despite all this no one seems to want to abandon the system of controls entirely. The latest change, placing the power of approval in the hands of the private Labor Foundation, goes so far in the direction of decontrol that the next step almost certainly requires complete decontrol or a return to more formal government controls. Which direction the trend will go only time will tell.

The British wage pause of 1948–50 and the Dutch periodic change of formula seem to make pretty clear the fact that no program can survive unless it is fairly flexible. The danger is that it will then become so flexible that it represents not control but simply recognition of what the parties would do without controls.

Even if a conclusion is reached that private organizations can modify their demands so that they more nearly accord with a desired government policy, there remains the question of whether labor and management organizations are capable of implementing their agreements. If one wants an unqualified "yes" or "no" answer to that question, the answer must be "no." The reason is clear. Since the government cannot deal with all employers and employees it must deal through their organizations. Such organizations do, in all of the countries in question, tend to bargain on a regional or industry basis, though there is always some plant bargaining. By definition not all of industry will be covered, but this may not be too serious because something approaching pattern setting tends to take place everywhere, and in some of the countries the bargained result is then imposed on the balance of the industry by government fiat. It is possible to assume organizational bargaining in conformity with the agreed pattern reached through discussions conducted under the aegis of the government and still find that the control program has been undermined by wage drift at the local level. As a matter of fact, drift may be so substantial, as in Germany, that workers lose interest in the results of collective bargaining. The net result is that national, regional, or industry bargaining may be a great help in focusing some central control on the negotiations, but that advantage may disappear through local changes. These local changes are often beyond the control of either the employer or labor organizations for reasons indicated in the country studies.

Moreover, wage drift is only one form of leakage from any national agreement that may be reached. The agreement assumes that but for local deviation the organization is in a position to enforce its commitment once it is made. Except in Holland, where the country is very small and the central organizations strong, there is grave doubt that either labor or management organizations can hold their constituents in line for any sustained period. Management organizations in the various countries seldom have any power of discipline over their members. Fiat and Olivetti in Italy have not folllowed the dictates of Confindustria, which is the management organization. British firms have persistently made local bargains which tend to embarrass the national bargainers.

Stated in terms of power, neither labor nor management organizations can promise adherence to any government policy agreement subscribed to by their representatives. Fortunately, power is not the complete answer to whether they can implement an agreement. A series of other variables will contribute to the answer. The cultural context in the Netherlands, where religious principles play so important a role, doubtless contributes to adherence to agreement there. And in Germany, where the workers are so disposed to accept what those above them say, the climate of opinion would seem to be more favorable than might be true in Italy, where there is a traditional distrust and cynicism about the government and its orders.

Dominant personalities can play a deciding role in whether policy will be implemented. This was well illustrated by the success of the wage pause in Great Britain during the reign of Deakin, Lawther, and Williamson.

The economic crises may be so serious that there will be no dissent, though the kind of crisis which will provide this kind of universal consent may seldom occur, and in our study shows up only in the desperate plight of the Netherlands in 1945.

Finally, organizations may get cooperation from their members on a limited basis by expending some of the "good will" capital which exists within the membership. Few organizations exist which do not have some group loyalties. These are not ties which can be utilized on a day-to-day basis without exhaustion, but they can, in an emergency, produce results. This came out forcefully during one of our conversations with a Trade Unions Congress executive in Britain. In response to a question about the TUC's capacity to implement any wage policy on which it might agree, he said: "If you mean does the TUC have the power to enforce agreement among its constituents, the answer is a clear 'no.' But you must remember that we have a reservoir of good will among our members and we can, on a limited basis, call upon it. This is the real explanation of what happened during the period 1948 to 1950."

PRESSURES ON GOVERNMENT

What has just been said relates to the problems of government in obtaining effective participation on the part of private interest groups in the formulation and implementation of economic policy. So stated there is some danger that the process will be viewed as a one-way street in which the government tries, with or without success, to persuade such groups to support a policy which it conceives to be best for the nation. Any such impression would, of course, be false, for the pressures clearly operate in both directions.

When cooperation on the part of private groups is sought some very practical threshold questions arise. One involves the estimates which such groups may make of their power to dominate policy formulation, and a second relates to the quid pro quo which may be exacted as the price of participation.

In Italy, for instance, the industrial giants, like Fiat, Montecatini, and Olivetti, have few fears of government planning because they are sure that they can, in the showdown, control the government.

("With two or three phone calls they can veto the appointment of a cabinet minister.") The smaller enterprises, represented in Confindustria, have more fears because they see planning as a step toward nationalization. The Italian unions are also ambivalent. Ideologically attracted to planning, they also see an opportunity to participate in broader economic decisions as to which they now have no voice. On the other hand, participation would imply some limitation of wage bargaining and this is unattractive.

In Germany the "Gremium" (a committee to make annual income projections, analyze economic tensions, and pinpoint threats to healthy economic development) does not carry the overtones of planning found in any of the other three countries. But it does contemplate an expert body whose pronouncements could have a significant impact on economic developments. Both unions and employers have favored such a committee, though the government has been lukewarm, to say the least. Labor, knowing that its power is weak and that its access to necessary statistical data is severely limited, sees the committee as a helpful device. However, it wants the members chosen by Parliament where the Socialist Party (supported by the unions) is influential. "Friendly" committee appointees would, in other words, be helpful. Management, too, supports the committee idea, but for different reasons. It believes that such a group would support resistance to wage increases. It wants the appointments made by the Minister of Economics, who is a conservative and who would be more likely to appoint men who are friendly to the business point of view.

In Britain the Conservative government badly needed the cooperation of the trade unions in 1963 if the National Economic Development Council were to have any chance of success. Though committed to planning principles, the unions were suspicious. The timing was not good for them because their own party, Labor, had a good chance to return to power. They were clearly in a position to seek certain concessions as the price of their participation, and this they did. The concessions which they sought, and gained, went to the makeup of the Council, its independence from the Treasury (which was thought to exercise too conservative an influence), and the right to discuss any subject.

In 1960, when the Dutch were having difficulties administering their productivity formula for wage increases, the government asked the Social and Economic Council to recommend criteria. The request made clear that it was not asking the council for a new system of wage determination. It will be remembered that the Social and Economic Council is a forty-five-man body, fifteen of whom are nominated and appointed by the government, fifteen by the central and other representative organizations of employers, and fifteen by the central organizations of workers. After two years of study the Social and Economic Council returned a report which ignored the government's request that it not get involved with the question of a new wage system, and suggested lodging supervision of the program in the private Labor Foundation. Despite its reluctance to do so, the government ended up accepting this recommendation, and it is this system with which the Dutch are now experimenting.

The power of private organizations to bargain with the government over their continued cooperation is not confined to the initial stages of the matter, as the last example, drawn from the Dutch experience, shows. On the contrary, there will be continuing interaction between the government and the parties.

One final point requires emphasis. It is that while the incentive for involving labor and management groups in the formulation and implementation of economic policy may spring from the government's desire to reach a consensus on wage-price policy which will otherwise be difficult to enforce, the discussions cannot be confined to these subjects. Planning, or "programming" as the Italians prefer to call it, will necessarily range far beyond wage-price questions. The Dutch have never deceived themselves about this. As a matter of fact, they continually emphasize to one who studies their system that it was never intended to be just a wage-price policy. Their list of objectives include: (1) full employment, (2) rapid economic growth, (3) balance of payments equilibrium, (4) price stability, (5) equitable distribution of income, (6) industrial peace in a framework of industrial democracy, and (7) economic planning to ensure an orderly, coordinated development of all the factors contributing to national economic policy.

In setting up the National Economic Development Council the British were equally clear that the scope of its inquiry could not be limited to wage-price questions — which were not even thought to be most important in terms of priority. The Chancellor of the Exchequer framed the charge to the council as one in which it would try to establish the "essential conditions for realizing potential growth and covering the supply of labour and capital, the trends of exports and imports, and the growth of incomes."

It is significant that the most serious interest in planning has come in all these countries during periods of prosperity, with unemployment virtually nonexistent or at low levels. The critical impetus for it has not been disillusionment with the existing economic and productive system, nor does it have much ideological relationship to Marxist interest in planning. Indeed, it is only where important management groups favor it that planning is being seriously discussed. In Germany, where there is little management interest in the idea, planning has not been considered seriously. The planning of the sixties is viewed by its business advocates essentially as a way of insuring the continuation of prosperity without disruptive side effects and as providing a setting of stability and predictability within which business decisions can be made with maximum confidence. The unions are torn, fearing controls over wage increases, yet hoping that planning might give them a greater voice in decision-making. While this essentially pragmatic politics goes on in the most influential groups, other interests allow their attitudes to be shaped by old and largely irrelevant ideological postures. In Italy, for example, small business and the employers organization that speaks for it (Confindustria) opposes planning because it smacks of Marxism, and the more doctrinaire Socialists and Communists favor it for the same reason.

If the critical pressure toward planning does in fact come from the more successful business elements and if their interest basically is in utilizing mathematical models in order to be able to make their own business decisions more rationally, it is probable that planning will go furthest where unemployment is minimal and affluence greatest. Only under these conditions can it be dissociated politically from the old, rigid ideological attitudes toward planning.

WAGE-GUIDELINES

Insofar as a wage program is required it necessarily involves guidelines, for without guidelines there can be no measure of control. Unfortunately, the problem of evolving guidelines is enormously complicated. There will be legitimate arguments over the cost of living, geographical and sex differentials, inter and intraplant inequities, fringe costs, productivity, merit increases, incentive systems, and a host of other things.

The postwar histories of the four countries include material on several of the above criteria, but the lesson, if any, seems to center on productivity.

As an economic principle, a wage policy geared to productivity is sufficiently unassailable to draw the limited approval of both Conservative and Labor functionaries in Great Britain. The difficulty is in application, and here one must record almost complete failure.

The Italian unions could not help but see impressive productivity gains in Italian industry since 1945. For understandable reasons they wished to share in the related gains. To accomplish their objective they hammered away at the government controlled IRI firms and at such giants as Fiat in an attempt to break down industry bargaining so that they could get at individual plants. In the bitterly fought 1962 negotiations IRI firms settled first, agreeing to plant bargaining. Fiat and Olivetti subsequently agreed to plant level bargaining. In the wage negotiations which followed after agreement on plant level bargaining, a 12 per cent increase was granted in the steel industry, where productivity was very high, and a 10 per cent increase was given in ship construction, where it is very low. The unions apparently felt that large differences would generate intra-union antagonisms. Whatever the motive, it is undeniable that the rhetoric and the end results were inconsistent. Given the tendency found in each of the other countries toward uniform wage increases, one's confidence that productivity bargaining will be based on the realities of the particular situation is not very great.

In 1959 Chancellor Adenauer asked President Blessing, of the Bundesbank, to try to establish criteria for putting wages on an objective basis. The Blessing Memorandum, published in January, 1960, favored tying wages to productivity increases, and estimated productivity increases for the following year at 3 to 4 per cent. The actual productivity increase for the year turned out to be 6.4 per cent, thus illustrating another of the difficulties in attempting to tie wages to productivity. There is no sure way of knowing in advance what the record will be, and retroactive adjustments are neither very feasible nor popular.

British governments, both Labor and Conservative, have issued a long series of White Papers and commission reports which have dealt with productivity as a wage criteria. Most recently the National Incomes Commission has been confronted with the problem. What it had to say in connection with some of the specific cases pending before it reveals one of the major difficulties in utilizing the productivity concept. Said the commission:

> The rule which is applicable to wage settlements in all industries in which greater productivity is achieved is . . . that the rate of increase of monetary incomes should be kept within the long-term rate of increase of national production. Translated into words which apply to the question what is to happen to the fruits of greater productivity, the fundamental rule will be that all wage settlements must reflect the overall national average increase in productivity and not the variations in the achievements of individual industries or firms.
>
> . . . If this rule is not observed and wages plus profits in those industries or firms which reach a high growth in productivity absorb the full fruits of that productivity, prices of their products will not be reduced and other industries or firms, not able to achieve growth, must either resign themselves to the status of poor relations or, what is much more likely, will have to submit to the pressure of their workers to bring up the amount of their incomes to the level of those which have been inflated by the appropriation of all the fruits of greater productivity.[1]

Having made the above remarks the commission was faced with having to decide in the context of three cases whether agreements reached between employers and unions were against the public interest. As to the electrical contracting industry agreement it was thought that the agreement was inflationary unless featherbedding practices, which it was argued were going to be abandoned, were in fact abandoned. The heating, ventilating, and domestic engineering industry agreement had much "to commend it," but "for the sake of agreement both parties seem to have allowed themselves" to take a bit more than productivity would allow. And the exhibition contracting industry agreement was just plain inflationary unless special circumstances, which were missing from the record, could be shown.

The dilemma is clear enough from the British cases, and so far no solution has been found. If productivity is to be the test, an unavoidable difficulty is that there are substantial differences between industries. If wage adjustments across industries are to be uniform, as they have tended to be in the past, they will be inflationary unless an average is struck. So far there has not been much disposition toward using the average. The problem is particularly

---

[1] National Incomes Commission, Report No. 2, presented to Parliament by Command of Her Majesty, July, 1963, pp. 6–7.

acute in the construction industry, for it is, as the commission said, a "sheltered" industry "not exposed to foreign competition" which when "coupled with the fact that about half of all work done is paid for out of public funds, induces in our view a more easy-going attitude to costs and efficiency than in cases where the end product of an industry has to compete in price and quality with a similar article produced abroad."

The Dutch, having started in 1945 with a system of wage controls which stressed a social minimum and sharing of their poverty, gradually moved toward more flexibility based on individual industries. Thus in 1959 they decided to permit wage adjustments on the basis of productivity in the various industrial sectors rather than on a national average basis. Employers would be permitted, however, to raise wages only on condition that they did not raise prices. The hope was that some prices would be reduced as the result of high productivity, and that this would allow room for higher prices in those industries in which productivity had not advanced so that such higher prices could in turn accommodate higher wages. Administered in this fashion the theory was that inflation would not result.

By 1963 the Dutch were prepared to concede that their productivity formula could not be made to work. Productivity figures by industry were simply inadequate. As a result the parties negotiated wage increases and then agreed upon productivity data which would justify the increases. If the Board of Conciliators refused to approve the resulting agreements, the parties were irked, and the board was without firm data to support its judgment. Moreover, there were certain industries, like construction, where some adjustment had to be made even though there were almost no productivity increases.

Given the theoretical soundness of productivity as a wage guideline, it may be that mechanical difficulties in administration can be overcome, but they are very great. Measurement is a tricky business, institutional realities such as one finds in the construction industry are unfavorable, and the bargaining problems require a degree of sophistication and self-abnegation which may be too much to expect.

SOME CONCLUSIONS FROM THE FOUR-COUNTRY STUDIES

Each of the countries subscribes to a common objective — the maintenance of full employment in a noninflationary economy. The approach to this objective nevertheless varies with the country, partly because each country is to a degree unique, and partly because the problem of how best to attain the common objective can be formulated in many ways. Indeed, there are those who say that it is impossible to have both full employment and a noninflationary economy. Starting with that premise the problem becomes whether one prefers a certain amount of inflation in order to have full employment, or a certain amount of unemployment in order to avoid inflation. And if one takes the view that full employment and a noninflationary economy are compatible, there is still plenty of room for argument about the relative importance and interrelationship of economic growth and wage-price restraint.

It becomes increasingly clear that the objective set forth above and the problem or problems which flow from it are, however formulated, primarily political in nature. In part this is because reputable economists are themselves in disagreement as to the proper approach to the problem, or even the exact nature of the problem. Inevitably the government is left with a choice among several alternative lines of action. The "government" is, in a democracy, not something which exists in the abstract, but the end result of political parties which vie for power. Such parties require political support and they get it largely from private pressure groups which approve their policies. Private pressure groups are organized to pursue somewhat limited objectives and are not under the same compulsion as is the government to respond to a variety of interests. In return for their political support private groups naturally expect a commitment to their interests.

As a general proposition business interests in each of the four countries will be found supporting Conservative political parties, and labor unions will be found supporting labor or Socialist parties. Whichever party is in power will find itself confronted with political difficulties in areas of economic policy. Specifically, full employment and a stable economy have great political appeal. This being so any government will be faced with the necessity for formulating a program to attain these objectives. In doing so, the government will naturally desire to retain the support of its principal backers, but it will be equally conscious of the necessity for support from the opposition; unless the program can be implemented without cooperation, it will surely fail.

Indirect controls — revaluation or devaluation of the currency, control of interest rates, monetary policy, tax policy, and so on —

have been utilized by all of the countries and have, it would appear, been generally effective. Their great virtue is that they are more easily enforced since the control mechanism is in the hands of the central government and compliance is fairly automatic.

Beyond indirect controls governments must resort to direct measures in attacking economic problems such as one finds in the wage-price area. Direct measures can, of course, run the gamut from simple appeals for self-restraint to a formal system of controls. In any case what is sought is agreement, for even a system of formal controls cannot survive serious and widespread opposition. Democracies are, in the last analysis, dependent on voluntary compliance with and acceptance of policies enacted into law.

One technique by which government officials try to directly influence wage-price trends is exhortation. Appeals, supported by statistical or economic analysis, are directed to the parties through public information channels in the hope that the parties will exercise self-restraint. Such appeals have been tried in all of the countries, and it is quite apparent that exhortation is not regarded as a serious control device. It serves to put the government on record "on the right side," it may have some effect in keeping things from getting worse, and it may help in creating a climate of opinion which will exercise a braking influence. Exhortation is a weapon of limited use. It has a role to play when the situation is not serious enough to warrant more vigorous measures, but is serious enough to be a matter of concern.

Beyond exhortation and before a system of formal controls, there is the possibility of using the very large segment of employment attributable to the public sector as a mechanism of control. Nothing in the experience of the countries which have tried this suggests success. If there is full employment, employees in the public sector will simply shift into private employment, and in any event there is a basic unfairness in deliberately restraining the public sector.

From exhortation and attempts at direct controls through manipulation of the public sector, one can take the broad jump to a system of direct legal controls administered, with appropriate penalties, through the courts. Each of the governments under study has resorted to this technique, but without enthusiasm and only under crisis conditions. Such a control system is demonstrably unpopular, hard to administer, and viable only so long as the crisis demands a tolerable level of acceptance. It may be fairly concluded that formal controls of this type will not ordinarily be used.

There is a step between exhortation and direct legal controls which is currently the object of great interest and experimentation. It involves economic planning in which private interest groups participate in both the formulation and/or execution of the plans. One sees it in operation in Italy in the Economic Programming Commission, in Great Britain in the National Economic Development Council, and in the Netherlands in the Social and Economic Council. It is much too early to tell how well the experiment is going, partly because the Italian and British versions are still so new and relatively untried. The essence of the idea is that the resources of a nation, like those of an individual, must be subjected to planned priorities if national goals are to be achieved. Authoritarian implications need not, it is thought, accompany such planning so long as its success is dependent upon willing cooperation of private groups having conflicting interests.

Economic planning at the national level necessarily extends beyond wage-price questions, yet it is with the latter that one finds most of the experience to date. A consensus in the wage area has been a subject of particular interest in Great Britain and the Netherlands, and to a lesser extent in Italy and Germany. The problems which have been encountered tend to fall into three broad categories: (1) the influence of social and economic events outside the immediate wage-price area, (2) the capacity of private groups to curb their own aspirations and to bind their constituents in so doing, and (3) the difficulty in formulating satisfactory guidelines for a wage policy. Much has already been said about these problem areas, but a few summary remarks may be justified.

Private organizations of the kind which represent labor and management spring into being in response to a felt need for power mobilized in the common interest of the members. When such organizations are asked to participate in planning which includes other interest groups it is self-evident that each will be required to sacrifice something of its own interests in favor of the whole. If the sacrifice can be said to result in offsetting benefits of sufficient value there may be no problem, but this will rarely be so clear as to permit no doubt. In any event neither labor nor management central organizations are monolithic in character. On the contrary, divisive influences are often strong within the organizations. What may be attractive to one member may be repulsive to another. The upshot of all this may well be that even a commitment from one of the private organizations engaged in the planning venture will not necessarily mean that its members will accept and abide by the judgment. One sees this clearly in Britain where management organizations have subscribed to governmental wage guidelines, and at the same time individual companies have engaged in local bargaining which greatly distorts the total wage picture. On the labor side there has been less disposition to accept wage guidelines in the first place, but strong individual unions have given clear evidence of rejecting such a position if taken.

The only sustained experience which one finds in any of the four countries with commitments by private organizations to a national wage policy is in the Netherlands. And in that case military occupation during the war and the shared poverty of the immediate postwar years made cooperation essential. This kind of catastrophic social and economic event is, fortunately, unlikely to repeat itself. Since 1945 the continuing trend in the Netherlands has been away from a centrally controlled system of wage increases. In no other country has the crisis been of sufficient proportions to obtain a firm commitment to a national wage policy in the first place.

Even if all other difficulties could be resolved, no country has yet succeeded in formulating wage guidelines which serve more than a temporary purpose. There is nothing surprising about this since the possibilities for wage adjustments in a free economy are never uniform. Workers, like others, prefer "more" and they do not feel the need of a consistent or uniform rationalization in order to get it. This is nowhere more evident than the trend in all of the countries studied toward local bargaining, which has the effect of altering national or regional bargains to the advantage of the worker.

Direct wage control programs such as Britain has attempted and the Netherlands has carried out are sometimes judged unsuccessful because they do not contain wages within the bounds of productivity increases. Such a conclusion may have a certain amount of validity from the economic standpoint, but it is evident that this is not so if a political judgment is applied. In the latter event success may be achieved if the timing of wage increases is changed, if there is reason to believe that without such an effort increases would have been even more, or if the climate of public opinion which is created is such that it is favorable to the government. (In this connection one remembers that public opinion polls showed Vice Chancellor Erhard's masshalten appeals to be popular even with German workers, although it is doubtful that wage bargaining was much affected.)

If what is said above is correct, one may expect governmental intervention in wage-price matters even though such intervention is less effective on the economic front than might be desired. Precisely because it is less effective, one may also expect continued experimentation with more comprehensive economic planning in which wage-price matters become only one part of a much larger inquiry. It is hard to predict how well such planning will succeed. The Germans are openly skeptical. The Italians are engaged in preliminary and exploratory sessions. The British are observing a moratorium pending the outcome of the coming election, and it is not at all clear what route further planning will take once the election is over. The Dutch have always confined themselve to short-run forecasts and the recent relaxation of wage controls poses some new problems for other segments of the economy.

FOOTNOTES ON AMERICA

Like its British and European neighbors, the United States has been concerned in recent years with full employment and the maintenance of wage-price stability. No attempt has been made in these pages to analyze the American experience, but what has happened elsewhere suggests some American comparisons which warrant comment. For the sake of both brevity and clarity, they may be listed as follows:

1. The American situation is unique in certain respects. A single dramatic example will illustrate the point. Like Britain and the Netherlands the balance of payments problem is of concern in the United States. But unlike those two countries, the problem does not arise out of an imbalance between exports and imports. On the contrary, it results from America's immense foreign aid and military support commitments around the world. The cure for the problem thus involves some entirely new considerations. Nevertheless, there is an area of mutual concern, for despite its strong export position the American government is worried about competitive price levels in world markets. This fear is abetted by high unemployment, plus a growth rate which has compared unfavorably with that of Western Europe.

2. It is evident that indirect controls have a political acceptability abroad which they do not have in the United States. This is not surprising in terms of changes in the value of the dollar, for nothing in modern American history has prepared the people for so drastic a step. But there is now ready acceptance in Great Britain and Western Europe of tax reductions, even in the face of substantial national deficits, as a constructive device for stimulating the economy and reducing unemployment. The American Congress has shown no evidence of being impressed by what has happened elsewhere in this respect. Tax reduction proposals remained linked to spending reductions, suggesting either a disbelief in the efficacy of the remedy, or a different view of the priorities which are appropriate in America. This point was put very nicely by the Chief Economist for the OECD in a speech at the University of California in the course of a conference on the subject of "Unemployment and the American Economy." He said: "Having concluded that European countries had no pre-eminent advantages in respect to the task they faced or the capacities at their disposal, I am led to conclude, by exclusion, that the major reason why most of them have done better [in terms of employment and growth] than the United States is that Europeans have been more determined that governmental capacities should be used. On this view, what European experience has to teach people in the United States is that you tend to get whatever it is that you want most." [2]

3. One of the clear lessons from abroad is that events are more important than the best laid plans in bringing about a national consensus. Moreover these events have to be serious enough to persuade people that there is a crisis which demands the sacrifice of self-interest. If this is so, and even the past American experience suggests that it is, one looks across the American horizon in vain in search of a crisis sufficient to unify the people as to economic matters. Even the tragic death of President Kennedy is unlikely to bring about a change in thinking on economic matters, though it may for a time rally wide support for a new leader. Unemployment, though high, is not likely to exert the required pressure, partly because it is highest among those who are weakest politically — the young who have not yet found jobs, and the minority groups. The danger of war is present, but in recent years it has always been

---

[2] *Unemployment and the American Economy,* edited by Arthur Ross (New York: John Wiley & Sons, 1964), pp. 160–161.

present and people have grown accustomed to living with the threat of war.

4. Implementation of a national wage policy may be no easier in countries which rely on national, regional, or industry bargaining than in the United States, where bargaining is predominantly at the company level. Theoretically one would suppose it to be an easier task to implement a wage policy where the number of control points is limited — as in national, regional, and industry bargaining. In fact, all the British and European experience shows a steady trend toward local bargaining which substantially alters the national or central pattern. In Germany this movement is so strong as to cause workers to lose interest in the national bargain. In Great Britain and the Netherlands it accounts for substantial wage drift. Under these circumstances a program of wage restraint will have to reach local levels to be effective anyway, and there may be less difference than observers have thought in the different systems of bargaining.

5. The formulation of wage guidelines abroad has been as difficult and as unsatisfactory in end result as in the United States. Productivity remains the popular favorite, except in application. The difficulties in calculating productivity on any except the broadest (and therefore least meaningful) base have not been overcome, the realities of bargaining power remain the more potent influence.

A social (living) wage may be a rallying point in times of poverty, but it proves inadequate in the affluent state.

Logically, a fair and equitable wage system may be said to require evaluation of jobs across industries. The Dutch system of controls operated in this direction, but the thought of trying to apply such a system to the immensely larger and more complex American economy overwhelms one.

6. In every country it is assumed that a viable economic policy involving wage-price restraint must have the cooperation of interested groups in the planning and implementation stages. This is but another way of saying that to avoid opposition one must involve private economic groups in the formulation and execution of the plan. Wartime controls in America have always involved labor and management groups, but on each occasion there have been those who felt that only the "public" interest should be represented in the control mechanism. The experience abroad is that a democratic government does not successfully impose restraints on private eco-

nomic groups without at least their tacit consent, and that this consent is gained through their participation.

7. Pleas from high public officials for restraint on wages and prices must normally be viewed as a political rather than an economic exercise. Rare exceptions to the contrary notwithstanding, such appeals are not demonstrably effective as economic control devices. Such appeals survive abroad, and one suspects they will in the United States, not because they are expected to bring about real compliance, but because they may cause economic changes to be less than they would otherwise be. Beyond this they are simply an essential of political leadership and must be weighed in these terms.

8. There is a movement abroad toward economic planning through collaboration between the government and private economic interest groups. Such planning is by no means confined to wage-price matters.

Insofar as there is an American counterpart of European bodies of this kind, it is probably found in a combination of the Council of Economic Advisors and the President's Labor-Management-Public Committee. Between them they have been concerned with such broad matters as economic growth, tax policy, the impact of technological change, foreign competition, price policy, and wage guidelines.

If there is a desire to go further along the road of economic planning in the United States, a way would have to be found to broaden the base of the present groups and to focus on overall goals. This would appear to be an unlikely prospect at the moment, but the economic continuum which runs through the affairs of Italy, Germany, Great Britain, and the Netherlands suggests caution in reaching any such conclusion. The notion that planning is necessarily undemocratic or authoritarian has been abandoned, and the key questions are whether it works and how it works. As to the latter, there is a variety of experiments in progress in the four countries which we have studied. The next ten years will have a good deal to say about success or failure in these areas. Policy-makers in the United States must watch with interest.

7   Wage-Price Decisions as Symbols

One theme that appears again and again in the wage-price politics of these four countries deserves more extended analysis, for it grows in importance as an explanatory factor as attention is focused upon organizational decision-making rather than upon economic trends alone. It is the use of wage-price talk, gestures, and actions to increase the political power, status, and maneuverability of management, labor, and governmental organizations and to win mass support for their policies and leaders. Repeatedly, behavior has served this political and organizational end even though it was much less clear that it was having the desired impact upon wage or price levels or relative shares of the national income. We are convinced that wage-price decisions are being shaped very largely, and sometimes entirely, by these noneconomic, organizational interests.

To suggest this is certainly not to imply that government, trade union, or company officials typically use wage-price policies unscrupulously to mislead their constituents. On the contrary, these officials, being representative of their constituents, no doubt share their anxieties, expectations, and assumptions about organizational acts and tactics and are typically eager to prove to themselves as well as their constituents that their work is worthwhile. Because the causes, and even the extent, of income changes are so difficult to know, it is natural enough to assume that the programs one has worked on have been effective. If they have brought few significant gains, it is always possible they have prevented significant losses that would otherwise have taken place. For the organizational leader to ask whether he has substantially affected wage-price trends, and to answer "Yes," is both natural and "politic." But to the student of wage-price decision-making it may well be the wrong question to ask. The question can rarely be answered objectively, and our findings suggest that regardless of the answer, decisions are consistently made in particular ways because of their organizational and political impact.

If that is true, wage-price decision-making can be explained only if we understand the role it plays in the larger political process. How have union, management, and governmental leaders been able to win political support and maneuverability so often through wage-price actions that had little demonstrable impact upon people's incomes?

A clue to the answer can be found in a number of recent studies that have detected a distinction between instrumental and expressive political acts.[1] These studies deal with different fields of public policy and do not use a uniform terminology to describe their findings, but they agree on some basic conclusions that help clarify the problem posed here. These can be summarized briefly. Some political actions demonstrably win tangible benefits for interest groups: money or other resources. Other actions, just as strongly supported politically, bring symbolic or intangible benefits: assurance that a group has social status, or reassurance that a group is being protected by the state from a widely feared threat. When a relatively small group pursues concrete political objectives and is organized to exert sanctions as a means of achieving them, it is likely to win tangible benefits. When a large mass feels threatened by developments over which it has little or no influence, it is likely to be easily manipulated and to be placated by gestures that bring little tangible benefit but do serve as reassurance.

In the making of wage-price policies, interests in symbolic reassurance are especially strong and especially easy to satisfy. Wages and prices become the focus of some of men's strongest hopes and fears. At the same time it is clear enough to everyone that future

---

[1] Harold D. Lasswell, *Psychopathology and Politics* (New York: Viking, 1930); Ulf Himmelstrand, *Social Pressures, Attitudes, and Democratic Processes* (Stockholm: Almquist and Wiksell, 1960); Murray Edelman, *The Symbolic Uses of Politics* (Urbana: University of Illinois Press, 1964).

income trends are largely unpredictable and uncontrollable. Individuals have little influence over them, and even unions and corporations are often at the mercy of unexpected economic developments. The mass public and the rank-and-file members of labor and trade organizations therefore look avidly for acts of organizational leaders and of public officials that promise to protect their interests in these unchartable and hazardous waters. Because they are anxious and because it is so hard to know what the real influences upon incomes are, they will usually interpret ambiguous acts and gestures as promising to give them the benefits they want. It is a long-established principle of psychology that in an ambiguous situation, men supply their own perceptions to suit their interests and psychological needs.

Our findings are reviewed now with a view to exploring some consistent patternings in the choice and change of organizational goals, in leadership styles, and in mass responses.

A logical starting point for this kind of analysis is the list of emotionally loaded slogans put forward in all countries as desirable guide lines for wage and price decisions. Sometimes particular objectives are recommended: increases in line with productivity, wage and price restraint, or the avoidance of inflation or unemployment. Sometimes particular procedures are advocated: economic planning or programming, codetermination, reliance on collective bargaining instead of wage drift, competition, direct wage or price controls. In all countries these terms are enthusiastically advocated by some interest groups and have often been adopted as official policy. Yet our studies show quite clearly that they cannot be relied upon to explain, describe, or control actual wage or price trends. Their coincidence with actual trends is always sporadic and short-lived when it occurs at all. They conform more often to Kenneth Burke's definition of the function of political rhetoric: "to sharpen up the pointless and blunt the too sharply pointed." The eagerness with which they are embraced in political discussion is usually in direct proportion to the flexibility private groups retain to observe them, stretch them, and sometimes ignore them.

Other forms of governmental and private action clearly do have a significant impact upon wage-price trends: monetary revaluation and devaluation, credit controls, large-scale fiscal interventions, monopolistic control of product markets, and labor shortages permitting monopolistic control of labor markets. To compare the rhetorical forms of wage-price influence listed in the previous paragraph with the tangible forms listed in this one is an instructive exercise. The latter do not rely for their effectiveness upon the co-operation of the general public. They are, in fact, insulated from mass influence, are not typically widely publicized, discussed, or understood, and do not arouse widespread political enthusiasms or antipathies. The former group, as will be shown in some detail below, play upon mass hopes and fears, and their function is basic-ally political rather than economic. Mass response is their very reason for being. They are expressive symbols, and the process of wage-price decision-making can be understood only if we recognize what it is that they express and what social functions they serve.

This distinction between instrumental and expressive acts in the wage-price field is revealing in the analysis of the wage-price actions of all three types of organization. We apply it now to unions, man-agement organizations, and governmental organs in turn.

II

Regardless of the absolute level of wages or of the amount of recent gains, we find unions in all the countries resorting to the same stylized rhetorical appeals and justifications. The unions' jus-tifications of their current demands for wage increases always either call attention to a common and widely feared threat (cost of living rise, inequitable sharing in economic growth, destruction of produc-tive facilities), or hold out the hope of equitable treatment of workers in the future (productivity as a guide line, fair shares, etc.). In either case these public statements, while ostensibly directed as arguments to management, are clearly intended to reach union members and potential members as well. It is doubtful, in fact, that experienced union leaders often expect them to influence managerial wage concessions, for there is ample evidence that managerial wage policies depend upon much wider and more concrete economic developments and power tests.

The justifications for wage claims do have a direct effect upon rank-and-file support for the union organization, however. They convey the message that the leadership is looking out for the mem-bership, protecting the men against looming threats and leading them to a brighter future. They are therefore to be understood as helping to maintain organizational stability for the union. This function of union rhetoric is all the more necessary where, as often happens, employers really wield the major influence in wage setting.

It is almost as useful when the unions have a great deal of bargaining power. Witness the continued use of the "productivity" justification by Italian unions in the early sixties as they happily claimed and won wage increases going well beyond productivity gains.

Union leaders must constantly be concerned about the willingness of workers to join and support unions. There were substantial shifts in union membership in the countries we studied, and it was especially noticeable that the inducement of workers to support a union wholeheartedly lessened when wage trends were being determined chiefly by management, as in Italy and Germany, or through political negotiation, as in the Netherlands. In such situations the union leaders naturally enough emphasized ideology, for talk of ideology keeps alive a sense of battle and a basis for organizational loyalty when the worker is not benefiting materially and immediately through his union membership. When, on the other hand, tight labor markets bring added bargaining power, the unions turn to bargaining, and ideology is soft-pedaled. Both Germany and Italy exemplified this trend in the early sixties.

A marked change in leadership style accompanied such economic and rhetorical shifts. In place of eloquent men who talked much of Socialist, Communist, or Christian ideologies but often had to accept managerial or political help in maintaining their own organizational positions, a new generation of leaders appeared. The new leaders were tough and militant, but they acted in behalf of concrete economic gains and had little interest in the ideological abstractions around which labor politics had centered earlier. The new style, like the old, served to induce workers to participate in unions, but a changed economic environment called for a new leadership posture. Workers whose real wages are improving need to be shown that it is the union that is doing it for them. They respond less enthusiastically to abstractions promising them a better world in the indefinite future.

In England and the Netherlands, where labor parties were in power for a time, still another organizational problem confronted union leaders: to win rank-and-file acceptance of a policy of wage restraint in order to help the government cope with a severe balance of payments deficit. The overlap in leadership between unions and labor parties typical of many European countries helps create this dilemma; and the common view among workers that labor parties represent their interests in some long-run and abstract sense even where they do not represent them concretely and immediately helps resolve it for a time. Where labor governments were in power, at any rate, unions have rather consistently worked for wage restraint, in talk and in action, and for relatively short time periods they have been able to win support among their members. It is unlikely that they could continue such a policy for long unless an emergency more serious than a balance of payments deficit persisted to keep the rank-and-file members quiescent.

Other developments described in our country studies further emphasize the key role of organizational loyalties in wage decisions. Wherever workers have had to rely for concrete benefits upon organizations other than unions, their attachments to the unions have weakened. Where shop committees have negotiated benefits above those in national or industry-wide contracts, or have dealt with grievances, shop committees and unions have always become rivals to a degree, even though both ostensibly exist to represent the workers. Where managements in Italy have negotiated with shop committees rather than shunning them or trying to break them, shop committee members have tended to see issues from management's point of view more often than union leaders with no day-to-day contact with companies. And where, under the German codetermination laws, union members have participated in plant management, they have also begun to see issues from the perspective of management. Clearly, union and worker goals and tactics are never fixed, static, or persistent. Always, they are a function of opportunities and of organizational ties and needs. A stereotyped picture of unions always representing current worker demands and displaying interests adversary to those of management oversimplifies and distorts the facts very greatly.

Yet this stereotyped image is itself an important aid to labor organizations in their constant effort to keep the rank and file loyal, and we can identify a number of devices that help keep the image bright. At British Labor Party Congresses votes are taken, ostensibly to determine party policy. In any organization voting is a powerful method of reassuring masses that they are the source of policies, but in the British Labor Party, as in many other organizations, this impression is a rather misleading one. The bloc voting system in fact assures that influence will be concentrated in an oligarchy. CISL unions in Italy sometimes ask members to indicate preferences on a checklist of possible bargaining demands, and here, too, the voting has little bearing upon demands or upon bargaining outcomes.

A common device for emphasizing that the union is involved in a bitter struggle with management is rhetorical emphasis upon the obstacles that face it. No matter what its recent successes have been, no union abandons its stylized allegations that the challenge is greater than ever, the times are critical, and the threat is formidable.

Most important of all, collective bargaining becomes the acting out of the leaders' persistence in the face of these obstacles. Even where, as in Italy and Germany through the fifties, management was often willing enough to make concessions beyond the unions' bargaining strength, collective bargaining served an important function for both sides. For the union it kept alive the image of a clash of adversaries and thereby made an appeal to the rank-and-file members. Dramaturgy is clearly a key element in wage decision-making.

There would be no point in the dramaturgy, the rhetorical justifications, or the acting out of labor-management battles if it were obvious to all workers exactly how much the unions had gained for them. That this is not obvious or even ascertainable is crucial to what happens. The interaction is complex. It is impossible to compare the relative gains of workers and management objectively or to know how much was won for the men by their unions rather than by market forces or managerial concessions. It is precisely this lack of objective reference points that makes it possible to create subjective ones: to manufacture images of the effectiveness of the union leadership and the relative power of union and management organizations. Thus economic trends and their accompanying dramaturgy bear little resemblances to each other, but the dramaturgy serves an important function of its own.

III

On the employer side organizational influences and noneconomic goals are equally conspicuous and complex. In all four countries the national employers associations represented chiefly the interests of the great mass of small- and medium-sized enterprises, in collective bargaining and in lobbying on governmental policies. These organizations have been conservative, consistently pressing to keep wage increases minimal and opposing economic planning, even when the larger enterprises in the same countries have conceded substantial wage benefits and have supported movements for one or another kind of planning.

In their conservatism the national employers organizations have reflected the sentiments of the managements of the smaller firms accurately. Given their relatively low profit margins and vulnerability to sudden changes in the market, the latter feel constantly threatened and therefore are likely to cling all the more tenaciously and uncritically to the maxims of survival they have long taken for granted: that wages eat up profits, that public controls hurt management, that planning is a Marxist tactic. Because the smaller employers do not normally have close personal contacts with public officials, they have little occasion to learn about the possibilities of influence and bargaining, and so their stereotyped impressions are not challenged. The bureaucracies of the management organizations retain their positions by reflecting and promoting these views, for the small- and medium-sized companies are their power base. Examination of increases in negotiated rates in the various countries suggests that the adamant wage-restraint stands of the employers' organizations had more to do with organizational cohesion and politics than with the outcomes of wage bargains. These outcomes were not too different in the various countries, and the differences that did appear were far more closely related to national labor surpluses or shortages than to the stands or tactics of employer organizations.

The managers of the advanced, profitable firms showed evidence in all the countries of looking beyond the immediate bargain to wider horizons: long-run influence over the unions themselves and increased influence for business in national and international economic policy. This contrast in behavior and motivation between large and smaller business is most conspicuous in Italy, with its dualistic economy and related ideological differences. In Italy big business consciously used wage concessions, union subsidies, and an "ideologies game" to win influence in the labor organizations, and it is sanguinely promoting the movement for economic programming on the assumption it can control it. In Germany, too, business has played upon the status-seeking of the labor movement for its own advantage, has periodically sought power tests it was confident it could win, has tied these tests closely to national politics, and is currently showing interest in an economic counseling body it thinks it can control. The same ambitions underlie the participation of British industry in NIC and NEDC and the economic planning bodies of the Netherlands. In all these cases the more successful sector of the business community has not shrunk from helping create and control decision-making institutions that mark a radical departure from conventional management-labor bargaining, and it has not hesitated to cooperate with old adversaries in the process. But the undercurrent everywhere of adherence by the old line employer organizations to classic opposition to unions and their wage demands and to negotiations that set minimal rates also helps the more profitable firms. It gives them a bargaining ploy in their negotiations with their newfound and still restive colleagues in the unions and the labor and Socialist parties.

It seems a tenable speculation that the past business success of the managers of large firms minimizes a sense of threat (even though it overhangs their less successful competitors) and maximizes their incentive to use political situations rationally and instrumentally for tangible gains in profits and in power. They know from experience that center-left governments are manipulable; that planning, programming, or economic advisory bodies mean whatever current political interests require that they mean; that codetermination need not mark the onset of socialism or even increased union influence; that governmental intervention and highly publicized planning programs can win worker acceptance of restraints they would otherwise resist. Managers use this knowlege to extend the power of their firms, for their own status is thereby enhanced as well.

For both sides, then, labor-management bargaining has often served as a convenient cover for political and organizational ploys. Its real significance appears only when it is recognized that the objectives of the bargaining parties have often gone well beyond striking a favorable wage bargain. In the 1950's at least, that end was often subordinated to much broader ones, involving the roles of management and labor in the national political arena. The actions, gestures, and talk of all the group interests involved have their functions, but they are often not the stated or ostensible ones. Union and employer organizations are often seen as shaping wage trends, whether or not this is demonstrably the case. Powerful managements, that can certainly influence them, often make concessions that are hard to explain in economic terms but that make a good deal of sense in the light of their organizational and political consequences.

IV

The actions of public officials are also more fully understandable and predictable if they are analyzed in this way. These officials must respond to the interests of groups that can wield sanctions: grant or withhold money from political parties; support or injure public programs through their business operations; perhaps help or hinder politicians' careers through social contacts or by swaying votes. At the same time governmental officials need to be sure that mass public opinion is with them, or at least not actively against them.

This is rarely easy, for the public official, responding to people's interests, typically faces incompatible ones. Measures that promote full employment are also likely to spur inflation. The stabilization guidelines or controls he hopes will protect consumers may also set off labor-management conflict and detract from free collective bargaining. If he tries to exercise exemplary restraint in setting wage levels for public employees, he may lose his best staff members. Ambivalence in the individual official is therefore the inevitable reflection of the political conflicts he has a responsibility to resolve. One way in which public officials everywhere respond to the cross pressures they face is to indulge in gestures to reassure both the public and themselves that their ambiguous decisions are effective; and the reassurances are a political necessity regardless of whether the economic effectiveness can be demonstrated.

Some forms of wage-price intervention directly involve the general public and are justified politically as responses to demands for protection against economic threats to the great mass of the people. Other forms, the so-called indirect controls, are not responses to immediate public demands and do not call for public cooperation in their enforcement or administration, but they do have substantial effects upon wages and prices and therefore upon distributive shares of the national income.

The direct forms of intervention have been relatively ineffective in preventing wage or price increases. Whether they have taken the form of exhortation, publicly prescribed guidelines, or ceilings, they have been ignored or evaded with sufficient consistency in all these countries that it is clear that evasion is a more likely response than compliance. Black markets and black wages appeared during the postwar inflationary crises of the various countries as a concomitant of direct controls, and they appeared later as well where, as in the Netherlands, there was a serious effort to continue controls. These forms of intervention call for the cooperation of the general public or large sectors of the public. The sanctions on which they rely are legal enforcement and the pressure of public opinion. Neither of these has often been applied in any significant measure. Indeed, no democratic government can for long enforce behavior which is strongly resisted by the public, so that where the pressure of public opinion is lacking, enforcement is likely to be absent, too, regardless of formal law or declared public policy.

There are some exceptions and qualifications to this observation. Sometimes so-called controls have really *described* existing behavior rather than calling for a change in it. Witness the price control program in the Netherlands after 1961 and many of the price regulations of CIP in Italy. Rent controls, moreover, have been fairly effective in many countries over long periods of time, and other ceilings have been enforced during relatively short periods of crisis stemming from a threat of runaway inflation. In these cases, however, very large numbers of people have been hurt or threatened with imminent deprivation, and so support for controls has been widespread and intense. Perhaps even more in point, rising prices in these cases threatened the economic position of the sellers, bringing some measure of support for controls even from them. Only a relatively small proportion of the population could afford to pay the rents that would be charged in the absence of controls. Normally, rising wages and prices have not meant immediate economic disruption, and they have increased the incomes of sellers without posing an immediate threat to their livelihood. In consequence neither the sellers nor the general public has succumbed to alarm.

Both the customary evasions of direct governmental intervention and the exceptions just noted reveal something of the political function of such intervention. It reassures an apprehensive public that the government is looking after its interests and shielding it from economic predation. Whether or not direct intervention interferes very greatly with economic market forces or prevents prices or wages from rising, all governments resort to it. They exhort businessmen and unions to exercise moderation when prices are rising and sometimes they suggest guidelines or prescribe price and wage ceilings. They do these things, then, not because they necessarily bring economic stability but because there are political advantages in doing them and because the public and the public officials alike find them reassuring. The high governmental official who urges wage and price restraint is conveying the message to the voters that he is on their side, for they are all consumers. At the same time he is conveying the message to businessmen and union officials that the ultimate decision is really theirs, and this, too, is a welcome and popular message, likely to bring political support from those who have the most money and votes at their disposal. An announcement that productivity gain or some other mathematical formula is to serve as a guideline for future wage-price increases has the same political advantage. It, too, reassures the public that the government is protecting it while also reassuring the parties themselves that they have little to fear, for they are aware that productivity or a similar formula is ambiguous and may serve as a justification for either party's position. In a sense such formulas furnish a terminology in which bargaining claims can persuasively be phrased.

Ceilings serve a similar political function. They have the form of vigorous governmental action in the public interest, but with the exceptions already noted they either describe existing behavior or they permit evasion to suit the interests of the groups involved. We do not suggest that these functions, messages, and evasions are deliberate or calculated. Normally they are not, and the fact that they are not makes it all the easier for the entire system to operate in the manner described.

The attempts at economic planning and the discussions of planning that have occurred in the four countries we studied are consistent with these observations about direct public intervention. In a sense the planning bodies have acted out governmental reassurances that the mass public is being protected in economic decision-making, while at the same time these bodies have responded sensitively to the interests of organized groups able to apply sanctions. The acting out doubtless serves the function of making the reassurances more persuasive. In the Netherlands it probably has done so; but in the British NIC the acting has been so poor and cacophonic that it simply made the pointlessness of the proceedings plain to all. The groping for a politically viable planning organization in Italy represents an early stage attempt to find a formula that will bring reassurance while protecting the interests of the parties involved; the British NEDC represents a later stage of the same attempt. Because planning involves more explicit intervention than the other direct devices, it seems to bring into the open the basic ambivalence among business groups, unions, and workers alike about economic stabilization measures.

Indirect economic controls are fundamentally different from the direct forms of intervention in the way they are formulated and enforced. It does not require the cooperation of the affected general public to change central bank interest rates or reserve requirements or devalue the currency. It simply becomes necessary for everyone to pay higher prices or higher interest rates, and evasion is not feasible. There is also far less publicity and general participation in the decisions to impose controls. Secrecy about the imminent imposition of monetary controls is often necessary in order to prevent speculation. In all countries central bank authorities enjoy considerable leeway in making these decisions, usually subject to a requirement that they consult specified representatives of credit institutions, of government agencies concerned with business and credit, and of the business community. The social and economic background of central bank officials also makes it likely that decisions about monetary control will take business interests into account; but neither labor interests nor those of consumers need be similarly considered, either formally or informally.

This decision-making structure suggests that monetary control programs serve a different political function from direct interventions. They do influence wage and price levels, often substantially, but with a minimum of general public involvement. Further, they are likely to accord major weight to the interests of the banking and business communities and especially to the balance of payments problem if there is one. This means they are likely to be biased in favor of deflationary policies that protect creditors and foreign markets and contribute to producing or maintaining a reserve of unemployed labor. Labor is thereby likely to suffer both through unemployment and through smaller wage increases. This is in fact the role that monetary policy has usually played in all four countries. Both the 1961 German currency revaluation and some Italian fiscal measures of the early sixties did meet with opposition from organized business. The German revaluation, however, was a move to restrain prices, ease the labor shortage, and protect the payments balance, and therefore involved a conflict between banking and export interests on the one hand and some other business groups on the other. The Italian case did not concern a major issue and involved a concession to small business in the South.

Fiscal policy has not often been used explicitly either as a stabilization device or to stimulate economic growth, and on political grounds it is understandable that it should not. Because fiscal measures require parliamentary action, any such general objective as wage-price restraint or economic growth is likely to be lost sight of in the concern of various blocs with specific appropriation and tax items that affect their constituencies. Logrolling, the fundamental process in all legislative bodies, thus works against this use of the fiscal power. This is one instance in which general symbolic values usually retreat before the claims of specific economic groups. Fiscal policy has accordingly been used to encourage German workers to save, to subsidize housing in all four countries, to benefit small business and the South in Italy, and to benefit big business and management through regressive tax policies in Italy and Germany. Britain's occasional austerity budgets do represent the exception: the use of fiscal policy to stabilize. This is apparently possible only when the balance of payments situation can be pictured as posing a national emergency and where party discipline is tight.

These observations suggest that private and public wage-price pronouncements, acts, gestures, and programs not only have economic consequences, but also wide and deep implications for social stability. Because this policy area is viewed with widespread and profound concern, the wage-price actions men read about and hear about become sensitive triggers of political unrest or of quiescence. Wage and price talk and action is typically tailored to this fact of political life. It often has considerable impact upon political and organizational loyalties, though its direct impact upon economic trends is more doubtful.

Its indirect impact upon economic trends may be substantial, nonetheless, for gestures that keep mass publics quiescent indirectly help organized groups influence wage and price levels by freeing them to exert what sanctions they can where sanctions count. Cartel arrangements and union pressures for large wage increases in tight labor markets are part of the same political transaction as symbolic gestures toward stability. Neither phenomenon would or could exist without the other.

Index

ACLI (Associazioni Cristiane del Lavoratori Italiani), 43, 45

Adenauer, Konrad, 86, 130, 131, 132, 139, 142, 280, 297

Administered prices. *See* Price policies

Administrative agencies, 3, 13, 70–71

Agricultural Wages Act of 1948 (G.B.), 176

Ahlener Program (Ger.), 130

Amalgamated Engineering Union (G.B.), 157, 166, 200

Ammassari, Giuseppe, *cited* 36, 37, 49, 51

AR (Antirevolutionaire Partij), 222

Arbitration. *See* Conciliation and arbitration

ASAP (Associazione Sindacale fra le Aziende Petrolchimiche e Collegate a Partecipazione Statale), 48, 56

Association of British Chambers of Commerce, 184, 195

Aufsichtsrat, 120, 122. *See also* Co-determination

Bad Godesberg Program, 88, 89, 130

Baffi, Paolo, *cited* 23, 66

Balance of payments, 66–69, 93–94, 108–109, 133–134, 147, 184, 199, 242, 246, 269, 274–275, 279, 280, 281–282, 304

Balkenstein, G. J., *cited* 224, 228

Balogh, Thomas, *cited* 216

Bank of England, 215

Bank of Italy, 16–17, 20, 21, 64, 65, 67, 69, 71, 284

Banks. *See* Bank of England; Bank of Italy; Bundesbank (Ger.); Central Bank (Neth.)

Batti, Luciano, *cited* 31

BDA (Bundesvereinigung der Deutschen Arbeitgeberverbände), 94, 95, 96, 104, 105, 115, 126, 128, 140

BDI (Bundesverband der Deutschen Industrie), 94, 95, 96, 114, 126

Beamten. *See* Public employees

BEC (British Employers' Confederation), 161, 162, 163, 168, 171, 184, 190, 195, 214

Bentley, Arthur F., *cited* 5

Berg, Fritz, 126

Bevin, Ernest, 182, 211

BHE (Refugee Party – Ger.), 87